P9-AQK-356

DECORATIVE ART OF VICTORIA'S ERA

By the Same Author
Folk Art of Rural Pennsylvania

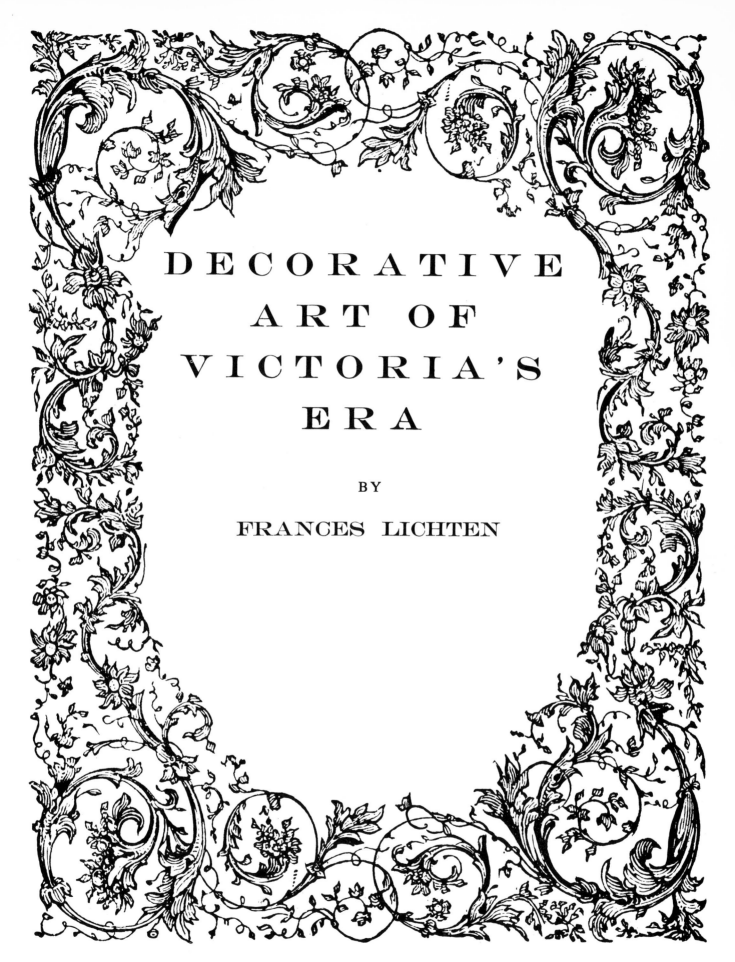

DECORATIVE ART OF VICTORIA'S ERA

BY

FRANCES LICHTEN

BONANZA BOOKS · NEW YORK

Copyright, © MCML, BY
CHARLES SCRIBNER'S SONS

———————

Printed in the United States of America

All rights reserved. No part of this book
may be reproduced in any form without
the permission of Charles Scribner's Sons

This edition published by Bonanza Books,
a division of Crown Publishers, Inc.,
by arrangement with Charles Scribner's Sons.
A B C D E F G H

TO
KATHERINE MILHOUS

ACKNOWLEDGMENTS

The author wishes to thank the following institutions and individuals for their co-operation.

THE ART INSTITUTE OF CHICAGO

CHESTER COUNTY HISTORICAL SOCIETY, WEST CHESTER, PA.

COOPER UNION MUSEUM FOR THE ARTS OF DECORATION, NEW YORK

FOLK ARTS CENTER, NEW YORK

FORT HUNTER MUSEUM, HARRISBURG, PA.

THE FREE LIBRARY OF PHILADELPHIA

THE HISTORICAL SOCIETY OF PENNSYLVANIA

INDEX OF AMERICAN DESIGN, NATIONAL GALLERY OF ART

THE LIBRARY COMPANY OF PHILADELPHIA

THE METROPOLITAN MUSEUM OF ART

MONTGOMERY COUNTY HISTORICAL SOCIETY, NORRISTOWN, PA.

MOORE INSTITUTE OF ART, SCIENCE, AND INDUSTRY, PHILADELPHIA

MUSEUM OF THE CITY OF NEW YORK

PHILADELPHIA MUSEUM OF ART

VALENTINE MUSEUM, RICHMOND, VA.

VICTORIA AND ALBERT MUSEUM

MR. AND MRS. PAUL AUMAN

MISS FLORENCE CANNON

MRS. FORREST DICKERMAN

MISS ELEANOR GRAHAM

MR. CHARLES HAGERTY

MRS. ROLAND DE HELLEBRANTH

MRS. SAMUEL LIFSCHEY

MR. OSCAR MAY

MR. WILLIAM RIEDEL

MR. EDWARD AUSTIN WALTON

MISS JULIA WILLIAMSON

CONTENTS

CONTENTS

DECORATIVE ART OF VICTORIA'S ERA

ALBUM 1

Of Destiny &
The Small Victoria Who Became
The Greatest Lady of the Land
Of Her Skills &
Of Those of Her Contemporaries
Of the Pretty Kickshaws
They Wrought with
Brush and Needle
Making the World to Blossom
With Their Own Flowery Handiwork
Of Samplers, Drawing Masters, Accomplishments, &
Lastly,
Of Berlin-work
All-pervasive &
All-popular

THE
PRINCESS VICTORIA

ALBUM ONE

❖

THE WORLD

OF

THE PRINCESS VICTORIA

HE gray English light falling through the lofty window filters down on a small child, busy at a table. Her pale and pretty face can scarcely be glimpsed, but the appealing curves of her bare neck and shoulders tell of great concentration. The twin ranks of her blonde curls bob and turn as she moves in rhythm with the scissors she wields, scattering snippets of gilt paper which gleam as they fall on the folds of her plain muslin frock. From among the litter of tinsel scraps, brushes, sketch-books and artists' tools—paraphernalia adored of children—she selects the paste-pot. Carefully she spreads the paste on the golden leaves she has just cut out and spaces them deliberately on the piece of work before her. This takes her entire attention.

With the application of the last clipping, the shoulders relax. The piece is now finished, and a prettily rounded arm topped with a pink puff of a sleeve displays it for the approval of a woman who stands quietly in the shadows bordering the window. The governess commends the young artist on her neatness, says she is sure the managers of the bazaar will value the donation highly, and suggests that the maker add her name to it. Reaching out impetuously, the little girl takes a gold pen from the china pen-tray. Under Lehzen's affectionate gaze, she sets her hand on the sketch in the center of the object and in beautifully formed letters signs it VICTORIA.

The handscreen—for that is what Victoria has just completed—is a popular decoration; in fact, no well-appointed mantel shelf is ever without one. Indeed, it is more than an ornament, for it serves as a graceful shield to interpose between a tender complexion and the too ardent heat of the fireplace. Victoria knew how to make all kinds of pretty trifles; "fancy ornaments" they called them. Her mother's lady-in-waiting showed her how to form small cardboard boxes and how to decorate them with her own careful paintings of flower clusters. Nothing provided a prettier container for a sentimental trinket—a lock of hair or a pressed flower—than these fragile boxes.

Overseas in the new red-brick houses of Charleston, New York, Boston, and Philadelphia, Victoria's American contemporaries, young girls of good family—the little Emmas and Marias, Penelopes and Harriets—were quite as adept as she in painting, cutting, folding and pasting. But few of their productions remain for us to examine, for these objects of frail construction in delicate materials have for the most part disappeared. Though the Emmas and Jemimas signed them in exquisite, tiny script, their graceful signatures have not been singled out by destiny. Victoria's name was imbued with a magic that has preserved to our time the bit of gilt and cardboard trivia fabricated so long ago in the old, shabby palace at Kensington by the little girl chosen by fate to become England's great queen.

When Victoria ascended the throne of England, she was almost unknown to her subjects, for she had been brought up in great simplicity and privacy. Even her name seemed an odd one to English tongues, a name borne by none of her regal predecessors, the Elizabeths and Marys and Carolines, the Charlottes and Catherines and Annes—all good English names and not at all like Alexandrina Victoria, that queer foreign combination which resulted from family bickering at her christening. Her family shortened the stately combination to "Drina," but the small girl preferred Victoria and began to use it as soon as she could print her first letters.

Her father, the Duke of Kent, brother of the Prince Regent who was soon to become George IV, seems to have had a prophetic instinct about his tiny daughter's future. Although there were several who held a prior right to the throne, the Duke, not at all unacquainted with the swift changes fate could interpose in the plans of princes, used to say to his family circle: "Take good care of the child; she may yet be Queen of England." The Duke did not live to see his prophecy come true. Before the little Drina was a year old he was no longer living, and by the time she was two, court circles had watched Death check off several other competitors to the throne. It was now quite likely that, if she lived, she would be Queen of England.

On her mother, the twice-widowed Duchess of Kent, descended the great responsibility of guarding and educating the heir to the throne. To face this task the plain-living, handsome, sensible Duchess was obliged to summon great courage. She resigned herself to living in England, a country where she was never completely at ease, for she was a German princess and her ways were German ways. Without hesitancy, she set herself to her important duty.

"The baby princess," recollected the ladies of her mother's entourage, "was a very pudgy infant." So greatly did she resemble her grandfather, George III, that with one voice they remarked, as they gazed affectionately at the fat baby waddling about: "There goes King George, in petticoats." She grew into a fair and pretty little girl adored by everyone about her in an environment almost wholly feminine, for there was neither father nor brother to add a salutary masculine touch.

Though Victoria seems to have had almost a superfluity of English uncles, all of them had gained such poor reputations that the Duchess took great care to keep her daughter away from them. Fortunately for the worried mother, her own brother, Prince Leopold of Coburg, was then living in England and could help with shrewd advice. It was he who suggested that the young Drina be kept in ignorance of her future position, so that she would remain simple and tractable. And it is generally believed that the secret was so well kept that Victoria did not learn she was to be Queen until she was eleven years old. To maintain this politically unsullied mind, the little girl was thoroughly guarded against unsupervised contacts. Until she actually be-

came Queen, she never slept anywhere but in her mother's room. When she descended the stairs someone always held her hand, and no grown-up ever spoke to her unless her mother or her governess Lehzen was present.

In Victoria's small circle, the governess was a very important personage. As plain, sharp-featured Fräulein Lehzen, daughter of a poor German pastor, she had come to England with the Duchess of Kent as governess to Feodore, the Duchess' daughter by her first marriage. When Feodore no longer needed her services, Fräulein Lehzen, whom George IV later made a baroness, was at hand to take over the supervision of the little Drina. Though at first she stood in awe of tall, thin Lehzen, Drina soon became devoted to her and later came to look on her as "her truest and best friend."

Although Lehzen was recognized as official governess, the Duchess realized that a male instructor would be necessary to guide so strong-willed a child. Before the little princess was quite four, she began the study of her ABC's with a tutor selected by her mother. This was the Reverend George Davys. As she grew older, other elderly gentlemen were added to her group of instructors. And since Duty and Obedience were written in capital letters in those days, she was soon taught the meaning of the words.

Victoria followed a schedule laid out with Germanic thoroughness and regularity. When at home she did the same thing at the same time, year in, year out. This close adherence to schedules inculcated in childhood set a pattern inflexibly maintained during her entire life. The hours set aside for diversion were apt to be lonely ones, for Drina rarely had a chance to talk to any one of her own age. To make up for the royal child's lack of playmates, her governess had to invent amusements. These were undoubtedly the quiet leisure pastimes in which all well-bred young girls were then instructed: painting little ornamental trinkets, making albums of pressed flowers, studying botany, and perhaps, as a test of endurance, even a trial at the lowly task of spinning.

If we could see today the handscreen signed by the young Victoria, it would be too modest an object to evoke the image of the sovereign of the British Empire, that imperious, stocky, unsmiling lady with the mournful upper lip—Victoria, Queen of the United Kingdom of Great Britain and Ireland, Empress of India. Yet Victoria's name became a synonym for the entire period in which she reigned. It was indeed a long period, for she was the titular head of her kingdom for sixty-four years, first as a fresh, innocent girl, then as happy wife and mother, next as disconsolate widow, and last as grandmother to practically all the then-regnant royalties. Towards the end of her reign, only the most ancient of her subjects could recall her predecessor, and it seemed as if no one could possibly take the place of the little black-clad widow.

Because she had been Queen for an incredible span of years, everything Victoria ever touched took on added importance, for she had become a symbol and her stately name a descriptive adjective. And *Victorian* was a most useful adjective to have at hand, of service to the fin-de-siècle and later generations to plaster on all manner of things they were setting aside—on certain inflexible patterns of deportment for which she had set the standard, and on certain moral attitudes which were passing in the rapidly changing world. A convenient word, too, to use in contemptuous repudiation of the vast flood of decoration, good and bad, which clung to the appointments of the generations just behind them.

Victoria's birth in 1819 and the birth of the industrial age were practically coincident. During her long life, she experienced as new and fresh marvels many things we now accept unquestioningly. Bravely she travelled on the railroad at a time when it was called "the steam demon" and when transportation by this method was such a novelty that her coachman, as a matter of form, insisted that he be allowed to mount the engine to make-believe he was driving. And this he did, dressed in scarlet livery, white gloves and all.

In her era the Atlantic Cable spanned the ocean; electricity brightened life, as did the telephone; the people received the ballot, and Great Britain reached its highest industrial as well as imperial development. The world changed more and more rapidly, but during all its speedy mutations Victoria presented to the whole world an example of character and dignity not often found on thrones. The Crown was again respected.

Victoria lived—in so far as her august position would permit—a private life of the greatest simplicity and domesticity; and as the fast-changing world gave no guarantee that her children would occupy in later life the same positions to which they were born, she had them taught to trust in themselves. Her four sons worked in earnest with the carpenters, and her five daughters learned to cook and to garden and were instructed in the useful and ornamental crafts as well.

In 1876, in order to commemorate the first century of American Independence, a great exhibition was held in Philadelphia. To the Centennial—as it was familarly known—the Queen of England consigned two exhibits, both the work of her own hands. Her personal contribution to the field of art was a group of etchings; to the crafts she sent two linen napkins, the flax of which she had spun long ago. The latter were indeed a quaint offering to be made by England's Queen to an exhibition based on the industrial progress of the world during her reign, but they may have been meant to convey a subtle lesson to a period which was rapidly shucking off many of the homespun virtues exemplified by the spinning wheel.

The life of the early Victorian woman was a curiously secluded one. Her horizon was sharply limited and she could do little to widen it. Shut in behind a stern wall of conventions, hypocrisies and pruderies, women neither expected nor were permitted much freedom of movement. Before the days of railroads they stayed tranquilly at home with their needles. As the day of the sewing machine had not dawned, everyone was taught the sewing techniques—from the highest lady of fashionable circles to the poorest peasant fortunate enough to possess one needle. Even the high position for which Victoria was being groomed did not exempt her from this practice. In the rigid schedule of instructions planned for the education of the ten-year-old princess, every Thursday from three to four was allotted to a charming combination of studies—to "read poetry aloud and needlework." There is extant today a large collection of the Queen's dolls, many of which were dressed entirely by the small Victoria. Early nineteenth-century instruction did not want children to look upon the needle as an instrument associated wholly with work and they were encouraged to use it also in their play.

Picnic on the Wissahickon. 1844. By American artist, W. Croome. Though this romantic spot is still used for the same purpose, ball-playing damsels in shorts have replaced poke-bonneted crinolines, and shouts supplant the garland-making and flute-playing.

In the pre-technological age, the education of the average girl still lumbered along a path that was already well trodden down in the eighteenth century. As customs, tastes and methods then were slow to change, no one saw any particular reason to execute a hasty right-about-face in matters well tested by time. The basis of formal instruction was, of course, the three well-known R's; even in the simplest schools children were taught to read (clearly, it was hoped) and to write beautifully. If girls failed to reach proficiency in the third R, lack of skill in arithmetic was considered of slight importance in females; they handled but few accounts. Beyond this elementary instruction, the only kind of "polite and finished education" obtainable for girls was that offered by Young Ladies' Seminaries. Courses in these establishments consisted chiefly in the study of "Accomplishments" and not much else. So old-fashioned does the term "an accomplished young woman" (that once indubitable stamp of high praise!) seem today that we have difficulty in grasping the importance it once held in the lives of all genteel young ladies. Sports and athletic achievements, then completely unthought of, now take up the time of the young person who, a century ago, would have been decorously applying herself to the instruction offered by embroidery teacher and by painting, music, French, and dancing masters. But applying herself not too intently, for no one expected to acquire more than a smattering of the arts; any really sound appreciation would have been deplored as an indication of decidedly unfeminine tendencies. And there was nothing that the average fashionable maiden dreaded more than to be called a "blue-stocking" or "blue"—the then derisive term for an educated woman.

Though they avoided really intensive study, young ladies set great store by their accomplishments and kept up the requisite practice hours long after they dropped every other pretense to mental exercise for these, unlike hobbies, were communal assets. A hobby was of value only to oneself and could be abandoned when it no longer held one's interest; an accomplishment, on the other hand, made one a factor in the social life of one's circle.

The early nineteenth century was a period which was obliged to depend for the greater part of its amusements on the performances of amateurs. From the present-day viewpoint, life was then incredibly dull. Except in the few cities there were no theatrical performances, no large social gatherings, no public places of entertainment. Victorian group diversions in which women could share were characterized by only slight activity. At home, one could read, talk, or "recline" in seemly fashion in the pleasant summer shade. If one's horizon became unbearably constricted it was possible in the more affluent circles to widen it by driving, riding, or boating. Sometimes a party would set out on that most adventurous of all Victorian pastimes, the picnic. These were occasions often filled with gay accidents which were the result of the inappropriate costumes in which the feminine portion of the picnic ventured forth—those fashionable crinolines which, on these rural excursions, were so awkward and mirth-provoking.

For persons with even the slenderest scientific bent, there was always botanizing. And no young woman ever passed up the chance to display her accomplishments in drawing and painting out-of-doors. The pursuit of these arts permitted a discreet retirement (even in those well-chaperoned days) from the main body of the social group in order to search for appealing subjects. A delicate maiden, sketchbook in hand, and a young gentleman bending admiringly over her work, composed a familiar and attractive picture.

Evening entertainments at home were given over to examining portfolios of prints and drawings, and—if the company were lively—to charades. The chief emphasis, however, was laid on music, for amateur music was then so much a part of the social fabric that it ranked in first place as entertainment; everyone came to social gatherings prepared to contribute his or her bit to the festivities. Therefore the Victorian young lady devoted much time to her musical studies. She learned how to stand gracefully by the piano as she sang one of the fashionable ballads, or to take her part in a duet. And how they loved "duettes"! With the skittishness of all amateur performers, they would let themselves be coaxed to the piano, where (after much protestation that they hardly knew a note of the selection, having just received it from the music master) they dreamily reeled off a piece which they had been practicing for months against such a contingency. And no matter how far they were from perfect, these exhibitions were always enthusiastically applauded by our polite ancestors, whose standards had not been established either by professional performances or by the present-day machine attenuations of the arts of virtuosi.

In that more contemplative era, the playing of the harp might almost have been ranked among the decorative arts, so pleasing a picture did the musician and her tall, golden instrument compose. The harp was in itself a flaunting decoration in any drawing room, a signet of both wealth and culture. As an advertisement of these intangibles, the harp was an accessory furnishing rarely overlooked by the nouveaux riches.

To know how to dance was considered another of the necessary "accomplishments," though opportunities to indulge in the practice were rare. Unless a local ball was organized about once a year, the skill the well-chaperoned young ladies had acquired lay buried. But dances and parties were uncommon diversions, to be viewed pleasurably long in advance and happily long in retrospect. To fill the interminable stretches of time in which no such entrancing distractions occurred, women and girls of the leisure classes were compelled to devise many pastimes in which they could lose themselves. For these they turned to "artistic" accomplishments, in addition to work with the needle. Even within their circumscribed sphere, women managed to extract a certain amount of competitive pleasure from needlework, outvying each other in fineness of execution. Occasionally, to demonstrate really superior abilities, women were stimulated to produce amazing tours-de-force. Needleworked copies of engravings fall into this class of marvels. With a startling fidelity the intricate lines of an engraving were reproduced on white satin in the most minute of black and gray stitches. So precise was the execution that it takes the closest examination to reveal the substitution of the silk stitches for the dots and lines of the engraver.

An interminable amount of time also went into the making of elegant knicknacks. It was an expenditure which women could always justify, as the financial outlay was negligible; many were put together from otherwise useless scraps of material. Such frivolities then constituted—in fact, still do—the type of article on which charity bazaars are based. At a time when there were no great department stores or shops, with their endless variety of choice, the *charity bazaar* was an important feature in the economic scheme and a dependable place in which to purchase both decorative and useful bits of handiwork. Nineteenth-century women, because of their limited opportunities for outside social contacts, doted on bazaars which offered them a triple attraction: a concentration of all the charms of a social function, of a shopping excursion, and of a trip to an exhibition. Easily entertained, women derived excitement from examining what other women had donated. Immersed in a warm flood of charitable emotions, they bought each other's gewgaws.

English bazaar managers were always elated when they could display a piece of work made by a member of the Royal Family. In Georgian and Victorian days the feminine members of these august realms donated many specimens of their handiwork. One of George

III's daughters, Victoria's Aunt Mary, "who amused herself daily with her needle," contributed her work so liberally to all charitable affairs that a writer of the day, musing on the subject of royal charitableness in general, said that "thousands in the humbler ranks of life" had reason to be grateful for her generosity. Accompanied by Lehzen, the little Victoria was permitted to visit a charity bazaar in order to purchase some Christmas gifts; this visit stood out as an unusual and exciting occasion in her routine life. Since she knew how to make fashionable trifles, she undoubtedly donated to such endeavors other pieces of her handwork besides the handscreen previously mentioned. A watch-case of yellow silk embroidered with pansies was cherished decades later because it had been worked by the great Queen Victoria when she was a fourteen-year-old girl.

American ladies were not behind their British sisters in enthusiastic support of indoor fairs. In 1828, the visiting Englishwoman, Mrs. Trollope, in her *Domestic Manners of the Americans,* presents a picture of such a charitable group at work: a delicately satirical portrait of the type of eleemosynary needlework then indulged in by ladies of the best American circles—Philadelphians, in this instance.

> Her free black coachman announces to her free black footman that the carriage waits. She steps into it, and gives the word, "Drive to the Dorcas Society." Her footman stays at home to clean the knives, but her coachman can trust his horses while he opens the carriage door, and his lady, not being accustomed to a hand or an arm, gets out very safely without, though one of her own is occupied by a work-basket, and the other by a large roll of all those indescribable matters which ladies take as offerings to Dorcas Societies.
>
> She enters the parlour appropriated for the meeting, and finds seven other ladies, very like herself . . . she presents her contribution, which is accepted with a gentle circular smile, and her parings of broadcloth, her ends of ribbon, her gilt paper, and her minikin pins, are added to the parings of broadcloth, the ends of ribbon, the gilt paper, and the minikin pins with which the table is already covered; she also produces from her basket three readymade pincushions, four ink-wipers, seven paper matches, and a paste-board watch-case; these are welcomed with acclamations, and the youngest lady present deposits them carefully on shelves, amid a prodigious quantity of similar articles. She then produces her thimble, and asks for work; it is presented to her, and the eight ladies all stitch together for some hours. Their talk is of priests and of missions; of the profits of the last sale, of their hopes for the next . . .

Many articles for bazaars were made by small girls who devoted much of their play time to sewing on reticules, bags, pincushions and needlebooks for these worthy purposes. To labor over such trifles came under the heading of "amusing works"—a term seemingly devised by grown-ups to encourage juvenile needlewomen to apply themselves to the production of minor objects which might, according to the undemanding standards of the day, have a faint claim to usefulness. In this class of needle frippery, pincushions and needlebooks take first place. The age had a passion for them, completely incomprehensible to present-day woman, no longer dependent on the army of pins which were once a part of the ritual of Victorian dressing. In that artless era such knickknacks ranked as most appropriate gifts, and no one was of such consequence as to be above receiving one. Victoria records in her childhood diary that she gave her governess "a white and gold pincushion," and, in the entry on her sixteenth birthday, she definitely states that her maid, Frances, gave her a pincushion of her own making.

These minutiae of needlecraft were usually flat, thin affairs conceived in many forms and styles, each characterized by the same underlying idea—a playful resemblance to something other than an obvious four-square pincushion. Found to be most delightful were those which concealed their function most successfully. Such whimsies might be shaped like a heart, a bellows, a swan, lyre, or guitar. The pin heads protruded from the edge of the piece in a series of points, forming a bit of added decoration. Inserting pins in this ordered fashion was considered to offer "a few minutes of amusing occupation for a little girl"—an engaging commentary on the precision then expected of the soft, fumbling fingers of the young.

But not even while "amusing" herself in this kind of play could the young worker escape moral instruction. As she worked out elevating sentiments in cross-stitch, the pious preachments were injected with needlepricks. While "Dieu me voit" and "Bless the Lord O my Soul" were Victorian girlish favorites for pincushions, a virtuous charge of an English orphanage stuck to her task until she had completed a trifle announcing the highly approved sentiment: "Religion is our Guide and Industry our Support." And one admiring young British needlewoman celebrated her young sovereign's accession by making a pincushion shaped like a bellows, the tube of which is a bodkin inscribed "Victoria born 24th May crowned 28th June 1838."

As we have seen by the handscreen, the young Victoria displayed considerable skill in drawing. When she was ten her drawing master was an elderly gentleman, Mr. Richard Westall, R.A., whose paintings, tepid as they now seem, were then much admired. Mr. Westall has left us a delightful painting of his young pupil engrossed in outdoor sketching. In a sense, this was a prophetic painting, for it shows Victoria engaged in a pastime which was to provide her much pleasure during most of her lifetime. At Windsor Castle there are hundreds of the Queen's sketchbooks filled with impressions of her travels.

In Victoria's childhood, education in the graphic arts differed but little from that offered to young ladies in the eighteenth century. To acquire an accomplishment the age did not consider a decided talent at all necessary. Private masters were on hand not only for princesses but also for commoners, ready to impart a practical knowledge of any or all arts. The drawing master was frequently not of the highest standing in his profession, but this was a comparatively unimportant matter, for most of his feminine pupils made but minor demands on his teaching abilities; generally they regarded the graphic arts merely as routines by means of which they meant to attain tangible decorative, and not intangible cultural, results. Consequently all they expected of an instructor was to be shown the techniques which would produce ornamental effects in current fashion, whether they were the latest methods of decorating a table or the newest tricks in making a wall decoration.

While all Young Ladies' Seminaries had their drawing masters, there were also private schools in the larger cities whose curricula were devoted wholly to painting and needlework. In the hinterland of America, there were persons who travelled about from place to place giving instructions in the same matters. In the ranks of these itinerant professors could be found both men and women, the latter obviously of a much more adventurous turn than the rest of their stay-at-home sex. From these peripatetic instructors ambitious girls in tiny villages learned how to make their chefs-d'oeuvre on velvet, their flower pieces, their brilliant red and green birds and their remarkable Scripture scenes in needlework. In their eagerness to apply themselves to fashionable artistic pursuits, these American girls were only following the cultural pattern set by the mother country. For no matter how stridently the young United States repudiated the political leadership of England, it was still dependent on her—at least for the first half of the nineteenth century—for guidance in literature and the arts. Later on, as it developed its own cultural

standards, the ability to draw and paint was not considered of paramount importance in an American young person's education. But in Great Britain, until recently, certain types of English ladies with characteristic national tenacity continued to view the practice of the graphic arts as a light and genteel pastime—an "accomplishment" which they pursued with unabashed persistence even in milieus frequented by professional artists. Doubtless they derived pleasure—though perhaps subconsciously—from the thought that in following their placid diversion they were carrying on an occupation long favored by their great Queen.

Early-Victorian young ladies kept their drawing masters busy. Equipped with the necessary materials and the necessary virtues of patience and docility, they flocked to classes. The drawing master supplied not only the technical methods but also the pictorial subject matter. With minds firmly fixed on the decorative possibilities of their endeavors they learned how to make figure drawings, portraits, landscapes, allegorical subjects; and, if these were found too troublesome for the modicum of ability they brought to the task, there were always innumerable and less demanding flower subjects which could be copied. The maidens were eclectic in their choice of medium; crayons, pencil, watercolor and even oils were tried—though the last medium was shunned by those who valued the delicacy of their hands or affected to be overcome by the pungent odor of turpentine.

On these genteel copyings the touch of the drawing master's hand was everywhere discernable. No one, least of all his pupils, raised the slightest objection to this professional embellishment of the pieces; indeed, it was something they all looked forward to in order that their feeble efforts could be made presentable and "fit to frame." From the very first brush stroke to the last meticulously placed accent by the master's hand, the pupil was conscious of sharing in the production of a "work of art" destined for a particular spot on the parlor wall. There it would grace the position chosen for it by an ambitious mother (in all probability the wife of a rising merchant) quite aware that nothing was more "comme-il-faut" for parlor decoration than a group of paintings executed by one's talented young daughters. Since such a woman was usually eager that her daughters obtain all the cultural advantages of those a grade or two above them in society, she always saw to it that they received instruction in all the "art accomplishments."

9

Philadelphia — L. A. Godey & Co. No. 112 Chesnut Street op. Post office

Ornaments for Ladies fancy Works.

As long as the general public held to the idea that the study of art was chiefly a young lady's "accomplishment," designed to enhance her social position, the professionals in the ranks of the drawing masters had hard going and the charlatans throve. Occasionally one of the gifted professionals would become so irritated by the attitude of his feminine pupils that he was provoked into expressing himself in print. One of these perturbed men, John Rubens Smith, in a handsome book on art instruction prepared in 1822, gives evidence of having been sorely tried. In his preface Smith could not restrain himself from making some pungent comments about pupils "who think that the art of painting is as simple as the art of dying [dyeing] and have no more difficulty in selecting from the preceptor's portfolio the picture that is to be painted than in choosing the garment they will wear from a tailor's book of patterns. To such contracted notions," he continues, "are to be attributed the many outrages on taste, science and common sense, we meet, in parlors, hung round with large pictures in gorgeous frames, furnishing by their confused jumble of prismatic colors, a glaring evidence of misguided talents."

The possibilities of drawing and painting for the domestic phases of decoration were endless. In the pre-machine age skilled artisans were kept so busy fabricating the major objects of daily use that production and decoration of the minor ones was usually left to women. Girls used their "accomplishments" to decorate all manner of workboxes, memorandum books and portfolios, letter-racks, small useless tables, and watch stands. These they painted with flowers and scrolls in a style then known as "Japan painting," purchasing or even renting the designs at the same "fancy shops" which supplied the undecorated articles. Most of the techniques which were concocted principally to pass time have been consigned to oblivion: such decorative potterings as winding bright-colored silks in intricate patterns on reels of different shapes. And no one today would ever dream of laboriously scorching paper in formal designs, then of further ornamenting it with flowers and cut gilt paper. In truth, no present-day pulp paper could be submitted to such treatment by fire and emerge (as did the tough rag papers) with enough substance left to be used for any artistic project.

Other early techniques, long neglected, have of late been revived, for they have been found adaptable to contemporary materials and decorative uses. Reverse painting on glass is one of these old-time crafts of which examples can be purchased today, as can certain lampshades ornamented in a manner already familiar in Victoria's childhood. Then it was called "Embossing on Cardboard." To achieve this old-time "embossing," a series of slanting incisions was made on paper, prepared especially for the purpose, with a sharp knife held obliquely; the cuts, arranged in ornamental fashion, raised the face of the paper slightly to make a shadowy decoration. Today the cuts are actual slits through which the light of the electric bulb gently and decoratively filters.

But no matter how much ornamental handwork was turned out by earnest ladies, these knickknacks were but the froth on the main wave of Victorian decorative preoccupation—a feverish devotion to a form of hand-worked textile known as "Berlin-work." By the time the wave ran its course, it had almost succeeded in covering nearly everything in its path with a woolly layer of this textile of tedious make. So widespread was the taste for it, so monstrous some of the ideas executed—with un-believable patience—that the term "Berlin-work" came to carry an opprobrium from which the Victorian era can never wholly disengage itself. While women were all a-flutter over canvas-work, crewel-work, or worsted-work (as it was also called), one notes the amusement they managed to derive from its various phases, and the fun they could extract from making repeated shopping trips with an equally interested friend to turn over the fascinating portfolio of patterns. The choice of subject was a vital matter, since a piece would be so long under way. Should they decide on that great favorite, dear Sir Edwin Landseer's "Bolton Abbey in the Olden Time," or on one of the many Scripture subjects which everyone always admired? Most of them frowned on Leonardo da Vinci's "Last Supper" as too intricate; its many figures presented such difficulties that it was at-tempted only by the superlatively ambitious. "Byron at the Seashore," "Robert Burns," "Young Lochinvar," "Laertes and Ophelia," were only a few of the favorites which young ladies worked out as stool or ottoman covers.

After the wool-work mania subsided in the large cities (at least in "the better classes"), it became epi-demic in the rural districts, where supplies were difficult to obtain. Girls remote from metropolitan sources tor-mented city friends to "match crewels," a time-killing occupation productive of overwhelming boredom unless the shopper was someone who shared the mania.

Miss Eliza Leslie, of Philadelphia, the outstanding woman writer of the period, always kept a sharp eye on the foibles of her fellow woman and was moved to com-ment on what she considered the "uncouth and absurd things which were the product of all this waste of eye-sight; sheer and idle folly!" As evidence of the engross-ing quality of the craze, she noted its progress in 1843, in a town whose name she omitted from her account: "Dogs, parrots, leopards, and indeed most animals are rather out of fashion. Flowers and fruit are quite gone by. All ————— seems to have taken chiefly to *people*. Nothing else will go down. Napoleon and Victoria are worked by the same persons, without distinction of party." Genuine votaries sat all day in silence before their frames, counting stitches, arranging colors, an-noyed at any interruption lest they make an error when peering in alternation from "a coarse and ridiculous picture on paper to one still coarser and more ridiculous on canvas," as Miss Leslie put it.

Until the nineteenth century, worsted-work was an aristocratic pastime only. Ladies executed pieces for furniture coverings and other useful and decorative pur-poses. Designs for such pieces were based on conven-tionalized forms and were drawn with a pen directly on the canvas.

The quality of the result was dependent on the artis-tic abilities of the needlewoman. For help in making selections of colors she had no other guide except her own taste. The technique used was one she had learned on her first samplers, which were of two kinds: practical and ornamental. On the practical sampler the small girl gained knowledge of methods and stitches needed in plain and fancy needlework. This was a laboriously acquired skill, practiced both in school and at home, for in those days educational precepts were well sup-ported by home co-operation, and plenty of volunteer mistresses were always about to supplement school instruction. In those days the girl-child was constantly admonished to sit up straight; to learn her tables or spelling; to practice her needlework; to sew on her shirt.

To finish a sampler put a powerful strain on childish patience. It is a touching evidence of the diligence then expected of children that so many samplers have come down to us, complete to the last, often crooked, letter. Occasionally we find some which were never finished. Today we can only speculate why they were left in that state. Was it through indifference, a tolerated rebellious-ness, or the premature death of the infant needlewoman? It must be sadly acknowledged that, in those days of youthful mortality, far too many young sampler workers did not live long enough to complete their pieces.

Grown up, the average sampler maker made little use of the cross-stitch sampler technique except to mark her modest linens. Only in well-to-do circles, as we have previously seen, was it used for broad ornamental pur-poses. Around 1810, however, this form of decorative art expression suddenly changed; no longer was it to be a technique reserved only for upper-class ladies. The ambitious young females belonging to the rapidly growing middle classes suddenly altered all this. Not unaware that they lacked cultural advantages, they were seized with a great urge to improve not only them-

Berlin-work patterns were engraved designs laid out on squared paper. Each tiny square, interpreted on canvas as a stitch, was colored in by hand—tedious work for which very little was paid.

selves but their surroundings. If it were possible and money could buy it, they, too, were going to share in the esoteric occupations of the class above them. This meant, among other things, decorative needlework, i.e. crewel-work.

To assist these uneducated needlewomen, the art of worsted-work had to become democratized. As they had no inherent taste which would enable them to select color and depict form, patterns had to be devised which would designate every tint. Equipped with one of these colored guides, canvas, the requisite number of matching skeins of shaded wools, and the ability to count, the worker could start out and be reasonably assured of the result, a matter formerly doubtful. On the shoulders of a print-seller in Berlin can be placed the responsibility for the overwhelming flood of Victorian wool-work, for it was he who worked out a method by which accurate patterns for canvas-work or worsted-work could be turned out cheaply. From the city of origin, they were always known as "Berlin-work patterns" and needlework based on them was almost invariably called "Berlin-work."

The print-seller's idea was only one of many bridges between the era of pure handcraft and the machine age. Although he used a press for part of the process, he depended on skilled colorists to complete the patterns, for no printing processes of that era, or indeed of any

other, could execute color work with the precision demanded by the eager purchasers of these working diagrams. So great was the demand for these patterns that the original enterprise quickly became very successful, a success which stimulated many other studios of *"Muster-Maler"* (pattern-painters) to set up in business. Not only German but other European industries expanded with this growth. Gainful employment for women increased with this fad, for they were now hired to fill in the designs on certain pieces, leaving only the background to be completed by the purchaser. These partially worked pieces became the foundation of a trade which, still operative today, allows European and even Chinese homeworkers the chance to earn a pittance to sustain themselves.

No serious objection could be raised to patterns which limited themselves to motifs already traditional: birds, flowers, and graceful arabesques. For several centuries women had found them aesthetically satisfactory. But when it was discovered that the technique of Berlin-work was capable of reproducing—even in its unavoidably stylized manner—all sorts of pictorial figure subjects and copies of famous paintings, the foundation was established for the future lack of esteem. After manufacturers obligingly dyed wools in most delicious gradations so that a needlewoman might make a tentative approach to the subtleties of color in the painting she was attempting to copy, women no longer regarded canvas-work as a textile admirable for covering chair and footstool. Instead, they insisted that the making of needlework pictures be considered one of the fine arts— a "sister art to painting"—and needlewomen looked upon themselves as nothing less than artists, plying a needle rather than a brush.

By 1850 the craze for Berlin-work pictures was so widespread that contemporary purists (for even in the midst of Victorian tastelessness there were some who maintained high aesthetic standards) began to rail against work which they justly considered to serve no useful purpose and, moreover, to show a woeful lack of artistic discrimination. The critics' jeremiads went unheeded; a quarter of a century later, we find them still stating this opinion. But to little purpose, for this business of supplying wools and designs was a profitable one which German industry had no intention of relinquishing. England, however, attempted to offer some competition. At the Great Exhibition held in 1851, she was displaying needlework patterns stamped in colors on the canvas itself, a method still in use. This innovation did away with the necessity for counting each minute square, though it demanded of the worker a bit more in the way of judgment. However, as it was a novelty, it was not adopted at first with sufficient alacrity to displace the German paper patterns. So the Berlin studios continued to load both Europe and America with endless gaudy designs, planned to suit every level of taste, expenditure, and competence in execution.

The day finally arrived when women gave up woolwork. This break was undoubtedly the direct result of new standards of taste, and it indubitably coincided with the wider opportunities opening up for women in social, educational and economic life. When the means of gaining personal financial independence and self-respect were offered to those who, longing for it, had instead bent with sad intensity over embroidery frames, Berlin-work pieces gradually disappeared from women's lives, never again to inspire the absorbed interest they once commanded.

Of recent years, Berlin-work (today known as "petit-point" or "needlepoint") has been revived, as it is recognized as an historically accurate textile to use with Victorian or Colonial antiques. But no one today attacks the piece with either the skill or the fervor once brought to it by all the craft's devotees. The contemporary feminine approach is both tepid and casual. Having severed themselves from the embroidery frame because it restricts mobility, women put in a stitch here and there—on country-club porches, on ocean liners, or in their own living rooms. Today few do more than fill in backgrounds on pieces imported with the ornamental details completely worked out. Nineteenth-century needlewomen who vaunted themselves on their ability to execute subjects of the greatest intricacy would be apt to regard the achievements of their descendants as evidence of sad incompetency. But the very fact that women today even attempt this time-honored needlework is a strong testimony to the survival of the pleasure all women once derived from their application to "this most elegant of female accomplishments."

BERLIN-WORK PATTERNS

Much Victorian handwork was based on copying designs laid out on squared paper. Famous paintings underwent this stylization, with scenes of mediaeval romance winning particular favor. "Franklin" is obviously designed to catch the American eye. To complete any of these large pieces took exquisite patience. Berlin-work, however, was not beyond the abilities of the disciplined schoolgirl, for there is a "Franklin" extant which is marked, "Presented by the pupils of the female department of Public School No. 2, Williamsburgh, N. Y. August 1, 1851."

Courtesy, Metropolitan Museum of Art

Parrot and Fruit in Sculptured Wool. Based, too, on Berlin patterns, this technique, long in style for cushions and fire screens, was called "raised work" or "reed stitch."
Courtesy, Index of American Design, National Gallery of Art

Beaded Bag, 1831. Copied from Berlin patterns, a bead substituting for each stitch.
Courtesy, Index of American Design, National Gallery of Art

From the collection of the Cooper Union Museum

SAMPLERS DURING VICTORIA'S GIRLHOOD

Sentimentality rather than piety began to infuse sampler design. Berlin patterns introduced less stylized buildings and a more naturalistic landscape. Sheep dominated the rural scene on samplers, and on needleworked pictures sheep took their place in tender family groupings. In the field of ceramics, they practically crowded out other fauna.

Above. English Elizabeth Parry worked out a View of Conway Bridge in 1836, but in general, Berlin patterns tended to obliterate such national characteristics in needlework.

Right. Decoration, executed in tiny beads by Mexican Dolores for her mother. 1836.

Lower right. French sampler. "Sophie Arcier. 1838."

From the collection of the Cooper Union Museum

Above and right. Courtesy, Metropolitan Museum of Art

Above. Christiana Baird's piece typifies sampler composition in the 1830's and 1840's. Probably English, but girls elsewhere were turning out similar examples.

Courtesy, Index of American Design, National Gallery of Art

PAINTED DECORATIONS

The accomplishment of painting was turned to both ornamental and pseudo-practical purposes. For decades, classical and scriptural scenes shared honors with bowls of fruit and flowers, all executed finickingly on white cotton velvet.

Courtesy, Index of American Design, National Gallery of Art

Below. Handscreens, set in pairs on mantels, were particular show-pieces for painting skills. Used to fend off heat, they were made of cardboard, centred with painted flowers or landscapes. The screen was bordered with shaded, gilt-paper scrollings and was mounted on handles sold for the purpose. The eagle, symbolizing the belligerent patriotism of the time, marks this piece as American.

Mantel Figurines, cut from thin wood and brightly painted, concealed holders for spills. The British Grenadier, a miniature, is copied from a life-sized cut-out, painted by Major Andre.

From the author's collection

Courtesy, Free Library of Philadelphia

In Victoria's girlhood, ornamental decoration was at its best on presentation pages of "Keepsakes" and "Gift Books." To design these pages was not beneath the dignity of prominent artists, and they were executed by engravers of equal rank. *Above*. Presentation page from "Friendship's Offering." London, 1834. *Below*. From "The American Juvenile Keepsake," 1840. 2¾ x 3½ inches. The tiniest gift book reserved space for owner's and donor's names.

Eagle. Woodcut. An essential in the stock of American typefounders. Philadelphia, 1849.

Above. Engraved Advertisement, 1820. A sample of the firm's work.

Courtesy, Free Library of Philadelphia

Decoration from Engraved Title Page. From Heath's *Book of Beauty*. London, 1838. A fine example of early Victorian design based on a traditional conception, The dawning of the era's eclectic tastes can be perceived, however, in the few frivolous details which are introduced into the classic pattern.

ALBUM 2

Of Royal Love &
Of Virtuous Royal Family Life
Made Known to All
By Facile Lithograph &
Solemn Steel Engraving
Of Scotland, Balmoral &
The Able Prince Consort
Of Landseer & Painting &
The Monarch of the Glen
Of Iron Stags on Lawns &
Of Stuffed Stags in Halls
Of Greyhounds on Gates &
Tartan-covered Sofas
Of the Botanical Marvel
With its Queenly Appellation
The "Victoria Regia"

ALBUM TWO

⚘

THE WORLD OF
VICTORIA AND ALBERT

"Thursday, 10th October [1839]

"It was with some emotion that I beheld Albert,—who is beautiful . . . really quite charming, and so excessively handsome, such beautiful blue eyes, an exquisite nose, and such a pretty mouth with delicate moustachios and slight but very slight whiskers; a beautiful figure, broad at the shoulders and a fine waist."

N words set down for only herself to see, in the mingled chronicle of her daily affairs, Queen Victoria of England admits to the pages of her morocco-bound diary that she has fallen in love. Albert, her cousin, seems even more remarkable than when she first met him. Then he had come a-visiting with his brother and his father, her uncle, the Duke of Saxe-Coburg-Gotha. To refresh her memories, she turns to her earlier diaries. Yes, here is the page: Wednesday, 18th May, 1836. Albert's first visit. They had played and sung and they had drawn and she had commented on the goodness, sweetness, and intelligence of his expression. But she finds that she was then equally impressed with a gift from her Uncle Ernest: a delightful tame Lory [parrot], much "larger than Mamma's grey parrot" with the most beautiful plumage of scarlet, blue, brown, yellow, and purple. How very young she had been—both the cousin and the parrot seemed equally attractive! But till then, she had met so few people her own age.

"It is quite a pleasure to look at Albert when he gallops and valses, he does it so beautifully," she writes, tilting her head, with its neatly arranged cylinder of fine plaits, over her diary. Indeed, she had had an excellent opportunity the evening before to feast her eyes on her future husband while she was obliged, because of the restrictions imposed by etiquette on her high station, to sit conversing during the more lively fashionable dances. Not for her was the fascinating polka.

Several days later she confided in her Prime Minister, Lord Melbourne, that she had made up her mind to marry Albert. The announcement must have come as a relief to the august gentlemen who surrounded her, for two years previously, when the eighteen-year-old girl became Queen, she had stated she was in no haste whatever to consider marriage.

In accepting Albert, the Queen was acceding to a plan which had been formulated by her Uncle Leopold, now King of Belgium, when both she and her future husband were still in their cradles. This gentleman had shrewdly arranged the most rigorous training for his nephew, Prince Albert of Saxe-Coburg-Gotha, so that he could be vaunted as an example of shining Coburg rectitude in the face of shameful Hanoverian slackness. In a field in which six other politically eligible swains had also been entered, Albert came out ahead.

Victoria's girlhood had been passed in a very critical period in English history. Satiated with a century and a half of Hanoverian reign, the country was ready for a moral change. The citizenry, the great bulk of which was excluded from any share in the government of the country, viewed Church, Government, and Crown alike with complete and cynical detachment. Much needed political reforms, long overdue, were instituted, and the Whigs, responsible for the changes, looked for a symbol to embody their ideas of moral reconstruction for the throne. They had not far to seek, for the symbol was close at hand in the fair heir-presumptive, the young

Victoria. To the Whigs this pure, unsullied young girl was a veritable gift from heaven.

Victoria was the youngest and freshest Queen ever to be crowned. No one could have offered a greater contrast to her immediate predecessors, her Hanoverian uncles, those vain, ridiculous, selfish old men. The very public which not long before had been rioting, went into affectionate demonstrations of approval of her, delighted to have a sovereign they might once again admire. With her accession, a new tide of thought swept the country: Georgian swagger went out of date and fashions in behavior changed. The newest model, that of "Sentiment and Feeling," was introduced, trimmed with modesty and also, unfortunately, with those other characteristics of prudery and hypocrisy with which the era would become forever associated. When Victoria mounted the throne, a standard inscribed with the middle-class virtues—respectability, duty, industry, sobriety, and morality—was raised over the Court, never to be lowered during the sixty-four years of her occupancy. From now on, the nineteenth century was to be careful of its manners.

It was 1840 when she allied herself in marriage with the virtuous and high-minded Albert. Victoria and Albert constituted a model couple. The middle classes adored them—for did they not typify that precious thing, a "love match," on which all doted? In the Royal Family's happy domesticity, the public could see a reflection of their own lives—somewhat heightened as was natural by the royal surroundings, but not to such a degree that kinship was non-existent. With the same regularity with which he visited the ordinary home, the stork brought babies to the royal residence. The public, peering through the railings round Buckingham Palace, were delighted when they could catch a glimpse of the Queen and Prince engrossed, exactly as were any middle-class parents, in their first baby. Those not fortunate enough actually to see this pleasant domestic picture could purchase many charming prints of the Royal Family. One of these color prints, obviously designed to publicize the bourgeois virtues of the Victorian court, depicts a heart-warming family scene. The dignified Prince Consort is down on all fours; the tiny Prince of Wales brandishes a whip as he tugs at the Prince Consort's cravat, while his equally small sister, the Princess Royal, holds fast to a dainty garland of roses flung round her royal father's neck. The Queen, who takes her proper Victorian place in this most unroyal

While Landseer (left) painted engaging scenes of Royal Family life, Winterhalter supplied the Court painter's expected glamour.

grouping, stands modestly in the background, balancing the family's newest member—a long-skirted doll-like infant—on her adored husband's back.

Constant recent improvements in printing processes permitted wider distribution of these pleasant pictures of royal family life. Without these new inventions in the graphic arts, without speedier means of transportation, publicity for the recent revolution in social attitudes could not have proceeded so effectively.

Before these mechanical improvements were made, printing was a slow and costly process. Several methods were used, all dependent on engravings made on wood or copper plates. Neither material was subjected to any but the most modest printing demands. Prints were naturally monochromes; if color was desired, it was added laboriously by hand. People who subscribed in advance to plates sometimes waited years to receive them, a delay which began to irritate the public who were now clamoring for pictures; the tempo of the world was speeding up, and leisurely methods of printing, adequate in the past, were due for a change. It came, in the shape of a brand-new process known as lithography or chemical stone printing. This invention of a Bavarian, Alois Senefelder, burst on the world in the early part of the nineteenth century, and its advent revo-

lutionized the graphic arts. The lithographic process provided faultless reproductions of an artist's drawings and was so simple in its essentials that from now on, anyone who could draw could produce a plate from which prints could be taken practically at once.

As the engravers, niggling at their costly copper plates, would not give way to this printing upstart without a struggle, a new invention—that of plating the soft copper with steel—fortunately made it possible for them to carry on their eventually-to-be-outmoded trade for some time longer. Through this invention of an American, Jacob Perkins, a much finer and shallower work was possible, and a far greater output of prints. These impressions, known as "steel engravings," were the height of Victorian pictorial elegance. Nothing so definitely and so promptly marked one a dignified member of respectable society as the possession of a group of them, handsomely framed. And no novelty was more welcome than the steel engravings which shortly made their appearance in all the best American publications.

The introduction of mechanically applied color to these monochrome processes was much slower in coming. As in other transitions from the handcraft era to that of the machine, methods used in earlier days were in part carried over. Any examination of publications destined for the community at large will disclose that, in the 1840's and 1850's, while the new has been adopted, earlier methods are still doing business at the same old stand. In magazines such as "Godey's," the fashion inserts were copperplate line engravings, entirely tinted by hand. In addition to these highly valued fashion plates, there were also handsome steel engravings and mezzotints, together with the first timidly drawn lithographs of flowers and birds, their delicate tones strengthened with hand-applied watercolors. For the really important illustrations of the best fiction, publishers had recourse to wood-engraving of varying artistic excellence. But we find, in addition, an occasional quaint woodcut—obviously from the hands of a cheaper craftsman—used to illustrate a minor feature. But even the homeliest woodcut was so tedious to execute that when, in 1842, the new weekly, the *Illustrated London News,* began to strew its text not only with the ordinary run of sketches but with actual pictures of *current events,* it was considered an exceedingly bold undertaking. Occasionally a reader would make a criticism of the portrayal of an event in which he or she had shared. The magazine was sensitive to letters which pointed out such inaccuracies, and felt, editorially, that the public should withhold adverse criticism about so impressive an achievement. And as we, who are completely under the sway of the camera and the half-tone screen, have no comprehension whatever of what then went into the making of a supposedly factual illustration which today seems quaintly unreal, let us range ourselves on the side of that august publication in the belief that its explanation to its public has even more value for us. With the great pride that the Victorians took in all their new inventions, their railroads and their printing presses, the *Illustrated London News* reminds its readers that the important events which the woodcuts illustrate took place "perhaps 200 or 300 miles away." Artists sketched the events on the spot, we are told, and the "sketches were sent to London, drawn on the block, engraved and printed in scarcely more time than was required to *travel* the same distance about 100 years ago!" Furthermore: "In order to gratify public curiosity, the engravers sat up two or three nights and"—the publishers remark, with the severity which seems then to have been an editorial prerogative—"charitable and reflecting persons would excuse instead of exaggerating the presumed defects."

In 1843, in a short-lived American publication called *Miss Leslie's Magazine,* mechanically applied colors

appear for the first time on a lithographed fashion plate. Editorial comment states: "We consider this another triumph in the art of lithography."

In England a really striking improvement in color printing was produced by George Baxter which he called "polychromatic printing." Baxter was interested in supplying cheap, artistic pictures for those who could not afford to pay much for pictorial art. Knowing that such contributions to cultural uplift would of necessity have to be produced mechanically, he used an ordinary aquatint as a foundation, imposing oil color on it by means of a printing press and a series of woodblocks, each charged with a different color. Sometimes Baxter used as many as thirty blocks. Though an improvement over hand-tinting, it was still a laborious method.

As all these improvements in the printing arts were coincident with Victoria's sovereignty, they probably were the means of distributing more of her likenesses over a wider area than that of any other ruler who preceded or even any who followed her. An acute interest in the Queen's personal appearance sprang up in all corners of the globe. Many early prints of the Queen were undeniable libels. This should occasion no surprise, for accuracy of likeness was dependent on the skill of the technicians who turned out plates for the graphic processes. These men worked from original paintings or drawings for which the Queen had posed. If the engraver's artistic calibre equalled that of the original artist, his work was likely to be an accurate transcription; the caricatures are from the hands of the lesser craftsmen, and often are copies of copies. The Queen was no beauty, though the Court painters, as was their wont, heightened her best qualities and softened the others. For a factual description of the young Victoria, one turns to the American periodicals. With what appears to be a deliberate frankness, a writer in "Godey's" in 1839 describes her as "rather pretty, rather dumpy, her features a little too large, her lips open (this is not very intellectual but I can't help that)."

The Prince Consort presented a great physical contrast to the Queen: she was short and he was very tall; she was plain, he was thought extremely handsome not only by the Queen but by unprejudiced observers as well. Though the English never liked Albert's shy and stilted demeanor, he was nevertheless a flawless exemplar of the burgeoning Victorian ideal of masculine good looks. His "beautiful nose," his "very sweet mouth" and delicate whiskers—attributes which so bowled over the Princess Victoria when he came to woo

—his stately bearing, all these constituted so perfect a picture of what was then considered male perfection that it is not surprising to find his physical characteristics stressed in the imaginative illustrations of the day. Indeed, the Prince might have sat for many of them.

In the third and fourth decades of the nineteenth century, the structure of society on both sides of the Atlantic was undergoing great changes. In England the hereditary aristocracy was being challenged by nouveaux riches industrialists, and in lesser degree the same thing was happening in the young United States. Brutalities and inequalities of the eighteenth century were being blasted away by the industrial age and the dawning of social consciousness. But as epochs are marked by notable events and not by man's arbitrary divisions of time, the eighteenth century did not cease on the day indicated by the calendar. It can be said to have persisted socially until Victoria's accession, and politically until the day when Jackson entered the White House. This event which signified the triumph of the common people proclaimed that the "government by gentlemen," as his followers called it, was over.

Many in this country who now found themselves with money and a voice in the management of their own affairs had only the most rudimentary education and no culture whatever. As a constantly expanding group these folk offered virgin soil in which to plant new social ideals. They looked about them for guidance. A pattern was at hand; the social design just established by

Pavilion designed by Albert for Victoria.

Victoria furnished a model which, if faithfully followed, would quickly help to stabilize American life. And though these confident followers of Jackson pretended to despise "Old World ways and notions," they were nevertheless permeated with an intense desire to reproduce all the established details of European living. None of its smallest items escaped them; they followed the fashions in everything with such fervidness that it might have been considered amusing had it not been done with such youthful earnestness.

In the picture of sobriety and domestic contentment offered by the English reigning house, there was indeed something which every family, no matter how modest, could emulate. Since the Queen frowned on drunkenness, so could the American Mrs. Joneses, and since the Royal Family paid its debts promptly, it became fashionable for others to do so. And who could lie contentedly abed in disregard of the picture of early rising set by the busy Queen and Prince?

While a summer pavilion was under construction in the gardens of Buckingham Palace, the royal young couple, with breakfast and morning prayers behind them by 9:30 A.M., could daily be seen walking out unattended to inspect the progress of the work. This summer-house was dear to Albert's heart, for he had designed it himself for the recreation of the Queen. As a great student of architecture, he delighted to use his knowledge for constructive purposes. Set on an artificial mound, Albert's romantic project was a fantastic creation sprouting with minarets, established in a setting which had become so rural, because of the Prince Consort's recent improvements of the Palace grounds, that it seemed almost incongruous in the midst of smoke-filled London. The pavilion contained three rooms, one Pompeian, one Romantic, and the third Raphaelesque —each a perfect expression of Albert's ideals. Each room was eventually decorated with fresco paintings executed by England's best artists, for Albert considered fresco the highest of the arts. The subjects chosen by the Prince depicted the loftiest and the most moral conceptions. Extracts from Sir Walter Scott adorned the chamber decorated in the Romantic style, and selections from Milton graced the Classic fresco inspired by his works.

Albert, a cultivated man, longed for the society of other intellectuals. In the subsidiary role of Prince Consort, he could not naturally be as content with his position as was Victoria. She found life completely satisfying in her triple role of wife, mother, and sovereign. The Prime Minister, Sir Robert Peel, recogniz-

From Milton's *Comus*. Fresco by Maclise in Queen's Pavilion.

ing Albert's abilities, made possible his entry into the world of arts and sciences when he appointed him President of the Fine Arts Commission. The position might have been tailored to order for the Prince Consort: it satisfied his love of art and his love of system, and it put him in contact with persons of distinguished achievements.

The Fine Arts Commission had come into being in order to raise the artistic standards of manufactured products. Thus, to give weight to its pronouncements, the Prince promised that both he and the Queen would range themselves behind its aims with the force of their prestige. If Albert occasionally appeared to lend his approval to ephemeral and foolish conceits, one must remember that as a practical man he was not unaware of manufacturing problems which frequently impose artistic restrictions on commercial productions. When making these concessions, he was denying his native good taste, which was really distinguished.

To range among the English artists and to invite the most important to execute the frescoes for the Queen's pavilion gave the Prince Consort much pleasure. And in making his selections, the Prince could not have avoided heading the list with the name of Edwin Landseer, for he not only was the Royal Family's favorite painter, but also was ranked as the greatest artist of the English-speaking world. In the productions which flowed with amazing speed from the brush of this petted darling of English fashion, the early Victorians could

find all the qualities by which they set such high store: great technical fluency, great feeling, and an unabashed sentimentality.

In 1824, when Landseer was twenty-two, he paid his first visit to Scotland and at once lost his heart to the rugged contours of the Highlands. Landseer was as one transformed; he had found the deer and stag. Henceforth these were to be his favorite subjects; no longer was he bound to zoos, barnyards, and stables for his models. In itself, however, Landseer's infatuation with the stags and crags of Scotland would not have been sufficient to keep the public's interest concentrated with such intensity on that rough and misty land. Behind this long-sustained attention was the additional publicity given to Scotland because of the Royal Family's attachment to the country. They, too, like Landseer, had fallen in love with the Highlands on their initial visit.

For Victoria and Albert this first trip, taken in 1842 after two years of marriage, was a romantic outing, a kind of honeymoon. German Albert, never too comfortable in England, felt delightfully at ease in Scotland; somehow it reminded him of home. Each summer the Royal Family returned there; year after year they became more attached to the quietness, the wildness, and the informality. Finally they purchased a small Scottish estate, called "Balmoral," which to this day remains one of the private residences of the British sovereign. When the almost annual increases in the family began to crowd the diminutive stone castle, the Prince began to plan a new residence for the Queen. As royal housing, nothing but a vast, baronial residence would serve. Though his first sketches were ready in 1848, the dream castle did not become a battlemented reality until 1855.

Neither politics nor bickering disturbed Balmoral's peace. Did not those timid creatures, the deer, approach so near the house at feeding time that the Queen caught a glimpse of them the very evening she arrived? From then on Victoria was attached to these wildings. She tried often to sketch them, but knew she could never approach the delicacy of line and alertness of poise which Landseer captured so beautifully; frequently, when she caught sight of a group of deer, she wished that he were on hand to limn them.

Since Albert's favorite diversion was deer-stalking, the public press from time to time felt impelled to describe this regional method of hunting. Even American periodicals called their readers' attention to its techniques, for they were quite at variance with the democratic American occupation of "going hunting for deer," the intent of which then was not primarily sport, but meat for the larder. As many popular prints also dealt with deer-stalking, Albert's own description of the sport is valuable. With his usual thoroughness, he analyzes its difficulties: "One has . . . to be constantly on the alert in order to circumvent them, and to keep under the hill out of their wind, crawling on hands and knees, and dressed entirely in gray" (in order that the hunters might blend in with the surrounding rocks). Victorian women were permitted as spectators of the hunt if they sat very quietly in the positions chosen for them. After viewing one such expedition with binoculars, the Queen wrote in her Journal: "Albert looked like a little speck creeping about on an opposite hill."

Many paintings and prints commissioned by her Majesty memorialized the prowess of the Prince as mighty hunter. But it was Landseer, more than any other artist, who made it possible for ordinary mortals, the world over, to participate (in imagination, that is) in this sport of the wealthy. The original paintings might be hidden in the stately homes of the fashionable, but engravings of Landseer's works were for many years keynotes of Victorian interior decoration. An American or British home was indeed out of touch with the times if it did not display a print of "The Monarch of the Glen"—that proud stag majestically sniffing the air—or "The Stag at Bay."

"The Stag at Bay," painted in 1846, was only one of many paintings of Landseer's which portrayed the death of these creatures. The tortured animal confronts the fierce hounds against a background in atmospheric sympathy with the event, for a thunderstorm darkens the sky in melodramatic fashion. How the Victorians, who wept so easily and so copiously, could contemplate these pictures of brute suffering with equanimity is a mystery. But sentimentality and cruelty are close bedfellows, and instead of shuddering, they seem to have delighted in the almost human expression of emotion with which the artist invested his stags.

Decorative tradition covered hunting-lodge walls with trophies of the chase, and Albert did not break with it. Heads of deer sprouted from walls of all the royal residences and even ornamented the kitchens of Osborne and Windsor. And though the actual mounted specimens—perhaps in deference to the taste of the ladies—were kept out of the drawing rooms, that did not prohibit the use of pictures of the same animals, particularly when they came from the hand of the Queen's favorite artist.

Victoria was as faithful to her happy memories of Balmoral as she was to her husband. Wherever she saw the pictured deer in her travels, she noted it in her Journal. In 1872, at Dunrobin Castle, she mentions the stags' heads spaced round the dark red walls of the dining room. "Behind one (a very fine one) gas pipes have been introduced, which light up each point."

With decorative hints such as these filtering over the sea, it was not long before unassuming American homes, utterly dissimilar in character to even the most modest of baronial residences, began to ape these traditional displays of noble sporting achievement. Soon mounted stag and deer peered gloomily from sombre red walls of innumerable American dining rooms or frowned upon the family from dark hallways, as permanent hosts to moth and dust. For fastidious housekeepers, desirous of being in fashion but unable to tolerate even the thought of such invitations to an ever-present pest, the manufacturers devised stag heads of incorruptible iron, which, as they posed no maintenance problem, were wholly satisfactory. They provided the sought-after mediaeval note and, exactly as in feudal days, they could serve as hatracks since antlers seemed formed for that precise purpose.

But it was not necessary for Americans to restrict their mannered interest in deer to an occasional glance at a stuffed head in their homes; nor were they obliged, as was the Queen, to travel to Scotland in order to catch infrequent glimpses of the wary creatures. Thanks to a

27

In 1847, an English novelty. The undoubted progenitor of the iron herd which took over the American Victorian garden.

miracle of domestication made possible by an enterprising branch of the iron industry, they could see on their neat grass plots these denizens of the woodland, at will. The taste for stag and deer immobilized in iron, sprang up in the late 1840's. From about 1850 on, tidy Victorian lawns were spotted with arrogant, chocolate-covered stags gazing blankly across sunny flower beds, and vast herds of deer roamed through every other phase of Victorian decoration.

Another interest of the Prince Consort's which had decorative repercussions in iron on this side of the Atlantic was the greyhound. The greyhound had for a long time been a fashionable as well as a sporting breed, but the sinuous tribe took on added lustre when it became known that the Prince's favorite, "Eos," a very famous specimen, had been painted by Landseer at the express commission of her Majesty. Moreover, "Eos" appeared again, this time in the Great Exhibition, as sculpture cast in zinc. This novelty caught the public's eye, and, only a year or so later, an enterprising American manufacturer was ready with copies in iron of this graceful hound.

To Victorian eyes a cast iron Newfoundland dog standing solemnly on a tiny grass plot was no artistic monstrosity or object of amusement; rather, it was a heartwarming symbol of canine devotion. As lawn decorations these ungainly iron beasts shared popularity with the iron stags.

When the Queen made her first visit to Scotland in 1842, she wore, as a tactful gesture, a dress and shawl of the Royal Stuart tartan. When Landseer painted a portrait of her clad in a skirt of this extremely gaudy plaid, he did the Queen and fashion no favor. The publicity given the royal costume implanted a popular taste for tartans which has bobbed up at intervals ever since. Before Victoria went to the Highlands, it is quite likely that no lady south of the Scottish border had ever been seen in anything so barbaric as a plaid. But the sober middle class modelled themselves on the Queen, and even her least publicized action was apt to influence its tastes. Enormous scarlet plaids became the vogue, one which raged virulently on both sides of the ocean. "Scotch Plaids," as the clan tartans were called, have recurrently become the standard wear for children ever since a far-from-fashionable Queen and her children first appeared in these distinctive textiles.

This lavish use of tartans by the Victorians was significant of the constantly growing interest the English displayed in the Highlands. Before 1750, England had given little or no thought to the region and its inhabitants. After George IV, hoping to win even a slight degree of favor for the House of Hanover, appeared in Edinburgh in 1822 with his great bulk clad in a kilt, England began to hear more and more about the Highland Scots. There sprang into fashion a spurious Celticism which, when used as a basis for decoration at Balmoral by the Prince Consort, evolved as a new theme in interior furnishings. In this residence, figures of Scottish Highlanders served as lighting fixtures. Every textile was indubitably Scottish and the Prince's untrammelled use of the tartan motif as a decorative feature poses the question whether anyone the length and breadth of Britain ever went in for plaids so solemnly and so heavily. Carpets and draperies were made of the brilliant scarlet Royal Stuart, or the dark green Hunting Stuart. Even the coverings of the drawing room chairs were selected by these sentimental dictates, and for this purpose the Prince's choice fell on the "dress Stuart," with its white ground crossed with color. Balmoral itself was equipped with its individual tartan designed by the Prince Consort. A quiet pattern of gray barred with red and black, it is reserved to this day for the sole use of the Royal Family. In the latter days of the Queen's reign, this "Balmoral" tartan replaced the gaudy Stuart in the Castle's drawing room. While this change may have lessened the amount of bright color, the plaid still created a startling effect on guests not used to the rec-

Drawing Room with tartans at Balmoral. 1882. *The Graphic.*

tangular patternings of the Castle's upholstery materials. As long as Victoria lived, however, tartans dominated the decoration of Balmoral, for she permitted no criticism of her husband's taste. In 1856 she wrote: "Every year my heart becomes more fixed in this dear Paradise, and so much more so now, that *all* has become my dearest Albert's *own* creation, own work, own building, own laying out, as at *Osborne;* and his great taste, and the impress of his dear hand, have been stamped every where."

The Victorian fashion for plaids affected even the field of ladies' needlework, and German manufacturers of patterns, sensitive to commercial trends, were soon ready with "new Berlin patterns of the various clan plaids which look extremely elegant, and are very correct." As a decorative motif, the taste for plaids fluctuates. Recently, the plaid motif (fortunately not based on the limited color range of the clan tartans) is again in vogue. Plaids appear not only on textiles used for decorating purposes but also on wallpapers; a taste which, despite all its boasted modernity, is oddly reminiscent of Balmoral, Victoria, and Albert.

The affectionate regard in which the Queen and her family were held showed itself in innumerable ways. Articles of most diverse or trivial character were named after them. The Queen's name is indelibly associated with a low, four-wheeled carriage, that once most popular vehicle, the "victoria." The term will be forever evocative of the era when beautiful ladies, their tiny parasols tip-tilted against the sun, took the air behind liveried coachmen in this vehicle, so perfectly designed for feminine display. Equally inseparable is the name of the Prince from a certain type of old-fashioned formal dress-coat, the "Prince Albert."

But Victoria's name is memorialized in far more permanent fashion by the world's greatest waterfall, Victoria Falls, in Central Africa, christened for her after its discovery in 1855 by Livingstone. And in British Guiana, the greatest of botanical wonders lay hidden from the world until 1837, when its discoverer named the world's largest waterlily the "Victoria Regia." England did not behold the lily until 1849, when it blossom'ed for the first time at Chatsworth, the estate of the Duke of Devonshire. To bring this exotic into bloom was only one of many notable achievements on the part of the Duke's estate superintendent, Mr. Joseph Paxton, a remarkable Victorian. For three years the lily had been sulking in Kew Gardens, refusing, in this alien climate, to thrive, much less to blossom. Paxton took up this challenge to horticulturists. In a tank which he invented to supply conditions simulating those of the tropics, the lily graciously consented to flower. Paxton then made a special journey to Windsor to present to her Majesty and the Prince Consort a leaf and flower of what was considered one of the world's great wonders.

As the notable event of the lily's flowering was well publicized, people came from all over to behold this golden-hearted marvel. No one fortunate enough to see its out-sized, multi-petalled, rose-white blossom and its gigantic leaves would ever forget it. The leaves, five to six feet across, resembled huge, floating, pale-green trays with neatly turned-up rims which disclosed the rusty crimson underside. But what caught the public's fancy more than the lily's beauty was the astounding fact that its enormous leaves were strong enough to support the weight of a child, a feature so striking that it was considered worthy of incorporation into nineteenth-century school geographies. Today memory, discarding geography's greater wonders, still holds fast to that lily.

The enormous publicity given this staggering specimen of the vegetable kingdom exercised no small influence on designers of the day. The lovely and poetic waterlily swayed and turned to embrace all kinds of objects, and was executed in all kinds of materials. Every Victorian heart was touched when the golden-hearted blossom was used to form the body of a cradle. And as the Victorian mind would immediately detect an analogy between the snowy whiteness of the lily and the purity of white marble, sculptors found it a perfect motif with which to ornament the fashionable white marble mantelpiece. Whole beds of waterlilies floated on Victorian floors, with the blue of the sky reflected enchantingly between the interstices of the lily-pads. Owners of such aquatic carpets walked on them proudly, totally oblivious to incongruities. As a motif for decorative arts, nothing was more obliging than the lily.

That the blossom was universally admired is indicated by the words of an unknown but not unperceptive art critic of the period: "Waterlilies—: for their newly discovered chief, the Victoria Regia, one of the most wonderful as well as beautiful of flowering plants, have with singular propriety, been the chosen model of not a few objects of manufacture woven, carved, or worked in metal, sometimes with admirable success, sometimes without a just understanding of the grace and delicacy of this exquisite plant."

Table Centrepiece. 1849. Designed by Prince Albert. After electroplating made it possible to execute objects of the utmost fantasy, the centrepiece often told a tale or set forth a whimsy. Prince Albert's design, made expressly for the Queen, is a triumph of marital sentiment over his native good taste. Today its details seem shockingly inappropriate for the purpose. On the pedestal of this miniature gilt civic monument, Albert shows four of Victoria's favorite dogs. Two stand over a dead hare; another pair, far more gruesome, alertly watch a live rat in a trap. A dead rat lies to one side!

Right. Chintz. Victoria surrounded by emblems of Great Britain.

Royalty, confronted by its likenesses, its insignia on all manner of articles, accepted them with royal equanimity.

Courtesy, Metropolitan Museum of Art

Tablecloth Border. 1851.
At Balmoral the Royal Family dined serenely on shimmering damask which depicted Prince Albert and his guests stalking the deer through thistles and scrollery tangles.

VICTORIA REGIA, THE QUEEN'S OWN LILY

The Victoria Regia and sinuous lesser members of the clan tempted designers into decorative excesses. As even the poorest among them could detect the analogy between blossom and a cup, between leaf and a saucer, cups and saucers were contrived from lily blossoms and foliage, contorted to fit the needs of the article. Though frowned on by persons of taste, these vessels in flower form delighted the sentimental.

The "Victoria Regia" Cot. 1851. Executed in papier mâché from design by an eminent sculptor. A Victorian infant born to wealth might pass its frequently all-too-brief span of life in such a rococo, poetic, unsanitary nest.

Courtesy, Index of American Design, National Gallery of Art

Extreme left. Waterlilies on American Parian Pitcher. C. 1853–1860.

Left. English Earthenware Pitcher. Decoration constructed of interwoven leaves with bud for handle. 1851.

Below. On Berlin-work chair seat and back, the Queen's lily dominates the floral garland.

Courtesy, Victoria and Albert Museum

THE PACKAGE LABEL

Recent progress in the printing arts enabled European exporters of fine fabrics to enhance their products with Labels of such artistry and elegance that they were sought for scrapbooks. Unmarred by advertising, these labels cleverly combined hand-colored lithographs with metallic embossing. The print was pasted in a stamped-out aperture. Such lavish use of handwork on mere labels is today inconceivable.

From the author's collection

DEER AND GREYHOUND

These royal pets featured prominently not only in the fine arts but also in every phase of decoration. Deer were cast in iron, shaped in terra cotta, sculptured in stone, molded in glass, and carved *ad nauseam* in wood.

Staghorn Furniture. Hamburg, 1851. Planned for hunting lodge or baronial mansion, these grotesque pieces attracted the sentimental because of their "appropriateness" — a false concept which persuaded many to set aside all standards of taste. The furniture also captivated Victoria, who ordered a suite for Balmoral made from trophies of "dear Albert's" prowess.

Deer were commonplace motifs in Berlin wool-work. Pattern offered in 1868 for use on sofa cushion or as centre of afghan.

Ceramic Ornament.

The greyhound makes its debut in Godey's, 1853.

Left. Cast Iron Greyhound.

Eos, the Prince Consort's well-known greyhound, posed for Landseer more than once. At the Great Exhibition a model of the hound, cast in zinc, attracted great attention. From then on Eos had a numerous (though unacknowledged) metal progeny. By 1853, Wood and Perot, Philadelphia foundrymen, were showing this stately greyhound as an ornamental setting for gatepost or doorstep.

Courtesy, Index of American Design, National Gallery of Art

Two Panels from Needleworked Carpet. Finished by 1840 in Canton, N. Y. In her embroidery the maker, Mrs. Eliza D. Miner, incorporated popular decorative trends.

Courtesy, Folk Arts Center, New York

Below. Stag Statuette. Made at Bennington, Vt., by United States Pottery. *C*. 1850. Mottled in yellow, cream, and gray-green. Stags and does sat sedately on whatnot or mantel.

Lower left. Garden Ornament. The alien chamois, with eye of glass, in cast iron.

Above and left. Courtesy, Index of American Design

Even in the most anti-monarchical interiors, the stag, symbol of royal privilege, loomed at every turn. In addition to the noble beasts of Landseer's ubiquitous engravings, antlered heads peered from forests of carven foliage which topped the great sideboards, peeked over picture frames, lurked in thickets of wooden scrollery on that most stylish article, the wall bracket.

Carved Wooden Picture and Frame, depicting field sports. When peasant craftsmen began to fill the demand for wall decorations of carved wood, the cervine tribe came into its own.

ALBUM 3

Of the Wide World &
How It Seeps into the Parlor
And Why—and Whatnots
Of Albums and Annuals &
Caskets of Love
Of Alabaster and Carrara &
Veiled Vestals
Of Kashmir and Carpets &
Walking in Jungles
Of Rosewood and Circassian &
Leopard and Thuya
Of Humming-Birds in the Hair
Of the Twisted Conch and Mother-of-Pearl &
The Many-chambered Nautilus

O Grandmother the tall lamp seems a little captive sun shedding its warm radiance on the russet-colored cloth of the sitting room table. Bits of the glow are ensnared by the thick frillings which edge the crocheted woolen mat on which the lamp stands, but there is plenty of light and space for everyone.

The illumination falls on Grandfather. In his comfortable high-backed armchair, he unfolds the weekly county paper, draws his spectacles from the case embroidered by his daughter, and proceeds to read aloud the choicest bits of village news; so brilliant is the light that he need not peer at the type. The family listen attentively. The lamplight touches Grandmother's face, picks out the lace-trimmed edges of her beribboned cap, flashes sharply from her knitting needles as she keeps them flying at the particular task of all grandmothers—the family stockings. It slides off the yellow heads of the children bent over their evening task—next day's lessons. The generous circle of lamplight encompasses Mother, comfortable in her low rocker. The lamp-glow catches her in white apron, her feet balanced on a pretty footstool, her lap piled full of her eternal mending.

The overhang of the heavy table-cloth moves slowly outward, propelled by a large gray cat, which leaves its favored shadowy retreat under the table to cross the carpeted floor toward a place even more attractive—the deliciously warm region of the iron stove.

Father enters the room, closing the door firmly behind him; he goes over to the stove, feeds its red gullet a few shovelfuls of coal, and then takes his place in the family circle to relax and meditate leisurely on his affairs.

Grandfather has finished his reading, and Grandmother is moved to reminiscence. "Things were not so easy in my day," she says. "At this time of evening, most of us would have gone to bed, for it was always cold and anyway there wasn't enough light for all of us to work by. Of course, there was enough to spin by, and if the children crouched on stools, they could manage to see enough to write. And although we had candles, they cost money, so we never burned but one or two at a time." She snuggles deeper into her knitted shoulder cape. "Really, this family has no idea of what life was like when we had to depend entirely on the fireplace. To be sure, the flames were pretty to watch, but in those days we could never move away from them. And now,"—she glances fondly towards the stove—"we sit and move about this room as we will."

If we accept the fireplace as the symbol of home life in the pre-industrial age, the symbol of the Victorian era should be the central, lamp-lit table. Today, except for special convenience, we no longer place a table in the centre of the room; in Victorian days, it was inconceivable that this space should be left empty. This placement was a significant witness of the changes which swiftly arriving inventions and discoveries were making in every phase of living. Among the blessings was the comparatively recent discovery of coal and of kerosene, which, together with very modest improvements in lighting, freed family life from the shivery periphery of the fireplace. For the first time, the average person could follow his avocations in hours chosen by himself and

"Greece" and "Georgia" typify the idealized world provided by engravings.

not dictated by the vagaries of Nature.

While the sitting room table stood for all that was warm and intimate in home-life, the parlor centre-table was the focus of its most formal aspects only. To leave the family circle and enter the parlor, unlocking the door, was like leaving a warm cocoon to enter the Wide, Wide World. Invariably, in the exact centre of this unlived-in chamber was a marble-topped table, the family's altar to the proprieties. Here was the stranger ushered, and for him, and for him alone, were the table-lamp and fire hurriedly lit. Awaiting the family, the caller pored over the virtually standardized objects spread out on the centre-table for his entertainment. Little piles of the newest annuals nudged souvenirs and mementos, and there was usually a sketchbook or port-folio of drawings to attest the ladies' artistic accomplish-ments. After a round of introductions, the visitor, in order to break the elegant ice of the parlor, would com-pliment the demure young ladies on their delicate pen-cillings, and, noting that many of the souvenirs were the evidence of travel, would compare notes on that educa-tional pastime with host and hostess.

As the nineteenth century never thought of the parlor table as anything but a showcase for cultural displays, nothing pertaining to daily life was ever permitted contact with its sacrosanct surface. In addition to the prettily bound books, however, and travel mementos, the light from the cut glass shade fell on a muddle of objects referred to generically by their owners as "cu-

riosities." Whatever their nature—perhaps a bit of min-eral, a historical souvenir, and a cluster of natural oddities from the immediate environment—the "curiosi-ties" were uniformly viewed with wonder and romantic speculation, for these articles were tangible evidence of that intriguing world which even then, in this subtle fashion, was penetrating the sacred confines of the Victorian home.

A custom of long standing decreed that a portfolio of engravings be allotted an honored place on the table. Romanticized interpretations though they were, such prints then furnished the chief means through which the average person could acquaint himself with the architecture, social customs, topography, and physical beauties of the world. Today we find it amusing to read of the great pleasure the Victorians experienced in look-ing over prints and engravings; it seems oddly stuffy as a social occupation, an inconceivable substitute for cards, dancing, or television. But in early Victorian days, a portfolio of prints disclosed to its rapt naïve examiners a world as exciting as the theatre, as unreal as a dream; it was almost as educational as a trip to a place itself; with none of the physical discomforts and hazards of travel. Above all, to study a portfolio of prints to-gether offered an easy means of breaking down shyness between the sexes, and, when the participants were not shy, one of the few legitimate opportunities for flirtation.

To display an interest in prints had been a mark of fashionable culture in the effete circles of the eighteenth

"America" and "Florence," strange and beautiful, stirred romantic curiosity.

century. In the nineteenth, the interest was taken over earnestly by the well-to-do middle class, who, in active revolt against the crudities of the era immediately preceding, turned—as they were instructed by their leaders in aesthetics—to Art, for its refining influences. In this transition period they were not interested in pictures which depicted the life about them; these would have presented a too vivid reminder of that which they were trying seriously to ignore. Realism, then synonymous with vulgarity, was not considered fit subject matter for art. To be sure, *Beauty* was their watchword, Beauty flawlessly moral in tone, but Beauty which could be found only in that which was remote in time and space. Sensitive to this popular trend, the new periodicals scrambled to outdo each other. Each month these magazines carried their quotas of delightful steel engravings which were carefully studied and then collected in portfolios by eager aspirants to "culture."

The Victorian "annual" or "gift book" was another type of profitable publication, evolved to meet this fashionable craze for engravings. No parlor table was without at least one copy. Since an annual was planned to be on view, its decorative features were given careful consideration. The paper was thick and smooth, the engravings of paintings were selected from the work of the best artists, and the watered silk or morocco bindings were designed pointedly to appeal to feminine tastes. Annuals, saccharine and trivial though they now seem, found place in the book reviews, jostling criti-

cisms of the works of the best writers of the day. In 1832, a reviewer acclaiming a welcome exception was moved to express his opinion of the banality inherent in almost every one: "Instead of a mock tour with a mockery of names and historical facts and incidents, and stale anecdotes and descriptions, vamped up from books, new and old, that all the world has read a hundred times over, we find a continuity of bona fide travelling sketches, redolent of freshness, truth, and originality."

The first example of an annual in England appeared in 1820, so they were generally referred to as *English Annuals*. This volume, called *The Forget-Me-Not*, had innumerable floral descendants, such as *The Aloe, The Harebell, The Lily*. In 1826, the first version of the gift book to appear on this side of the ocean was brought out by a Philadelphia publisher and patriotically named *The Atlantic Souvenir*. Of excellent quality, its illustrations and literary contents were entirely the work of Americans. But many publishers were little concerned with originality and put together annuals for every variety of taste, from whatever source they could pirate the materials. There were Juvenile Keepsakes, Patriotic Gift Books, Books of Beauty which featured pretty girls, annuals with a pseudo-botanical slant, and those with a religious appeal, besides the great number based on romantic fiction and the maudlin verse which flowed so freely from the slender gold pens of Victorian gentlemen. Indeed, the field was taken over by ladies.

41

Annuals were planned as chaste gifts for the young Victorian female so nothing was ever included between their pretty covers which would cause any young lady the faintest blush. From certain viewpoints, however, volumes prone to excessive sentimentality were considered objectionable. When seventeen-year-old Princess Victoria lists the annuals among her Christmas gifts, there are no such ambiguous titles as *The Pearl* or *Affection's Gift,* and *The Casket of Love.* Only those based on the beauties of nature or the wonders of the world were thought fit reading for the young scion of the Royal House: the educational *Finden's Tableaux,* comprising prints dealing with wholesome subjects such as "National Character, Beauty and Costume"; Heath's *Picturesque Annual for 1837, Friendship's Offering,* and *The Holy Land* (the latter beautifully illustrated, she notes in her journal). Sentimental and sugar-coated and flimsy though they undoubtedly were, the annuals probably did their bit to eradicate provincialism. In imagination their readers travelled everywhere: to Persia, to holy Jerusalem, or to the classic ruins of Greece, Rome, and Thebes. Colored engravings of birds and exotic flowers provided an entrancing introduction to natural history. Even works devoted primarily to literature, such as the American *Graham's Magazine,* featured exquisite drawings of this type.

From its very inception in 1842, the *Illustrated London News*—that periodical of the new bourgeoisie—laid stress on the strange areas of the world, those distant lands whose products, once the countries were subdued, would be coming into the world markets. Proudly the journal presented its readers with articles on such fascinating subjects as the customs and appearance of the Circassians, the Pasha of Egypt, the overland route to India, the Khyber Pass. Many Victorian occupations and interests were but the outward demonstration of the eagerness to amass, not only wealth and material goods, but all the variety of vestments in which culture clothed itself. Collections of prints demonstrated one's interest in the whole broad world of art; collections of pressed flowers and seaweeds showed a leaning toward natural sciences, no matter how shallow; scrapbooks— and how they loved them!—an interest in education and literature. No aspect of this instinct to collect is to be decried if we recognize it for what it was—the first stirrings of curiosity about the world at large. When travel became easier, the Victorians became inveterate collectors of souvenirs of their journeyings. Because of this mania for accumulating, their homes of necessity took on the character of museums, for the early Victorians had no other place in which to house the curiosities and objets d'art which they so avidly brought together. In the first half of the nineteenth century, public museums and great collections figured practically not at all in general life. The few museums extant were composed of an amazingly heterogeneous mass of objects assembled with no more discrimination than was displayed in the average Victorian home, a place where, in lesser degree, the curious, the strange, and the exotic simply piled up.

Those prevented by circumstances from garnering travel souvenirs could nevertheless follow a phase of collecting at home. They could, and did, make scrapbooks—and what scrapbooks! So many-faceted was the appeal of scrapbook-making that most Victorians were caught by one or another of its enchantments at some point in their lives. Before cheap printing, libraries, and public education did away with any need for scrapbooks, they were a homemade substitute for the cultural facilities offered by these institutions. But not only were they educational; they also were satisfying to the ego, for a superb example permitted its maker to bask in the approval of his or her social circle—the conning of scrapbooks being another of the recognized forms of Victorian entertainment. Much of the pleasure derived from examining these literary and pictorial miscellanies lay in the deliberately muddled character of the contents: they were unpredictable, therefore fascinating. To assemble their haphazard items from whatever source was available undoubtedly exercised the same charm on a certain type of individual as did the making of "crazy-quilts" in the latter days of Victoria's reign. It offered amusement to the industrious, the sentimental, the neat, and the thrifty—in fact, to all those who liked to keep busy but who found the scientific, orderly approach not only mysterious but actually distasteful.

After weekly and monthly periodicals began to enter the home, each with its mass of information, with every installment quite as novel and interesting as the one which preceded it, the character of scrapbooks was materially altered. No longer was there need to clip and hoard, for the publishers would see to it that the fascinating flood was sustained. The making of scrapbooks now descended from its former adult level to become an amusement of children. And clipping, as a pastime, itself received a deathblow when manufacturing lithographers, sighting in the scrapbook a new field for business, brought out pictures expressly made for pasting in albums. Never before had the printing presses produced anything so cheap and attractive.

While the allure of the earlier scrapbooks was assumed to be based on their literary and artistic value, that of these new, brilliantly colored scrapbook pictures was avowedly a sensuous one, planned to catch the eye, not only of the child but of the undemanding adult in whom the collecting instinct still surged. Highly embossed and, for the most part, of an enchanting realism never before attained, they were, in addition, exquisitely glossy and smooth to the touch. Stamped out with dies, their forms were clear and definite; sensory stimuli which no small exploratory fingers ever rejected. With what delight the unspoiled children of the 1870's and 1880's turned the pages of scrapbooks again and again to pore over the familiar forms of puppies, bunnies, and kittens which tumbled eternally from boots, baskets, and Easter eggs. And with what absorption they studied the unfamiliar contours of the strange elephants, giraffes, tigers, and kangaroos turned out by the same considerate printers for their express amusement. Lithographed pictures were provided to suit every taste—whether it leaned to the coy, the sentimental, the humorous, the romantic, or the historical. By 1885, as the fad wore off, assortments of "beautiful embossed pictures," (enough to fill a book) could be had for a dime, a price which indicated that another pastime—one which two centuries before had held the interest of the cultivated—had now descended in the social scheme as far as it could go. Only children could extract any pleasure from working with such precollected items, for even the excitement of assembling them oneself had been taken away by this phase of business enterprise. And the pleasure of pasting—a dubious one at best—was not sufficiently engrossing to furnish any long-lasting attraction even to the young.

But before the Victorians completely relinquished their interest in the scrapbook, they were stimulated to collect "trade-cards," an early and modest scheme of mercantile advertising. To acquire a collection of trade-cards required at least a show of effort on the part of the collector, although they were easy to obtain since they were distributed by business firms to all comers.

Scrapbook collections permitted only the display of two-dimensional objects. For those given to a fondness for the concrete, the Victorian "whatnot" or *étagère* came into being. This piece of furniture—never to be dissociated from the era—was frankly a sentimental showcase for the display of collections.

The whatnot held a perennial fascination for Victorian children who were frequently told "to look with your eyes and not with your fingers," an injunction they dutifully tried to follow as they peered—hands safely clasped behind their backs—at the strange enchantments spread out on its many levels. In homes where a member of the family had followed the sea or had travelled, whatnots were cluttered with delightful and decorative baubles: a flask of sand from the Sahara, a nodding mandarin from China, trifles brought from faraway Ceylon and India, the leaning tower of Pisa in alabaster, bits of carved ivory and minerals, spiralled shells and scented sandalwood, all forms and textures strange, exciting, and captivating. Occasionally a careful or much petted child would be allowed the privilege of handling these cherished curios, and through such contacts would receive an education in sense-impressions which no peering at specimens in a museum could ever approach. Indelibly engraved in the author's memory are the color and markings of a cross-section of petrified wood from Arizona's great forest, the heft and texture of a bit of natural asbestos, the prickly roughness of a dried star-fish, the pleasant smoothness of Japanese carved ivory—impressions imparted early in life by means of the trivia on a whatnot, of which not a bit of the original vividness has been lost.

Although the Victorians worshipped the idea of Home and expected to find their pleasures within it, at the same time they could not help revelling in all the fascinating objects, materials, and textures which the great, bouncing world of commerce was bringing across the seven seas and depositing right on their own doorsteps. With much gusto, they introduced the names of strange places and foreign substances into their conversations, a trend which was at once reflected in the exotic names bestowed by the fashion designers on ordinary cloaks and mantles. Scottish tartans had already been popularized through the agency of the Queen.

In Victorian days no salesman of an "imported" article failed to lay particular stress on that then almost universal fact. And never was an "imported" object mentioned by its proud possessor without the adjective indicating its place of origin. No pair of vases was ever referred to simply as *vases;* if they happened to be a pair of the tall, carved Italian vases so long a feature of Victorian mantelpieces they were always "my *alabaster vases.*" The Victorians found *alabaster* a lovely word, with its haunting suggestions of waxen whiteness

Among the Queen's commissions were statues of the royal children, posed in symbolic attitudes. The Princess Helena made a tender "Peace," the Princess Louise, a graceful "Plenty," Prince Arthur, "The Hunter," Prince Leopold, "The Fisher."

and its curious translucency. To authors of popular fiction of the day, it was a godsend, for it furnished them with the perfect cliché: an "alabaster" or "marble" complexion or bosom was the almost inescapable description for the pallor then so greatly admired and often acquired at great sacrifice of health.

The bust and pedestal of Carrara marble was an inevitable accompaniment of nineteenth-century gentility. The proud owner of this elegant appurtenance (which coquetted or brooded in the corners of Victorian parlors all through the Queen's long reign) might not know the title of the sculpture, but we can be sure she knew the foreign word "Carrara" and savored its musical quality as she displayed the charms of this newest bit of furnishing. Victoria, who admired marble greatly, always had her sculptural commissions executed in the chilly immaculateness of "Carrara."

Public squares, parks, and gardens were dotted with white marble statues proclaiming their sentimental or historical stories. And, in the library of the Victorian home, busts of Shakespeare or Dante, in marble or plaster, perched high on ornamental brackets or on top of towering bookcases. Occasionally likenesses of Franklin, Petrarch, Milton, or Sir Walter Scott supplanted those great immortals. In the engaging phrase of the period, these busts were supposed to give a "finish" to the room.

The "Veiled Head," and other marble sculptures of this type, were great favorites in middle-class circles. This form of tour-de-force first appeared at the Great Exhibition in London. Visitors to that amazing display may shortly have forgotten most of the decorative details shown there in international profusion, but they never forgot Monti's "Veiled Vestal." With magical craftsmanship, the sculptor had fashioned what appeared to be a marble veil of the utmost transparency, through which one could catch glimpses of the kneeling Vestal's pure features. "The Bashful Beggar," offered by a competitor, played with the same idea. Another familiar piece is the type in which the intractable marble was worked with incredible skill to resemble the openwork of lace. Female heads surrounded with these lacy marble frills were in common use as decorations up to the turn of the century. Not accepted by the best taste of the day, they were nevertheless extravagantly admired by the general public, which is forever fascinated by "tricks in art."

But even this type of virtuosity did not content the Victorian sculptor who regarded the virgin purity of

44

the marble itself as a challenge. His predecessors, Michelangelo and Canova, had found its unsullied whiteness quite adequate to express their grand and noble conceptions. But the nineteenth-century sculptor, spurred by the era's passion for embellishment, set out to gild its lily whiteness and—quite literally—touched up his pieces with color and gold. In 1847 the English sculptor Gibson produced a marble statue of Queen Victoria, the perfect Roman matron, both in pose and costume. To enliven its blank whiteness, he added touches of color to the Grecian borders of the robe and realistic accents of gold to the crown. Since neither the Queen nor her image, apparently, could be wrong, the English critics gulped slightly and swallowed this innovation—one which was then startling, as the ancient Greek fondness for colored statues had been completely forgotten. But when a similarly tinted statue of Phryne —a subject which in itself was open to criticism on the grounds of immodesty—was shown a few years later in the French Section of the Great Exhibition, British critics pounced on it with considerable glee and censored the French sculptor, Pradier, for "the bad taste of ornamenting the hem of the garment with a red border and fingers with gold rings, which contrasted painfully with the otherwise colorless marble."

In the full orchestra of ornament with which the Victorian experimented, the classic and its rather restrained patterns played but a minor part. In the field of textiles the major part was taken by innumerable variations on a strange theme—an Oriental motif which, quietly emerging from one of the more distant corners of the earth, eventually came to dominate the minds of both designers and public for over a half century. This motif, generally referred to by its Victorian admirers as the "palm" or "pine" design, was the feature of the Cashmere or Kashmir shawl. As the height of feminine elegance, that article of woman's apparel held its position from the time of the Napoleonic Wars to about that of the Franco-Prussian struggle. While the fashion for shawls raged, the average woman was stirred to such emotional depths by her desire for a Cashmere example that today the feeling can be comprehended only if it be compared with the agitation which fills certain feminine bosoms at the sight of a good mink coat. And in truth, the Cashmere shawl *was* the "mink coat" of its period, and prices were comparable; genuine specimens ranged from $500 to $5,000, enormous sums in those days, but intelligible as expenditures when we realize that women were then judged not only by their dia-

monds but also by their shawls. The wives of nouveaux riches California gold miners vied with each other in the sums spent on these masterpieces of the East Indian craftsman's art, and women who had never previously heard of India, much less of its province Kashmir, bandied these exotic words about with great glibness.

A genuine Kashmir (or Cashmere) shawl was woven of the fine down-like under-wool of the Tibetan goat. It was bound to be a luxury, since a good example often represented the year's entire output of three or four men who toiled long hours to produce, at each day's end, perhaps no more than one-quarter inch of textile. Real Indias or Cashmeres were executed in several manners: they could be woven on looms in small segments which were sewn together with such precision that the joinings were imperceptible, or they could be fabricated in one piece. India was also known for its embroidered shawls which were distinguished by a ground covered with needlework in rich, minute patterning.

As early as 1750, the first examples of this elegant accessory of apparel might have been observed in England, displayed on the backs of a select few, ladies whose husbands were directors of the East India Company which imported a few pieces from time to time. The rich distinction of these shawls aroused a general desire for them, and English weavers were fired with the idea of imitating them on the power-driven loom. By 1805 the first shawl woven on a machine was achieved in Norwich, a fortunate circumstance not only for Norwich, but also for the manufacturing town of Paisley, for it provided the latter with a new stimulus to its moribund textile industry of fine cotton weaving. As a result, women to whom a genuine India might be a luxury forever unattainable could now be swathed in the handsome substitute presented by the loom-woven Paisley. With such acclaim was it welcomed by the Victorian feminine public that the demand created for that Scottish town a business enterprise which in its heyday exceeded $5,000,000 a year, then an enormous revenue. On her very first visit to Scotland, the Queen herself wore a "splendid shawl of Paisley manufacture," an act of royal courtesy which not only did much to aid the British textile trade but possibly stiffened the resistance of innumerable Victorian males beset with insistent demands for a genuine "Cashmere." Beleaguered by their ladies, heads of families could and undoubtedly did reply, with all the weight of royal example behind them: "The Paisley shawl is good enough for her Majesty! It ought to be good enough for you!" And with such ease did the term Paisley become a commonplace of everyday speech that it has ever since been used as the label for the forms peculiar to the genuine Cashmere —the Indian "palm" or "pine." To this day they are known as *Paisley* and not as *Cashmere* patterns.

When shawls were in high fashion, women practiced all kinds of economies in order to gratify their longing for this particular type of ostentation. Even on social levels where outright ownership was completely impossible, the feminine world managed nevertheless to appear draped in this costly wrap. As an example of this sort of conniving, let one consider the English factory girl of the period who, on her small earnings, could never have saved enough to purchase a shawl, yet contrived to walk out in one at every week-end. One Saturday she bought it on credit, wore it on Sunday, pawned it on Monday, and redeemed it again the next Saturday. And though she never attained the actual ownership of it, she wasted enough money in these weekly maneuvers—grumbled Victorian moralizers—to buy an entire and more suitable wardrobe. After shawls went out of style, several succeeding generations of women, awed by family traditions of their original cost, carefully preserved them. In spite of this care, there are far fewer shawls in existence today than there should be. Their disappearance can be laid to a fashion which made its debut in the 1880's and burst forth again in the 1920's. This fad for transforming the Paisleys, and even expensive Indias, into fitted wraps, draperies, and chair coverings, destroyed innumerable examples of the Oriental and English weavers' art. And oddly enough, in the Kashmir of today these textiles once highly important to the province's commerce are unobtainable.

It is worth noting that the mid-Victorian public's attachment to the Oriental taste in textiles at first went no further than shawls. The wearers of the latter displayed no willingness to adopt Oriental patterns in floor coverings. Though the manufacturers could, from the outset, have introduced excellent imitations of Turkish and Indian carpets, they hesitated to do so, for they were catering to a great new public, many of whom had never owned a carpet. When at length the purchase was made, the low-toned designs of the Oriental rug had no charms for a woman who expected her new, flowery carpet to add the final touch of ornateness to an already elaborate interior.

In acceding to this taste for the florid, the designers eventually exhausted the possibilities of roses, flowers, and birds, and looked about them for fresh, generously scaled forms. Curious motifs, indigenes in the stranger corners of the world, suddenly burst forth amid the botanical familiars. Representations of real palm trees— not the conventionalized "palm" of the shawls—made jungle patterns on lace and muslin curtains, and their tropic fronds were sharply etched on glass door panels.

For those who romantically yearned to stroll in far-off isles, the designers proffered a substitute: exotic carpets which featured enormous fringed banana leaves and other outlandish vegetation, interspersed with alien gaudy birds. Other jungle motifs invaded the muffled precincts of the home. The fierce leopard was tamed by the carpet manufacturer to lie down peaceably on the hearthrug, and the noble lion was demeaned for the same purpose. To see one's tender infant sprawled before the fire on one of these no-longer-to-be-feared beasts was undoubtedly a titillating sight to Victorian parents.

The use of other exotic products was made fashionable. Good old English oak was shoved aside, and im-

Silver Table Ornament. On opulent dinner tables, palm trees, Orientals, and sphinxes celebrated the expansion of Empire.

ported mahogany, once the most aristocratic of woods, was supplanted by new types of lumber brought in from the four corners of the earth. Most favored was Rosewood, the commercial name for quite a few varieties found in the tropics of both hemispheres. In mid-Victorian days, no well-to-do home was without its parlor suite and piano of this dark, red-brown wood, and no one in those days ever referred to these important decorative possessions without the qualifying adjective. "Rosewood" was inseparably linked with piano and parlor-suite, an indication of the great value set by its owners on this particular material. To contribute to surface patterning, other foreign woods were imported. From the region of the Black Sea came Circassian walnut; Leopard wood and Violet wood came from British Guiana; golden-brown *thuya,* finely speckled and swirled, was from Algeria and Morocco. Prettily named Tulip-wood, rose-colored and striped, and coming from Brazil, adjoined Amboyna and Ebony from the East Indies in the cabinet-makers' shops. The latter was a favorite for pianos and piano keys. In the 1860's, fashion took over the names of these tropical woods and women went clad in colors named *rosewood* and *logwood.* As a further adornment for the formal parlors of the West, India sent a mass of decorative articles made of sandalwood. Victorian ladies kept their most cherished letters in caskets of this scented wood, and pierced and ribbon-threaded fans of the same material exhaled their delicate perfume on many a whatnot shelf after their journey across the several seas. On this innocent repository, objects made of sandalwood showed no trace of the competitive struggle which once took place for this important article of commerce. In early days, the search for sandalwood caused more bloodshed than did even the whaling trade.

In the 1860's the Empress Eugenie appeared, wearing humming-birds as ornaments, a fashionable precedent which created so great a demand for these bits of ornithological jewelry that hunters in far-off Central American and South American jungles found a new kind of livelihood in collecting these tiny marvels.

As exotic and collectible objects, shells, with their intricate frillings and rhythmic flutings, could hardly have failed to attract a public which invariably preferred the elaborately detailed to the simple and unadorned form. In the great range of shells assembled from the Pacific for the embellishment of Victorian life, one ranked above all others in public favor. This was the "pearly nautilus." Poets and painters celebrated its nacreous lustre, and we find it used as an appointment in harmony with the romanticized versions of feminine beauty so popular in the days of steel engravings. To enhance its rainbow hues, the nautilus was often carved with elaborate decorations. The monks of Bethlehem specialized in this art, and a reverential interest was attached to the carved nautilus which was a souvenir of a journey to the Holy Land. The age found the delicate, shifting hues of mother-of-pearl both mysterious and fascinating, and indulged itself without stint in its passion for objects wrought of this substance. Mother-of-pearl, the lining of pearl-mussel shells from which pearls themselves develop, was used as inlay on furniture and was the essential part of the painted ornament on articles made of papier-mâché. It was cut into jewelry as well as buttons, and was worked into such elegant feminine accessories as card-cases. Every correct table setting included a set of fruit knives with mother-of-pearl handles. When eventually fashion lightly turned to other fancies and materials, the livelihood of the collectors at the source—the far-off Arabs of the Red Sea and the romantic Polynesians—was tragically affected.

To the Victorians, shells were admirable material with which to border flower beds. Though they preferred the elaborately curved conch shell for this purpose, they were not above using the humble clam to set boundaries to their horticultural efforts. To women who could not tolerate the untrimmed, the tidy edging of clamshells, outlined against the soil's rich brown, was quite as necessary as the scalloped border to their petticoats. And when these scalloped petticoats sallied out into the garden with a sound soft as the rustle of the wind on the sand dunes, they brushed against the pretty pink lining of the great carved conch which served to hold open the door—a humble task for Beauty.

THE WHATNOT ADDED INTEREST TO LIFE

Whatnots or *étagères* were magnets which attracted all manner of curios, ornaments, and family memorabilia.
Left. Characteristic Whatnot of simpler type, its shelves stepped back gently to its crowning ornament, Victoria, in ceramics.
At bottom. The most luxurious Whatnots were fantastic arabesques of rosewood with mirror-backed shelves.

Searfaring men, journeying to the world's far corners, returned bearing shells as gifts. These women viewed as ornaments for whatnot and centre table. Besides making collections and learning how to paint them in careful compositions (lower left), women were encouraged by their periodicals to study the scientific nomenclature of shells—a subtle encouragement of broader female education.
Above. The interest in shells is reflected in a textile design for upholstery material, presented in 1853.

Courtesy, Index of American Design, National Gallery of Art

Left. An example of mosaic inlay (*pietra dura*) could usually be found, together with shells carved with cameos, among the whatnot's curios. Both were Italian crafts.

Courtesy, The Metropolitan Museum of Art

From the author's collection

Courtesy, The Valentine Museum, Richmond, Va.

THE SCRAPBOOK ADDED COLOR AND CLUTTER

The collecting of embossed Scrapbook pictures was a major craze. German lithographers produced them in a countless variety of subjects. To choose and dissect individual motifs from the large sheets in which they were clotted together was one of the pleasures of scrapbook making. The tinier examples of these pictures were used to decorate album pages or visiting cards.

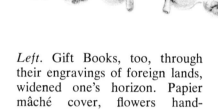

Left. Gift Books, too, through their engravings of foreign lands, widened one's horizon. Papier mâché cover, flowers hand-painted on black and pearl.

As in today's greeting cards, the assortment of sentimental devices was endless. A slight search disclosed a pictorial expression for every emotion or sentiment.
Below. Sheet of Alphabet — for monograms.
Left. One-quarter of sheet of birds.

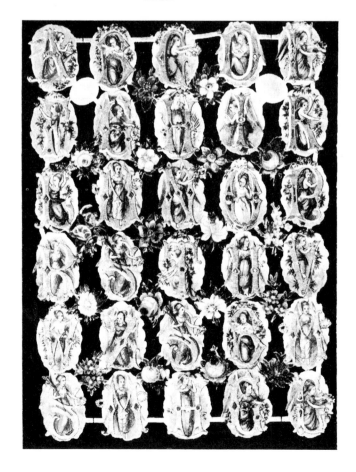

All examples from the author's collection

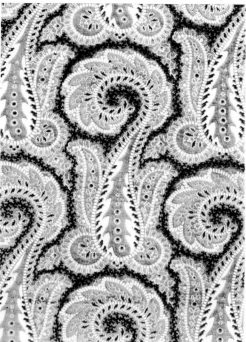

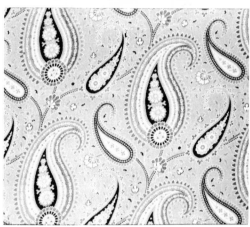

Courtesy, Metropolitan Museum of Art

For a time a curious Oriental form, introduced to the West by means of the Cashmere shawl, was ubiquitous. Imitations made in Paisley, Scotland, of that costly article fastened the town's name to the motif, completely obliterating the botanically inappropriate term originally applied to it, the Indian "palm" or "pine." Archaeologists, aware of the same form on the ruins of Persepolis, stressed the pattern's likeness to the Oriental cypress, its tip swayed by the breezes.

Left. Shawl Pattern, developed at Paisley. 1851.

Above. Printed Cottons. Russian. Late 19th century. Finding the soil congenial, the motif continued to flourish on the textiles of the West.

ALBUM 4

Of the Romance of Living in the Past
Or in Scotland or Turkey without
Setting Foot from the Home
Of Early Antiquarians in General &
Of Sir Walter Scott in Particular
Of the Romantic Novel &
Knights and Ladies and Ruined Abbeys
Of Battlemented Wooden Castles &
Castellated Cottages
Of Machine-made Gothic
Of Jigsaw and Iron Traceries
Of Morayma, Clemira, Arzelia, &
The Oh-so-Saxon
Adelgitha

ALBUM FOUR

THE WORLD OF ROMANCE

Why does fair Margaret so early awake,
And don her kirtle so hastilie;
And the silken knots, which in hurry she would make,
Why tremble her slender fingers to tie;
Why does she stop, and look often around,
As she glides down the secret stair;
And why does she pat the shaggy blood-hound,
As he rouses him up from his lair;
And, though she passes the postern alone,
Why is not the watchman's bugle blown?

The ladye steps in doubt and dread,
Lest her watchful mother hear her tread;
The ladye caresses the rough blood-hound,
Lest his voice should waken the castle round;
The watchman's bugle is not blown,
For he was her foster-father's son;
And she glides through the greenwood at dawn of light,
To meet Baron Henry, her own true knight.

Sir Walter Scott
The Lay of the Last Minstrel. Canto II

AT a time when the world of reality was moving forward at a pace never before known in history, when railroads and steamships were altering the very texture of humanity's thinking, the Victorians were concentrating all their artistic and literary interests in the World of Long Ago. This world, with no existence except in the minds of its creators, caught and held the Victorian imagination for decades. The fragment of Scott quoted above is excellently furnished with most of the chief components of this retreat; the main actors—the ladye and the brave knight—hold the centre of the stage, but fully to round out the décor one should add some mossy turrets, shafted oriels, and hawthorn bowers, and accent it with a dash of latticed windows and dungeon halls. If equipped with these properties, any picture of feudal times, no matter how fantastic, could find an enthusiastic audience. For the Victorians, as a group, were sublimely gifted in ignoring life; with one's mind fixed on the past it was impossible to see the sordidness, the horrors, which choked the everyday world about one. It has been hinted that the Victorian mind escaped into the past because it could not face the world in which it lived; the idea had not yet taken root that present unpleasantnesses could be dealt with. Only that which was far away in time and place was fit subject matter for artist as well as author—only the picturesque, the foreign, above all, the mediaeval. This false and sentimental attitude so influenced all the arts that only in the last half century have its dictates been wholly relinquished in favor of the realistic and the functional.

The exigencies of modern life demand, and the public generally accepts, the doctrine that use dictates the form. But in other times form and style were at the mercy of many influences; they might result from the taste and whimsy of a ruling monarch, from interests stimulated by archaeological discoveries; or the taste of the public might even undergo radical alterations because of the powerful influence exercised on it through the works of its favorite authors. Today the printed word unsupported by illustration would have no effect whatever on decoration; to affect ornamental styles, it must be accompanied by pictures, for the latter convey a definite impression which the printed word does not. Early in the nineteenth century, however, before the world had become indifferent to the flood of printed material which now pours from the presses,

53

Decorator's Sketch for wall treatment, 1827. To satisfy the public's
demand for romance, walls were painted with traceries and ruins.

the writers of the day, particularly several of the great Romantics, had a definite effect on the arts—one which designers proceeded actively to forward.

Just recently we have witnessed a fashion in decoration which was introduced through the filming of an enormously popular novel. *Gone With the Wind,* while quite as romantic in its way as any of the early nineteenth-century novels, could have altered absolutely nothing in the contemporary scheme of furnishing as a written work unsupported by any picturization. But its translation into a film resulted in the public's adoption of many incongruous bits of old-time décor, the worst of which is a plague of lamps of extreme hideousness. These resurrected Victorian lamps—known today as "Gone With the Wind lamps"—should have been allowed to remain in the forgotten corners to which they had been consigned half a century ago, after gas and electricity had rendered them out-of-date. But their appearance amidst the florid furnishings of the film's Victorian settings carried a terrific impact to a public not equipped to judge the period, one with which they

had for the most part no close affiliations, either in memory or by inherited background. Eager to possess what seemed to be charming relics of an appealing past, they went searching for duplicates of the lamps. Soon the manufacturers obliged with new, electrified versions of these gaudy, bulbous articles, and today we are confronted with a revival of something which is, in its way, as remote from present-day living as were some of the decorative throwbacks of the Victorians. For this retroversion, the antiquarian film must bear the whole responsibility.

In the first half of the nineteenth century, however, when the entire world displayed a sudden interest in the Gothic style, this odd vagary of fashion could be traced, not to pictures, but directly to the romances of Sir Walter Scott. If one did not know its sources, this trend in decoration would have seemed an inexplicable retroversion in a world on the march. As the undoubted pioneer of the whole Romantic movement, Scott created an entirely new public for novels, one which, now that books had suddenly become cheaper, developed an

Her Majesty's Private Dining Room at Windsor. In 1847, the *Illustrated London News* reports on its superb decoration.

unlimited appetite for his enchanting re-creations of chivalry and of antique times. So powerful was the effect of his literary works on the imaginations of his readers that it is not at all surprising to find them setting aside the dignified neo-classic styles which were still in favor at the time of Victoria's birth—a date which coincided with the publication of one of Scott's great romances, *Ivanhoe*. The middle classes now began to look agreeably on an era which they had hitherto regarded as shrouded in horrid melancholic gloom: a mediaeval abbey, once viewed with dread and superstitious awe, now became a thing of pilgrimage and picnics.

With great gusto the Victorians intertwined the Gothic with the strands of their daily lives. It became not only the fashion in architecture, but it influenced the styles of furniture, the designs of fabrics, wallpaper, painting, decoration, and illustration. Furthermore, the Gothic altered trends in travel, and its effect was noticeable even in the appellations fastened on defenseless girl-children at their christenings. But the taste for the Gothic was supported not only by the middle classes; it

met with approval in the highest circles as well. When the Prince Consort was selecting subjects for the mural decorations to be installed in the garden pavilion at Buckingham Palace, earlier described, it was practically foreordained that he should choose, at least for the chamber allotted to the "Romantic" style, subjects taken from the works of Sir Walter.

While Scott's was undoubtedly the most popular contribution, other scholarly antiquarians—religious, literary, and artistic—delving in the same field, added greatly to the factual knowledge of the Gothic. One such antiquary was John Britton, 1771-1857, who, though obliged to earn a living as a singer, waiter, and writer of popular songs, developed so great a love for the hitherto neglected beauties of English mediaeval architecture that his efforts resulted in a series of great illustrated works. These books were of a new type, for Britton dramatized the poetry, the charm of ruins and ancient monuments and inspired his readers to journey forth to see the relics for themselves.

Equally important was the passionate zeal of a still

The "Fatal Letter" and endless other prints depicted for the sheltered the dangerous life of maidens who lived in castles.

earlier searcher in the field of literary antiquities who, in one volume, Percy's *Reliques of Ancient English Poetry,* caught the quintessence of all mediaeval romance. This collection of ancient ballads would never have been preserved for the world if their editor, Bishop Percy, had not rescued them, literally, as "brands from the burning." Seeing a housemaid attempting to light a fire with what was, to her, nothing but a worthless collection of old manuscripts, he snatched them from her hands. In 1765, he presented their antique cadences to the English-speaking world.

The sentimental absorption in the life of former times continued to grow—a trend that was reflected in a flood of new novels and of periodicals which specialized in what were then known as "Gothic" tales. And the field of art was utterly dominated by the pictured aspects of the same life. The early Victorian artist was sure of appreciation only when he confined himself to subject matter based on the more glamorous aspects of the mediaeval past or when he presented an imaginative picture of life as it was supposed to be lived in the Scottish highlands. These artistic works so accurately mirror the literary influences of the day that the engravings of paintings which filled the annuals and new magazines might

have served just as well as illustrations for Scott and Percy. And since pirating was a widespread practice, these pictures *were* frequently pressed into service by publishers in need of a few engravings to furbish up a new edition.

Though the Victorians may have displayed but little interest in the life of their contemporaries less fortunately situated, they were thoroughly apprised, through these works of art, of the more attractive and disinfected aspects of mediaeval existence. That life, as shown in the steel engravings of the day, was usually enacted against a backdrop of a Gothic castle, veiled in a haze which covered all unpleasant crudities. Maidens peered from castle towers while they awaited the return of knightly defenders, or waved to their noble lovers as those gentlemen in armor left for the wars. Other touching subjects in the ladies' annuals depicted kirtled damsels immured in dungeons or kneeling in prayer at cloistered shrines. Occasionally, when not at their almost perpetual orisons, the forlorn ladies sat with their companions in their traceried bowers wringing their lily-white hands.

The influence of this type of engraving soon permeated the arts of decoration as well, particularly those which lent themselves to facile reproduction of the subject matter of the prints, such as needlepoint, amateur paintings in young ladies' albums, and professional embellishments on papier-mâché.

From the very first, Scott's literary efforts brought him honor. His *Lay of the Last Minstrel,* which appeared in 1805, sold more rapidly than any other poem had ever done. The beautiful ruins of Melrose Abbey which it celebrated became a place of pilgrimage and the subject of endless engravings and bits of applied art. Since Sir Walter had once suggested that

"If thou would'st view fair Melrose aright,
Go visit it by the pale moonlight;"

pilgrims to this literary shrine were enchanted if they caught a glimpse of the abbey at its most dramatic, or were desolate if, after having made the tedious journey, the Scottish climate destroyed (as it usually did) their opportunities for poetic reveries. But if their jaunts were disappointing, the alert British manufacturer of papier-mâché was ready with a substitute for lost moonlight, one guaranteed to shimmer permanently. For such sentimental romantics the industry turned out all kinds of small accessories and pictures decorated with mother-of-pearl abbeys and castles, gleaming with moon-lit radiance, eternal and unchanging against a ground of midnight black.

As Scott's romances flowed with great regularity from the presses, the fervor for things both mediaeval and Scottish never lacked fuel to keep it alive. Drawn northward by the glamorous embellishments which the novelist had thrown over his beloved countryside, more and more English travellers flocked to Scotland. So fashionable did such pilgrimages become that the rates of travelling by post-chaise were increased. Each traveller returning from a visit to the bare, gray, heather-covered hills added his enthusiasm to the growing interest in legendary lore. To the Victorian mind, Scotland and the works of Sir Walter were indivisible: sight-seers turned his writings into guide-books. When Victoria travelled with Albert in the region, a copy of Scott travelled with her, and she notes in her journal that she read to Prince Albert the first three cantos of the *Lay of the Last Minstrel* "which delighted us both," as well as selections from *Marmion* during the same journey.

Even Scott's literary and artistic contemporaries were drawn to the scene of his labors, in particular to Abbotsford, his great baronial residence, and on it based many paintings and descriptive articles. Situated on its bare moor, Abbotsford took more than a decade to build; it was not completed until 1824. The supervision of this long-drawn-out construction gave the great author much pleasure—he viewed the building as "one of his air castles which he was reducing to solid stone and mortar." Melrose Abbey, which he had long been mining for literary inspiration, now furnished him with decorative material as well, for it became a rich quarry from which he dug out choice bits of Gothic sculpture to incorporate into the fabric of his new mansion. Descriptions of Abbotsford appeared in the very early days of publishing, even in the then remote American journals. By 1834, the genteel readers of *Godey's Lady's Book* were made acquainted with details of its furnishings, and other articles elsewhere stimulated an interest in the Gothic style. A writer in a "keepsake," *The Anniversary,* brought out in 1829, floridly describes the establishment which was probably the grand-daddy of the whole Gothic Revival. How the Americans of the period must have revelled in this picture of something which was totally different from their own simple wood and brick houses! "The house," says this anonymous writer, "is more than one hundred and fifty feet long in front, as I paced it; . . . has a tall tower at either end, the one not the least like the other; presents sundry *crow-*

Scottish scenes, prettily presented, provided background décor for readers of Sir Walter's poems and historical romances.

footed, alias *zigzagged,* gables to the eye; a myriad of indentations and parapets, and machicolated eaves; most fantastic waterspouts; labelled windows, not a few of them painted glass; groups of right Elizabethan chimneys; balconies of divers fashions, greater and lesser; stones carved with heraldries innumerable. . . ." These were details which, in less elaborate form, could be found incorporated in the Victorian house all through the period.

Scott was undoubtedly the first person in the public eye to start the vogue for antiques. As the great pile was so long under way, he had plenty of time to search for material suitable for his purpose. In 1822, he wrote to a friend: "Had three grand hawls since I last wrote to you. The pulpit, repentance stool, King's seat, and God knows how much of carved wainscot, from the kirk of Dunfermline, enough to coat the hall to the height of seven feet: supposing it boarded above for hanging guns, old portraits, intermixed with armor, etc. It will be a superb entrance gallery . . ."

As Abbotsford's fame spread, total strangers made contributions of antique fragments. But in his reconstruction of mediaeval times, Sir Walter encountered the usual difficulties, for he ran out of material and it was necessary to find more to complete the job. Since no one in the 1820's had yet set up in business as a dealer in antiques, the mediaeval woodwork had to be searched for elsewhere than in shops. Fortunately, Scott's agent located in a lumber yard an ancient porch covered with carved (and *whitewashed*) panels, which had been acquired from a recently dismantled prison in Edinburgh, the Tolbooth. Happily for Scott, the owner of this relic willingly exchanged it for a sum which would enable him to pay for a replacement.

The novelist's predilection for old black oak and rich color was in marked contrast to current taste, which dictated that both walls and woodwork be painted only in bright, cold tints. Fashion, however, also accepted painted simulations of rare materials, such as marble. Where construction demanded authentic material, as in doors and wainscoting, the genuine oak was used, but where strength was unimportant, as on ceiling and cornice, plaster modelled and painted in frank imitation of that honest timber was generally employed. Therefore when Sir Walter ordered the library walls to be *decorated* to look like stone and the woodwork to be *painted* in exact likeness of English oak, he was following the taste of the day. And, so that there would be no doubt as to the exact effect he desired, he suggested to his decorators that the woodwork should appear somewhat "weatherbeaten and faded, as if it had stood untouched for many years." Thus did Sir Walter lend his approval to "antiquing"—that method of faking the appearance of age which, even today, has its innumerable admirers. None of Scott's visitors was aesthetically disturbed by this union of the genuine and the spurious;

so they bestowed quite as much admiration on the painted facsimiles of carved oak picture frames which surrounded authentic oil paintings previously built into the walls, as if they had been wrought by the chisel rather than by the decorator's brush. Such examples of *trompe-l'oeil* were then considered delightful; today they suggest nothing as much as old-fashioned painted stage sets.

To enhance the rich hues of the genuine as well as the perfectly imitated oak, the wallpaper selected was of crimson—that depressing hue which was to afflict the walls of Victorian dining rooms the rest of the century. Other mediaeval decorative ideas incorporated in Abbotsford appeared in interior furnishings elsewhere all through the century—ceilings embellished with heraldic shields, somewhat illegible black letter inscriptions as borders in libraries, and dolorous windows of stained glass.

With the décor for libraries established by the greatest literary light of his time, none of Scott's imitators ever dreamed of departing from the sombre gravity of his scheme. To the newly rich, none too familiar with books, the possession of a Gothic library, dark with panelling, carried an almost overpowering aroma of mediaeval scholarship. As the century wore on, the painted imitations of carved ornament might become amusingly out of date, and would then be replaced by actual traceries of very golden oak. But bits of ornamental glass—the debased descendants of mediaeval glory—continued to scatter their kaleidoscopic hues over the walls and woodwork of houses of every grade, from those of the wealthy in Scott's day to those of the most modest in President

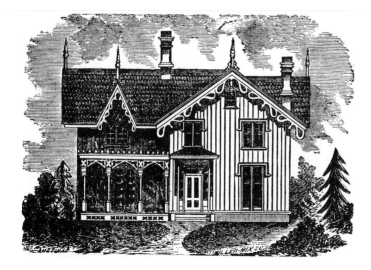

Everyone could have a Gothic dwelling. The farmer's home was of wood, bursting out in gables and thin, jigsaw scrolleries.

The suburban dweller ordered a Gothic cottage, stuccoed, many-gabled, enhanced with fences and verandahs of cast iron.

Garfield's time.

Since Abbotsford was viewed by all classes of persons, the taste for the mediaeval idea in furnishing spread like wildfire. By 1827 a set of furniture had been made for Windsor Castle in this new-old style. In the same year, its designer, Augustus Charles Pugin, presented the public with a book of colored engravings depicting furniture designed in the "Gothic manner," aimed to please "gay and lively fashionables." So linked has the Gothic become in the present-day mind with the ecclesiastic that it is difficult to realize that in Victorian days persons lived from choice in houses which were built to look like Gothic castles and attended to their religious duties in churches constructed along the lines of Greek temples.

To the English Victorians, the name Pugin became a household word. It was not, however, due to the influence of the elder—Augustus Charles Pugin—but to that of his far more famous son, Augustus Welby Pugin (1812-1852), whose work is permanently associated with the Gothic Revival. The younger Pugin, an architect, was a passionate devotee of the mediaeval way of life. Ignoring the fact that old-time craftsmanship was no longer available since modern inventions had destroyed the need for it, Pugin campaigned in lively fashion against shams and substitutes, but with little result. As he grew older, he began to suspect that it was indeed impossible to return to earlier ways of living, and undoubtedly he regretted the flood of atrocious Gothic which resulted from the style which he and his father had done so much to foster—a flood which nothing could stem. "Cheap deceptions of magnificence," he writes in 1841, "encourage persons to assume a semblance of decoration far beyond their means or their station, and it is to this cause we may assign all that mockery of splendour which pervades even the lower classes of society. Glaring, showy, and meretricious ornament was never so much in vogue as at present; it disgraces every branch of our art and manufactures."

Despite the scarcity of good architects, the taste for the new fashion developed quickly in the United States, and by the 1830's there were many examples of the style. The Gothic was thought to be particularly well suited to the American countryside—a region characterized by the "wilder, romantic and more picturesque country where the hand of man has been only partially laid on the forest. This type of terrain," says A. J. Downing, the greatest American arbiter of architectural taste in the first half of the nineteenth century, "supplies the appropriate background for a style which sprang up among the rocks and fastnesses of Northern Europe." Mr. Downing's affection for the Gothic was responsible for innumerable examples of the Old English Cottage, and of residences in the Castellated Style, as the domestic specimens imitative of castles were then called. Like mushrooms, they popped up on every hill in the more cultivated regions of the country, for country estates were then a fashionable indulgence, and the Gothic, the only style then considered appropriate for rural living.

In 1836, a traveller, describing his initial train ride on New Jersey's first railroad, indicates the early flowering of this taste: "Our ride to Philadelphia over the Camden and Amboy Railroad and up the beautiful Delaware was truly delightful, especially the latter. New

In the staid aggregation of Philadelphia's Georgian red brick and white trim, this exotic residence attracted much attention.

Wealth commanded a castellated stone villa, with parapets, towers, and the lancet-shaped windows of genuine old castles.

and beautiful scenes continually opened to view—with fine country seats, built in imitation of Gothic castles, with towers and battlements standing amid a fine growth of trees of every kind. . . ." To be sure, the make-believe castle might be but a wooden one, stuccoed the color of gray stone, with the mortar of non-existent joints neatly painted on in white; the roof-line, however, was gratifyingly that of a castle, complete with machicolated parapets and embrasures. Turrets concealed the chimney flues, and every window was uncompromisingly lancet-shaped.

Downing, reflecting the Victorian admiration for home life, regarded the Gothic as the style most capable of expressing "the quiet domestic feeling of the library and family circle." In addition he thought that the exterior of a well-designed Rural Gothic Villa ought to convey its owners' "strong aspirations towards something higher than social pleasures." To the more frivolous, he allotted residences built in imitation of the Classic and Italian periods, styles which he considered suggestive of "the gay spirit of the drawing room." In his choice of Gothic for use in the country, however, he urged restraint on his clients and deprecated a too florid imitation of ecclesiastical motifs in such rural dwellings —advice the American admirers of Romantic architecture must have found difficult to accept, so eager were they for embellishments.

Pugin, shocked by the absurd examples of castellated architecture which he saw on every hand, came out flatly in 1841 with the statement that "Ancient architecture ought to furnish inspiration but imitators produce ridiculous results." Any architect living in England, rich in authentic examples of the mediaeval, might well wince at the depressing imitations which he saw everywhere about him. But in the whole vast stretch of America there was not the slightest trace of ancient Gothic architecture to which the sensitive might point as a deterrent to those who were about to perpetrate some fantastic outrage on good taste. Without such critical restraints, American contractors, sure of the demand, went on building their gimcrack castles and cheap cottages, for the desire to own a house built in the Gothic style had descended to those possessing even the most modest of incomes. Carpenters who built these toy "Old English" cottages soon discovered that sharply peaked gables, applied wherever they could tack them on to the thin board construction, were sufficient to convey the Gothic idea. And if, to the many gables, they added an edging of mediaeval tracery cut with a scroll

saw, their undemanding clients, ignorant of the heavy, hand-carved vergeboards of the ancient English cottage, were enchanted with their gingerbread imitations of this handsome architectural feature.

As the nineteenth century moved into its sixth decade, the craze for the Victorian Gothic house must have reached its utmost in absurdity, for we find it dealt with by the writers of the day. James Russell Lowell accepted the challenge offered his pen by the sight of a ridiculous wooden castle, set on an unshaded, mathematically squared lawn patterned with flower beds of equal geometrical perfection. His good-natured satire called "The Unhappy Lot of Mr. Knott" was published in *Graham's Magazine* of April, 1851.

> "My worthy friend, A. Gordon Knott,
>   From business snug withdrawn,"

was the subject of the verses. Lowell continues

> "And, since no man, retired with pelf,
>   The building mania can shun,
>   Knott, being middle-aged himself,
>   Resolved to build (unhappy elf!)
>   A mediaeval mansion.
>   *   *   *
> Whatever any body had
> Out of the common, good or bad,
> Knott had it all worked well in,
> A donjon-keep, where clothes might dry,
> A porter's lodge that was a sty,
> A campanile slim and high,
> Too small to hang a bell in;
> All up and down and here and there,
> With Lord-knows-whats of round and square
> Stuck on at random everywhere,
> It was a house to make one stare,
> All corners and all gables . . ."

Since the scroll saw quickly produced crude approximations of what was formerly the result only of laborious handwork, Victorians were tempted to use this substitute for woodcarving everywhere. But it was far from being the only means by which they satisfied their insatiable love of fussy design for when its possibilities were exhausted they were not at all baffled, since the recent application of cast iron to the purposes of ornamental building construction opened up new fields for decorative display.

Designers for this product brought out patterns calculated to attract the eye of the romantically inclined. No longer need the owner of a new Gothic mansion enclose his velvety lawn with anything so commonplace as a white picket fence. Now he could purchase fanciful cast iron traceries, as Gothic in detail, if not in material, as that of the most ornamental of ancient stone or wood carvings. As additional mediaeval garnish, the foundrymen stood ready to supply porches and verandas patterned in formal Gothic trefoils or quatrefoils, as well as garden pavilions—the latter affairs being frivolous counterfeits of the flamboyant traceries of a cathedral window. Over these lacy structures, the Victorian maidens coaxed vines to grow, to simulate the antique arbors of their sentimental reveries. And if the solemn English ivy, accustomed to a support of honest stone, refused to clamber over a deceitful edifice of iron, the light-minded native vines were found to be more accommodating and made quite as satisfactory if less poetically evocative green draperies.

As a sense of incongruity was no component of the staid Victorian mentality, this make-believe mediaevalism was permitted to tincture every phase of life. In the 1840's, even fashion was touched by the Romantic idea, and women added to the crinoline what was then called a "Gothic" corsage. This was a style in which the lower edge of the bodice was curved into a sharp descending point, an inspiration unquestionably derived from the lancet arch, whose line, inverted, it precisely paralleled.

Not even the changes which took place in fashion, in home decorations, and in architecture satisfied the cravings of the intense Romantic for further alliances with the Long Ago. Sentimental novel-reading mothers, immersing themselves still deeper in the world of their imagining, saddled helpless girl-babies with the names of their favorite heroines. In 1843, the writers for the ladies' magazines were producing heroines named Morayma, Clemira, Orinda, Zemira, Glaphyra, and the oh-so-Saxon Adelgitha. Though a woman sensitive to public opinion might hesitate to select quite such fantastic inventions, realizing that her neighbors and family might consider them frankly outlandish, she yet approached them as closely as she dared. Women who lived beyond the duration of this craze went to their graves labelled for all time with the evidences of this fashion. A quick glance at the marble, flower-wreathed stones in the early Victorian section of any old cemetery will disclose that women bearing such names as Arzelia, Ermina, Rejessa, Markina, Clarimond, and Diademia once lived and breathed—sad creatures of fact, not sentimental exotics of fiction.

In addition to these touching examples of Victorian rebellion against the commonplace still visible on tombstones, many specimens of the Victorian Gothic residence are extant, both in city and in country districts: the substantial stone and stuccoed mansion as well as the wooden farmhouse and cottage, their eaves still supporting the remnants of the once-so-fashionable edging of wooden lace. Where the battlemented stucco castle stands deserted, once trim trees and shrubs crowd jungle-thick, and push exploring fingers through broken windows of many-colored glass. In the dark of the moon, fog drifts about the ruined toy-like turrets. Morayma's or Arzelia's bower is given over entirely to bats and rubble, and the thrust of strong vines has pushed apart its delicate iron traceries.

In truth the decaying structure conveys to the present-day observer the same sense of horror and mystery that the mediaeval ruin conveyed to the popular mind. Lacking the patina which the mellowing touch of time and nature gave to the ruins of the middle ages, the abandoned *Victorian Gothic* domicile, its shoddy fabric disintegrating before one's eyes, has today become the artistic and literary symbol of "the haunted house."

THE GOTHIC TOUCH WAS INESCAPABLE

When A. J. Downing, the arbiter of architectural taste, showed Americans how easily a plain country house could be transformed into a romantic residence, by adding gables, verandahs, diamond-paned windows, and a coat of fawn paint, he gave great impetus to the building mania of the 1850's. Amusingly enough, many of these farmhouses altered a century ago have been restored again to their white, pre-Downing state.

Photo by Oscar May

While there was nothing unique in churches and public buildings modelled on the Gothic, a guard's shelter in a public park (*above*) and a marble-cutter's yard are quaint examples of the neo-Gothic's pervasiveness.

Left. House at Gambier, Ohio. Excellent example of what were denounced by some as "fancy houses."

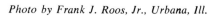

Photo by Frank J. Roos, Jr., Urbana, Ill.

Photo by Oscar May

The character of Gothic tracery was such that, without alteration, it could be translated from wood or stone carving into the molded forms of iron or terra cotta, though the limitations of the molding process stripped it of its original vivacity of execution. Tracery confronted one everywhere: on garden benches and urns, on formidable entrance gates to minute grass plots. These gates bristled with pinnacles and crawled with crockets. *Above.* Cemetery plots were enclosed with foliated traceries of iron.

Left. Gothic patterns applied by early American foundrymen to wood-burning stove. *C.* 1820.

Courtesy, Philadelphia Museum of Art

Photo by Oscar May

Courtesy, Index of American Design, National Gallery of Art

THE GOTHIC DOMESTICATED

The Bookcase or Secretary, scaled for lofty ceilings, could hardly escape a touch of Gothic; its very height was an invitation to the style's aspiring lines. Openwork tracery topped elegant examples and covered glass door panels. By the 1840's Americans were so familiar with Gothic details that even the simplest country-made furniture was almost certain to display some hint of the pointed arch. (See bookcase doors in contemporary engravings, *c.* 1845, showing middle-class appointments. p. 115. Illustration from children's story, detailing the charms of housework.)

Courtesy, Index of American Design, National Gallery of Art　　*Courtesy, Chester Co. Historical Society, West Chester, Pa.*

The Victorian Gothic chair was planned for style, not comfort. While it gave the home a desirable Gothic note, it was at the same time the beloved accessory of the daguerreotypist's studio, for it provided that busy man with an elaborate background detail. His clients, anxious to be recorded for posterity, disregarded the inconvenience of the knobs and turnings against which they were so stiffly propped.

"Cottage Pianoforte" of English manufacture, shown in 1855. Both its material (walnut) and its lines are reminiscent of church pews.

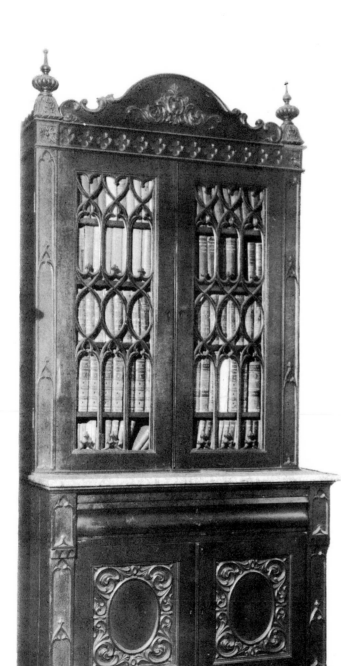

Courtesy, Index of American Design, National Gallery of Art

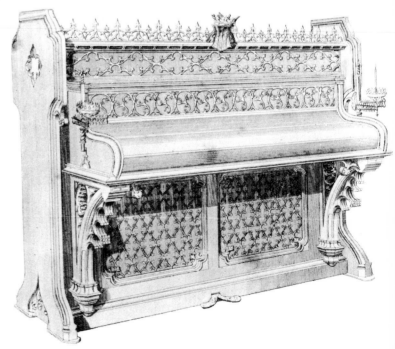

In 1827, a Gothic Commode was the newest thing for drawing room decoration.

Parlor Stand for richly colored foliage. Gothic arches provide a romantic support for vines.

Right. Sideboard. English. Shown in 1851 at the Great Exhibition. In perfect harmony with the spirit of the time. Designed for use in mansion styled in Gothic. The construction details, while providing bold contrasts in light and shade, practically did away with all storage space.

Above. "Carpenter Gothic" Sideboard. Simplicity of line, though tolerated, was not considered to have any particular merit.

From the author's collection

Above, top of page. Printed Cotton Hangings were striped with Gothic balconies and barred with heraldic charges.

Left. "Gothic Pattern" Wallpaper, printed from wood blocks. English, *c.* 1840–1850. The modish wall was covered with an upward surge of pointed canopies and slender columns.

The Gothic flourished on the printed page. Initial Letters from L. Johnson, Typefounders. Philadelphia. *C.* 1850–1860.

Courtesy, Victoria and Albert Museum

ALBUM 5

Of Victorian Eclecticism &
Of How All Things Became Domesticated
Except the Sphinx
Of Tombs Despoiled &
Hieroglyphics in a London Fog
Of Obelisks
Of the Necklace of Pharaoh
Worn by Dowager and Debutante
Of the Beautiful Lord Byron
With Whom Zoë, Myrrha, Olimpia
And All the World Fell in Love
Of Lord Elgin &
The Rape of the Parthenon
Of the Latter Days of Pompeii
Of the Battle of Goth and Greek
For the Possession
Of the Victorian Soul

THE Victorian world domesticated everything, making household pets not only of the Newfoundland Dog and the Spaniel, but also of the gods of the heathen. On the sacred altar of Home they placed their varied offerings—that geographic-historical mélange in which they delighted.

In the works of the English Miss Mitford, who in the 1830's wielded a gentle but occasionally delicately barbed pen, we can catch a glimpse of a contemporary interior. "Rosedale Cottage," she writes, ". . . is overdone with frippery and finery, a toy-shop in action, a Brobdignagian baby-house. Every room is in masquerade: the saloon, Chinese, full of jars and mandarins and pagodas; the library, Egyptian, all covered with hieroglyphics, and swarming with furniture crocodiles and sphynxes. Only think of a crocodile couch and a sphynx sofa! They sleep in Turkish tents, and dine in a Gothic chapel . . . Now English ladies and gentlemen in their everyday attire look exceedingly out of place amongst such mummery . . ."

Of all ancient cultures with which the early Victorian designers played—and they had a go at all of them—the only one which seemingly baffled them was the art from the land of the Sphinx. We already know how they watered down the arts and crafts of the Middle Ages, so that the lofty Gothic became the plaything of the boudoir. They had long been toying with the arts of classic Greece, arts which they found equally malleable for nineteenth-century uses. Only the Sphinx, with whom they had just become acquainted, refused to become part of the family; she showed a

definite unwillingness to lie down on the Victorian hearthrug with the Victorian pug-dog. All fashion's attempts to make an indoor pet of this desert creature were doomed to ridicule. Today, with libraries filled with publications recording the world's art and archaeology, it is evident that no additional finds, no matter how remarkable, can ever again color public taste to any marked degree. But the early nineteenth century was a period when the antique world, just awakened from its long sleep, began to disclose its beauty and mystery. Then each discovery, even the slightest, fed the public's curiosity, nourished its love of romance, and, as a corollary, was apt to be reflected after a short time in its surroundings. A publication on the arts of Egypt or Greece was then important news, a thing discussed not only in libraries of scholars but also in the drawing rooms of the fashionable.

When the field for antiquarian research was suddenly broadened in the early decades of the nineteenth century, this opportunity came as an accidental offshoot of progress. Men who went about feverishly building railroads uncovered with their cuts and tunnels many earlier forms of man's ways of life. Further impetus to the inquiry into man's past developed when a new class of persons—thanks to industry—found themselves with more money than they could use, and, in addition, an embarrassing amount of leisure. Many of these rich industrialists turned to collecting, and, since archaeological fields offered these dilettantes a fashionable interest, they vied with each other in accumulating material. A prize from any field was always the subject for much publicity. If, in their scramble for antiquities, they or their agents caused much damage, these parvenus must still be credited in part for the mass of early nineteenth-century archaeological material from which the modern world derives much of its knowledge of ancient cultures.

Furthermore, recent improvements in printing were making possible magnificent publications of the arts of the Greeks, of the Middle Ages, of the Italian, the Oriental, and the Egyptian. These appeared suddenly, one treading on the heels of the other. Contemporary designers, overstimulated by such artistic wealth, produced results often really shocking in their tasteless assemblage of incongruous details. But this could hardly be otherwise, for they had as yet no possible opportunity to familiarize themselves with any of the guiding principles which lay behind the arts of these ancient civilizations.

Their deepest pitfalls lay in the hieratic art of the Egyptians, but the subject of Egypt could hardly have been evaded for it was one which, at the junction of the eighteenth and nineteenth centuries, had great appeal for the civilized world. To comprehend this absorbed interest on the part of even the average citizen would be difficult if one were not aware that it had been aroused both by politics and by war. In 1798 Napoleon sailed right under the nose of Nelson's fleet and embarked on a military expedition into Upper Egypt, an action which turned the eyes and the armies of Britain upon him. In 1801, as a result of the defeat and subsequent departure of the French from the land of the Nile, certain antiquities were ceded to the British, among them the famous Rosetta Stone, which had been discovered in 1799 by a party of Napoleon's engineers engaged in digging a trench. At a time when England was just beginning to learn of the existence of Egypt (for before this campaign of Napoleon's even its name was known to only a few) the arrival in London of the Rosetta Stone with its mysterious hieroglyphics provoked intense curiosity.

Then, in 1804, appeared the first publication to acquaint the world at large with the actual appearance of Egypt and its arts—the work of the Baron de Dominique Vivant Denon. Imbued with an overwhelming interest in art and archaeology, Denon had begged to be allowed to join the group of French savants whom Napoleon had already invited to accompany the military expedition. The scientists later published the results of their finds in a series of magnificent volumes —the *Description de L'Egypte*—a work which can well stand as the permanent monument of the Napoleonic

venture. But Denon's account, illustrated and written in a lively manner, had come earlier, and its copperplate engravings depicting "so distant a portion of ancient history" aroused in the public a hankering for this "description of embellishment." It may be that the Baron was one of the first archaeologists to travel with a military expedition, for he records his difficulties, both in the text and in an illustration which serves as frontispiece. This shows him in the Napoleonic uniform, shabby and rumpled, flanked by his horse, his folding stool, and his colored attendant. In the background are the ruins of Hieraconpolis which he is sketching, and the near foreground is occupied by a group of camels and their drivers. Denon drew only at the army's convenience, whenever they made camp or halted a few moments to give the infantry a rest. His drawings in his *Voyage dans la basse et la haute Egypte* reveal a masculine, factual, and unsentimental world. In order to give scale, tiny figures of natives and soldiers are set in contrast to the gigantic monuments he was depicting. Even the Sphinx is submitted to this scientific approach: a group of men stands on her head and a ladder leans casually against her flanks.

After the French capitulation, the current pasha threw open the country to European travellers, and a fierce competitive traffic in Egyptian antiquities began. New accessions were constantly arriving in England. In 1815, a Pharaoh took up his residence in London, and any citizen visiting the British Museum could now confront the great image of his Majesty, Rameses II, face to face. In 1820 a facsimile of the tomb of another Pharaoh was exhibited in Egyptian Hall in the same city. It was then known as "Belzoni's Sarcophagus"— for its original occupant, Seti I, had not yet been identified.

The first decorative inspirations derived from the contemplation of these archaeological wonders seem weighted with an immense solemnity—the Victorian architect, if not the Victorian designer, was sensitive to the portentousness of Egyptian art and used it for equally serious purposes, calculated to move the beholder to thoughts of death. Nor did he miss the correspondence of catacombs with the idea of prisons; therefore prisons styled in the Egyptian manner breathed forth their gloomy implications, even in the United States. Furthermore, the new suburban cemeteries bedecked themselves with embellishments taken from this mortuary culture. Planners of these projects were given to impressive entrances constructed on the lines of

Egyptian temples, and miniatures of these same edifices served as mausoleums within their confines.

As the years passed by, forests of small Egyptian obelisks sprang up to puncture the sky above the cemetery's calm. The first Victorians found the obelisk especially intriguing and romantic because of the undecipherable symbols patterning its surface. Stories about these curious monuments, published from time to time all through the era, always attracted readers. One of the "Cleopatra's Needles," as the obelisks were commonly called, was presented to England by the Pasha in 1819, the same year that the first attempt to decipher the Rosetta Stone (the key to the inscriptions) was published. In 1831 another of these great monuments was presented to France and was erected by 1836. To the great shame of England, the gigantic pillar destined for that country lay in an Alexandrian ditch until 1877, the convenient prey of souvenir hunters who chipped off fragments for their whatnots. In that year means were devised to transport it to London in a cylindrical vessel especially constructed for the purpose. The following year New York City received its own obelisk, and the difficulties attending the removal and the erection of both "Needles" again turned the public's attention to the land of the Sphinx. Again the decorative arts reflected the event; but the revival of the Egyptian style in the 1870's seems to have been confined to the minor arts, particularly those fabricated in metal—jewelry, clocks, and silverware.

Each new flurry of interest, however, was mere curiosity. No Victorian writer was sufficiently stirred by this hieratic and characterful art to enter imaginatively into the distant world from which it had been wrenched and to dramatize it so movingly that the public would desire further evidences of it in the background of their everyday lives. The Pharaohs lacked a poet, and so the taste for the Egyptian flickered feebly and died out, not to appear again until the third decade of the twentieth century when King Tutankhamen, an insignificant Egyptian monarch, became a contemporary celebrity. Egyptian designs suddenly blossomed out on textiles and on bits of decorative trivia; but the vogue was a short-lived one and soon faded as the desire for further novelties supplanted it. Though King Tutankhamen had a far better press and unlimited publicity, his effect on the decorative arts of the twentieth century was slight, if the results are compared with those evolving from the interest in Egypt shown in early Victorian days.

To be Egyptian was to be modern. Cemetery Entrance, 1852.

The Gothic and Egyptian in amiable conjunction. Moyamensing Prison, Philadelphia, 1838.

Waterworks in Philadelphia, details taken from Nile temples.

There remains only one influence which this amazing discovery can be said to have made on present-day taste. Ever since King Tutankhamen's personal adornments were exhumed, a barbaric note has reigned in the fashions for costume jewelry: necklaces are today bolder and heavier, and women's fondness for many large and ornamental bracelets is one which parallels that of the King's contemporaries.

The Victorians were great readers of verse. Theirs was an age which delighted in metre, even apart from content. Through Sir Walter's eight-syllabled measures they had been able not only to indulge themselves in the pleasures of sing-song rhythms but agreeably to acquaint themselves with the historic Scottish past. And when the works of Lord Byron, quite as popular, succeeded in diverting romantic interests from the mediaeval to the Grecian world, the reading public was intoxicated. Through the magic of these two authors, the Victorian reader could swing happily back and forth through the ages and across the world. No frontiers, no dangers were encountered in these imaginative travels.

Had the first half of the nineteenth century been able to invent a personality which would characterize

PORTRAIT of the YOUNG GREEK.
To whom Lord Byron addressed his Poem of "Maid of Athens ere we part"
From a Drawing by Guard by permission of Capt. Le Mesurier.

its romantic ideals, it could not have improved on Lord Byron. His beauty was that of the Apollo Belvedere (a tribute paid him by a masculine, not a feminine contemporary); and the extravagant life led by this dissolute young man was the very stuff of romantic fiction on which his readers secretly—and oh, how secretly!—gloated. Even his abode might have been a figment from the imaginative art and literature of the time, for it was nothing less than a ruined abbey.

It was in 1808, when he was twenty, that Byron came into the estate of Newstead Abbey, which was in great part uninhabitable. After refurbishing a portion of the edifice, he moved into this lordly domain, and from it there began to issue fabulous stories of his caprices. So powerful was Byron's impact on his age that the Abbey itself became the subject of many steel engravings, and even of sentimental pilgrimages. The threadbare terms the poet uses to describe this ancient ruin, "its mouldering turrets," its "grey-worn towers," its once "smiling gardens," its "damp and mossy tombs" epitomized the aspects most dearly cherished by the sentimental, who fed on this depressing stuff and clamored continually for more. Byron loved to be thought mysterious and melancholy, all of which added to the glamorous haze through which sedate Victorian misses viewed this beautiful, exotic young man.

When he came of age, Byron set out on his travels. His writings, reflecting his journeyings, served as romantic guide-books by means of which his many readers received a generous education in the customs and scenery of the "gorgeous East" and in the classical monuments of forgotten corners of the world. The effect of his metrical romances on the culture of the day was enormous. Long after his premature death, artists and engravers were kept busy illustrating his works. Imaginative portraits of Oriental beauties and contemporary Greek maidens now competed in the annuals with forlorn Gothic damsels. And in 1837, for his bereaved admirers, there was published a beautifully illustrated volume appropriately entitled *Le Byron des Dames*.

Byron's influence, like Scott's, was felt in other than literary and artistic fields. Many a girl-child who grew up bearing a melodious but strangely un-Anglo-Saxon name could credit it to this craze for Byron. The poet was unquestionably responsible for such fancies as Genevra, the pleasing Medora, Leonora, and Lesbia, as well as the Turkish Haidee and Zuleika, and the utterly classic Zoë, Myrrha and Olimpia. Florence, now commonplace, can probably also be traced to his works.

Such exotic appellations were the living testimony of many an isolated romantic's revolt against the humdrum texture of her daily life, a revolt in which even the humblest participated. What pleasure and spiritual stimulus must many an aspiring but poverty-stricken woman have experienced as she murmured to her infant the musical syllables of its Byronic name—the poetic key which unlocked the bright world of her imagination!

Though Byron's appreciation of the great monuments of the classic age was fervid, it partook of none of the qualities which went into the making of a connoisseur of the antique. Those who were stimulated by his writings to express an interest in the classic arts themselves, and wished to pursue their studies further along artistic lines, would have been defeated except for an occurrence which fortunately deposited a portion of the greatest Greek art right in England itself, at just about the time Byron set out on his voyagings. In 1807, the first fragments of the Parthenon, the so-called "Elgin Marbles," arrived in London and were put on display. Assembled by the Earl of Elgin, ambassador to Turkey from 1798 to 1802, this so-called "rape of the Parthenon" created a sensation. Elgin had been asked by a Scottish architect, anxious to learn more about Greek antiquities, to bring back pictorial records and casts of classic art. Receiving permission from the Turkish government, Elgin started the undertaking as a public service. But making drawings and castings did not suffice to appease the collector in him. Bitten by a desire to outdo the savants who had accompanied Napoleon into Egypt, he began to crate up the actual fragments themselves. The British were later subjected to extensive criticism for this spoliation. They felt it to be unjustified, for at that time it was common practice for the ordinary traveller to knock off a fragment or two from ancient sculptures as a souvenir. In extenuation of such vandalism it must be said that neither the Greeks, nor their overlords the Turks, viewed their antiquities with any appreciable respect. Eventually the Elgin collection of marbles—which constituted in a sense (as their collector pointed out) a preservation, not a spoliation—was purchased by the English government and placed in the British Museum for the edification of all lovers of classic art.

Other examples of the art of the ancients were soon made available. During the French administration of Naples, the first book on the excavations of Pompeii was brought out in 1812 by F. Mazois. It was a magnificent and costly publication. Soon it was followed by another and much less expensive volume prepared by Sir William Gell, an artistic dilettante. When these initial investigators first began their studies, it was difficult to obtain permission to work. Authorities at Pompeii refused to allow visitors to make even the tiniest sketch, preferring to keep the pictorial recording of the excavations as a local monopoly. Foreign professional artists were forced to wait three or four years for a drawing permit, and witnessed, while they waited, many beautiful and fragile wall-paintings speedily fade and crumble on exposure to the elements. This circumstance was regretted by both Gell and Mazois, who, with their own pencils, toiled long and earnestly to save for posterity as many of Pompeii's rapidly deteriorating treasures as possible. Gell's work, appearing in 1817-1819, gave the average English student his first glimpse into the life and arts of that remote era, and his volumes became the standard textbook to which the creative designers of the period turned whenever they wished to study what they called the "Grecian." It was a term used loosely. So popular were the adaptations of antique forms that "Grecian" was a common adjective which the writers of the day, whenever they needed a fashionable term, found convenient to fit to all manner of attenuated interpretations of the classic. Houses, furniture, even the silken frivolities of the upholsterer, all bore the "Grecian" tag.

The Pompeian is a transitional style lying between the Greek and the Roman—one whose charm for the nineteenth century was based in all probability on its engaging elaborateness, its romantic and historical

Pompeian Suburban Villa, visualized for Godey's readers, 1853.

evocations, and above all on the comparative ease with which its interesting and somewhat decadent motifs and arrangements could be translated into contemporary decorative language. Now, for the first time in history, as a result of the Pompeian discoveries, designers could derive inspiration from actual domestic interiors and accessories, instead of being forced to adapt the austerities of Greek and Egyptian public monuments to such lesser decorative purposes as furniture for which the ancients had left few models.

The painted and decorated walls of the Pompeian interior were turned and twisted to fit a great variety of Victorian demands. Eventually the vogue for painted walls died out and was supplanted by the taste for less costly wallpaper. Even then Pompeian ideas still held sway in certain parts of the house, as the style was one eminently suited for halls and vestibules of Victorian dwellings. *Pompeian red* was a color which, for a long time, ranked high in nineteenth-century decorative schemes. And the Victorian division of the wall space into three sections: the dark dado or base, the middle section, and the upper portion—the frieze— was a style indubitably derived from a close study of Pompeian art.

The first few decades of the nineteenth century witnessed a lively battle between the two architectural styles then struggling for leadership: the Grecian and the Gothic. Both styles had their defenders and both marshalled convincing arguments. For two centuries past the champions of the Classic had been supported by fashion. The taste for the "Grecian" had first sprung up at the time of James I, when various great English mansions were built along classic lines. Since fashion's stamp was attached to the "five orders," those who aped their betters demanded cheap imitations of the Classic. Somewhere and somehow, the idea had developed in the minds of this line of architectural imitators that the possession of a Grecian villa or country house clothed its inhabitants in a mantle of classic scholarship and good taste. This silly snobbishness kept the Classic style in favor until it was used on such insignificant social levels that its defenders could no longer present any sensible argument for its adoption. The battle crossed the seas and was fought—though over less magnificent examples—in the young United States, which, with its passion for novelties and its determination to try everything, built houses first in one style then in the other. A. J. Downing, earnestly trying to instill some principles of taste in the raw American public, was exceedingly critical of the use of the Classic for American domestic purposes. "Fifteen years ago," he wrote in 1838, "there was but one idea relating to a house in the country. It must be a Grecian temple. Whether twenty feet or two hundred feet front, it must have its columns and portico. There might be comfortable rooms behind them or not; that was a matter the *severe* taste of the classical builder could not stoop to consider. The roof might be so flat that there was no space for comfortable servants' bedrooms, or the attic so hot that the second story was uninhabitable in a midsummer's day. But of what consequence was that, if the portico were copied from the Temple of Theseus . . . ?"

Cottages and country houses, he rightly argued, should express simplicities inherent in their surroundings; they should not be miniature wooden caricatures of the Parthenon set down amidst the alien roughnesses of our as yet none-too-developed landscape. Such structures, with their overpowering wooden porticos, he labelled "temple cottages."

The early English architects felt that the style selected for a house should be chosen for a certain effect on the imagination of the beholder. Since in those days one lived architecturally in either the classic or the mediaeval world, the pro-Gothic faction argued reasonably that no *Englishman* could be moved by the sight of a replica of *Greek* architecture, no matter how faithful the copy, for he had had no previous opportunities on his native soil to develop any emotional attachments to the style. In the whole length and breadth of Great Britain, or of America for that matter, they averred, there were no classic ruins, not a vestige of an ancient Greek temple or villa. The Grecian style, therefore, must always remain an alien one, redolent of dusty scholarship. But—continued the supporters of the mediaeval, now on defensible grounds —everyone in England had innumerable emotional ties with the Middle Ages. No one who dwelt on England's historic soil could escape the many surviving examples of the Gothic. Where was there a citizen who could not find embedded in his memory rich sentimental recollections of antique buildings: the ancient ivy-wreathed parish church, the quaint square of the market town bordered with venerable dwellings, the ruins of the castle which dominated the village?

From our present-day viewpoint, it is obvious that the frippery-loving Victorians would eventually range themselves on the side of the mediaevalists and the

Gothic; the scales were so heavily weighted in their favor by romantic picturesqueness. The alteration produced by this switch from the neo-Classic to the Gothic resulted in some amazing architectural monstrosities. Those financially able established new pseudo-castles on gently rounded elevations, trusting hopefully to invoke in the spectator his romantic memories of castle-topped crags. Those enamoured of this fashion, but able to afford only a remodelling job, altered the simple lines of their Grecian houses with gingerbread trimmings. Scratch the Victorian casing and the Classic is frequently discernible just beneath the surface.

As the taste for the Gothic increased, the self-styled "restorers of the antique" found themselves more and more on the defensive, but to little avail until, just when the Classic style in architecture was about to be completely swamped by the neo-Gothic, a new stimulus for the former was provided by Byron's writings. On both sides of the ocean, those swayed by fashionable trends pretended to share with their favorite author the sympathies for the woes of struggling Greece, and found new reasons for attachment to the current manifestations of its arts and architecture. They harped incessantly upon the "exquisite simplicity" and harmony inherent in Grecian forms and gave their patronage to architects who came forth with fetching analogies between Ionic volutes and ladies' curls.

Though the supposed supporters of the Greek taste paid profound lip-service to all that related to the classic orders, these designers made not the least attempt to understand the spirit of the forms which they copied so faithfully. Moldings might be styled with meticulous accuracy, the capitals of columns might be most faithfully reproduced, but beyond this they did not venture. As a result of this piecemeal approach, anything styled "in the Greek manner" in most cases turned out to be in very bad taste, without character, and, naturally, without unity in the conception.

Nevertheless, from the point of view of a designer of

1826, one who was draughtsman to his Majesty, King William IV, the products, emanating from his and other pencils given over to the "Classic," were beyond criticism. In his *Cabinet Maker and Upholsterer's Guide,* George Smith, obviously unafraid of any competition to the "Grecian" (though Pugin's first work on Gothic furnishing was to come out the next year), remarks that "Perfection, it appears, was reserved for the present period, in relation to ornament and domestic embellishment." Despite this enthusiastic championship, the "Grecian" lost and went underground for some decades, only to reappear again in the degenerate eclecticism of latter-day Victorianism. This time it was styled, by the French designer Liénard who introduced it, the *"Neo-Grec."* As a fertile source of inspiration, Liénard seems to have been especially useful to designers of architectural details and interior furnishings; many examples of this late style can still be noted in the substantial construction of old-fashioned houses.

That Liénard went to the classic for inspiration can eventually be deduced: close examination of the sombre-hued brownstone buildings, walnut furniture, and mantelpieces of the sixties and seventies discloses attenuated presentations of certain familiar Greek motifs: the projecting heads of goddesses, the columns, the faintly perceptible forms of swag and vase and anthemion. But to such an anaemic and ghostly state have they been reduced by the designer and the processes of industry that the relation between the Victorian "Neo-Grec" and the antique is barely perceptible. Changes in color have also obscured the source of inspiration. The Neo-Grec was presented not in the soft ivory of antique marbles or the modulated tones of terra cotta or bronze associated with Greek art, but in the lugubrious browns, liver-colored marbles and shiny blacks which were the latter-day Victorian decorator's choice for interior construction purposes. Thus transformed beyond much possibility of recognition, the "Grecian," that once lusty growth, was finally withdrawn from the nineteenth-century scene.

Cast Iron Table. Greek inspiration. 1851.

Courtesy, Metropolitan Museum of Art

Printed Textile. Though sadly debased, the merest suggestion of capital and column satisfied the admirers of the "Grecian."

Anything termed "Grecian" was accorded great deference. As the Greeks left no domestic dwellings, designers of furniture and accessories turned to other examples of Greek arts for inspiration, selecting details with little regard for unity.

Above. Couch Sofa and two Chairs, designed "in the Greek taste." From George Smith's *Cabinet Maker and Upholsterer's Guide,* London, 1826. A work whose influence was soon reflected in pieces by American cabinet makers, such as Duncan Phyfe.

Below. Graceful Chairs in the approved taste of the 1840's.

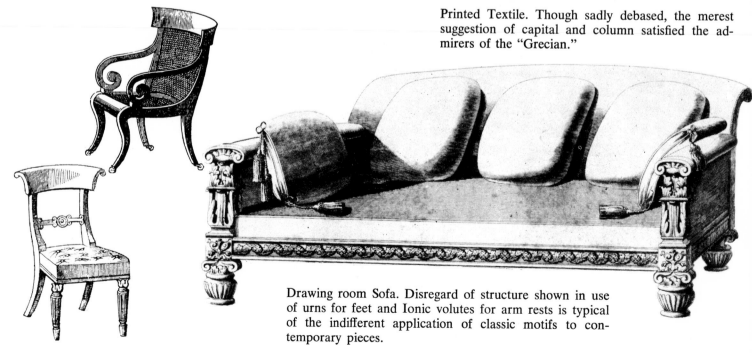

Drawing room Sofa. Disregard of structure shown in use of urns for feet and Ionic volutes for arm rests is typical of the indifferent application of classic motifs to contemporary pieces.

Mass-produced articles "in the Grecian style" were occasionally introduced into the prevalent jungle of Italianate scrollery. The cool classic lines of these objects of daily use pleased the discerning.

Centre. The fancifully ornamented walls of Pompeii supplied inspiration for wall decorations in the nineteenth-century house.

Above. Staffordshire Washbasin and Pitcher. 1851. Decorated with figures taken from Flaxman's drawings. Though Flaxman, who once designed for Wedgwood, died in 1826, his influence persisted. Designers depended on him for neo-classic inspiration, and, for some decades after his death, parlors on both sides of the Atlantic boasted ladies' stilted copies of his drawings.

Top, right. Claret, that nineteenth-century British beverage, was poured from jugs shaped like antique ewers.

Centre. Cut Glass pieces engraved with the chastest of Greek borders demonstrated that beauty and utility could be united.

Below. By 1850, elegantly formed tureens on classic models were obtainable in Britannia ware—a popular metal which ousted pewter.

77

NIGHT

MORNING

Courtesy, Art Institute of Chicago

Thorwaldsen's "Night" and "Morning."

Of all the works of the Danish sculptor Thorwaldsen, his "Night" and "Morning" were the most beloved. Their very presence in a home was a signet of culture. They were reproduced as plaster plaques or as photographs, their delicate graces silhouetted against a black ground. In the form of plaques they were the outstanding preference of those whose tastes leaned toward the classic. In these more austere establishments their whiteness was sometimes accented by tendrils from a frieze of ivy, whose living green was trained to border a room.

Left. The pretty nymphs were also caught in the all-pervasive web of Berlin-work and were executed in silvery-toned beads against a solid color of one's own choosing.

From the author's collection

On a Hand-Blocked Cotton of early nineteenth-century make, animal-headed gods stared out placidly at a world which stared back, profoundly interested in their mysterious forms.

Upper left. Egyptian Decoration. 1827. The world of Victoria's childhood accepted every decorative idea presented to it, appropriate and inappropriate. After confronting a flood of such conceits—the aftermath of recent interest in Egypt—an English writer on architecture, J. C. Loudon, warned the public "never to adopt, except for motives more weighty than a mere aim at novelty, the Egyptian style of ornament." Nevertheless, whenever Egypt made news (as when the Suez Canal was opened in 1868), the arts reflected the event.

American Clock, French Silver and Enamel Tea Service, German neo-Egyptian and neo-Greek Jewelry. *C.* 1868.

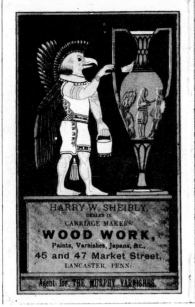

From the collection of Charles Hagerty

THE GRAPHIC ARTS
MEET THE SPHINX

Plate from "Osiris" Fish Service.
Limoges China. 1886.

WE COME FROM THE MUMMY'S LAND TO BRING YOU GREETINGS TO-DAY   IF YOU THINK US A STRANGE LOOKING BAND REMEMBER WHERE WE CAME FROM & PRAY

Courtesy, Free Library of Philadelphia

After color began pouring from the lithographic presses, designers frequently turned to Egypt for inspiration.

Above. Greeting Card. Prang Company, 1883. Egyptian cherubs were so astounding an idea that the card apologizes for their singularity.

Top row. Trade Cards. *C.* 1880. Horus, the hawk-headed, with brush and can of paint, serves to advertise the varnish industry. And royal Cleopatra becomes the handmaiden of a flavoring-extract concern.

Below. Greek and Egyptian mingled form Victorian ornament.

ALBUM 6

Of the Crystal Palace &
Royal Dreams Materialized
Of Industry, the Machine &
The World's Spread of its Wonders
Of Flowers Made of Beetles' Wings &
Gas-jets Formed like Lilies
Of Garden Urns of Iron &
Of Furniture Glamorous with Pearl
Of Catafalques of Walnut, Bedight
With Gilt and Ebony
Of Marble for Everyone
Of Shepherdesses of Parian &
Of China Besprinkled with
Field Flowers Scattered by
The Delicate Fingers of
Dedicated Females

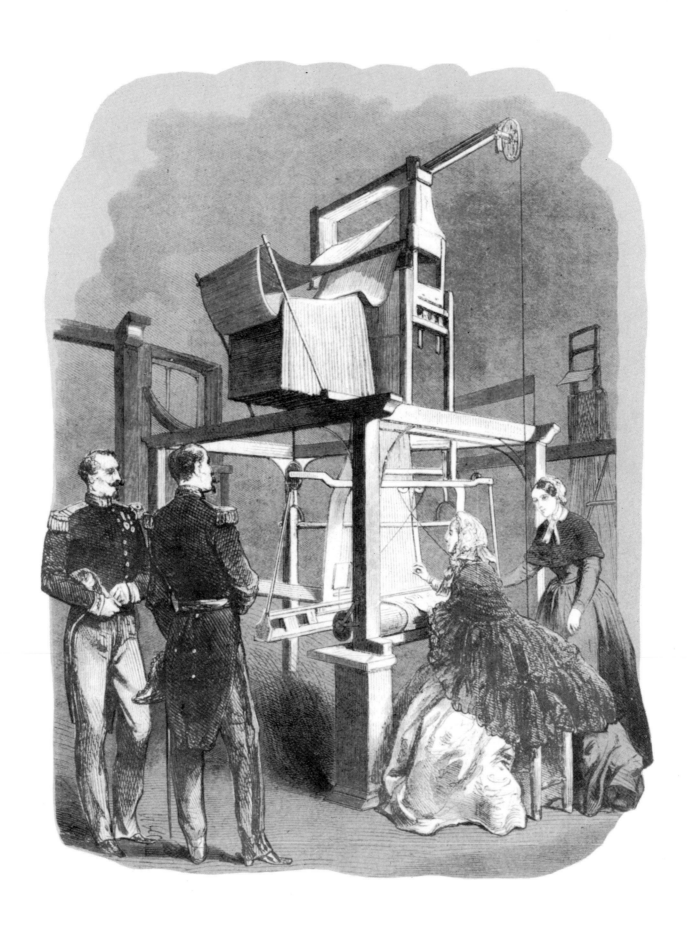

ALBUM SIX

❧❀❧

THE WORLD OF INDUSTRY

HEN the Victoria Regia un-furled her incredible leaves and was finally brought to flower on English soil, the flower-loving people of that tight little isle welcomed it as one more marvel of the amazing age in which they lived. To them it was a convincing symbol of the world about them—a world in which everything was unfolding almost before their very eyes: industry, transportation, ideas, empire. And so it would seem fitting that Mr. Joseph Paxton, the man who had nurtured the Queen's lily into bloom, was to be the person from whose easy pencil sprang the idea of the Crystal Palace, that equally incredible creation which sheltered the first "International Exhibit of Art and Industry."

On its completion, fame—for the second time inspired by the lily—came unsought to Paxton. In his design for the great glass shell, Paxton says, "Nature was the engineer." Marvelling at the way the lily supported its gigantic leaves, the engineer-gardener made a careful study of the structural principles on which Nature had built this wonder. Finding them successful in a new building which housed the demanding lily itself, he applied them again to the Crystal Palace, that fortuitous fairy-tale name bestowed on the edifice by *Punch*. Though it was meant as a mocking appellation, it threw a romantic glitter over what might have been considered simply a humdrum manufacturing show if it had been called by its sonorous official title.

The Crystal Palace was the magnificent materializa-tion of a cherished dream of the Prince Consort's: his conception of a method by which the nations could get together in friendly fashion, forget national jealousies and hatreds, and, by exhibiting their respective achievements, study and learn from one another.

The world's initial attempt at co-operation in the arts of peace was indeed stupendous—a palace of the Arabian Nights evolved by magic on England's sober soil. This edifice was put together from standardized units—an idea then quite as novel as was the material of which it was constructed. Its extent was so vast (1900 feet long and over 400 feet wide) that its far reaches were lost in a blue haze—the only building in the world in which *atmosphere* was perceptible! This effect was the result not only of its gigantic scale but of the artistic efforts of Owen Jones, the outstanding art decorator of the period. This gentleman applied certain hitherto neglected principles of color to its decoration, and, by painting the roof girders the blue and ivory of the cloud-hung English heavens, he created the effect of airy insubstantiality which fascinated all beholders.

Probably nothing has surpassed this mass spectacle of luxurious elegance. Entranced by the sensuous beauty of the assembled arts of the world, poets and writers burst into print. Thackeray wrote both a serious ode and a humorous set of verses in its praise. For a description which is worth quoting for sheer effulgence, let us turn to a work by an American, one Samuel Warren. The verbal arabesques of his *The Lily and the Bee, an Apologue,* undoubtedly catch the visual

83

intoxication, but a little of his prose must suffice, for the work in its entirety today is almost unreadable.

> "There was music echoing through the transparent fabric. Fragrant flowers and graceful shrubs were blooming, and exhaling sweet odors. Fountains were flashing and sparkling in the subdued sunlight [Author's note: the light was tempered by a thin curtain over the whole structure]: in living sculpture were suddenly seen the grand, the grotesque, the terrible, the beautiful: objects of every form and color imaginable, far as the eye could reach, were dazzlingly intermingled: and there were present sixty thousand sons and daughters of Adam, passing and repassing, ceaselessly: bewildered charmingly: gliding amid bannered Nations—through country after country renowned in ancient name, and great in modern: civilized and savage."

On May 1, 1851, the Queen, in pink and gold brocade, opened the Exhibition in a ceremony which, for splendor and pageantry, was said to have surpassed even her Coronation. The sight of the vast ensemble was tremendously moving, not only for the emotional Queen, but for all present. Victoria records her own feelings in her private diary: "The great event has taken place — a complete and beautiful triumph — a glorious and touching sight, one which I shall ever be proud of for my beloved Albert and my country. . . . Yes! it is a day which makes my heart swell with pride and glory and thankfulness!"

The world is still in "dearest Albert's" debt, for it was he who first called the public's attention to the need for better design in industrial products. At the time when Victoria was growing up, designers endowed with discrimination no longer existed; the long period of the Napoleonic wars had also deprived England of skilled craftsmen. Since the industrial arts had no leadership, grotesqueries in unbelievable bad taste were all that the enfeebled invention of the age seemed capable of producing. At first this utter degeneration in design was hardly noticeable because of the general rejoicing in the marvels of the industrial age. But, as the machines turned out more and more rubbish, the lack of taste became more and more evident. Though the era believed thoroughly in the forward progress of human affairs and prated piously of the greatest good for the greatest number, business men bent every effort towards the removal of restraints to their economic ambitions, firm in their conviction that the prosperity of manufacturing was all-essential to the well-being of the community. In 1846, this fashionable political economy won its way into the clear, and with the removal of restrictions on manu-

factured goods a further flood of English factory-made trash swept through the markets of the world. England was well in the lead with shipping and practically monopolized the textile and hardware trades. Since she had no competitors, and her goods sold in the farthest corners of the world, why should her industrialists trouble themselves about such aesthetic vaguenesses as the good or bad design of their wares? In fact, most of them found satirical amusement in the idea that serious concern should be wasted on the subject; they sneered at what they called "meditated muffineers and planned pokers."

This attitude the Prince Consort found extremely disturbing. From the earliest days of his marriage, Albert had been taking great delight in visiting industrial plants, for he was perennially intrigued by all processes of manufacture. Most of the royal entourage might pay but perfunctory attention to the wonders displayed, but Albert, a tall, elegant figure in search of information, could be observed bent over workmen in metal-working plants, in papier-mâché factories, and in glass works. As he was a discriminating person, he must frequently have been outraged by the manufactured atrocities shown him on official tours with the Queen.

Since a sense of the artistic had, for some decades, been practically lacking in the English, those able to purchase the new products of the machine accepted them uncritically. On the other hand, the aristocrat could remain serenely unconcerned about the flood of tawdry machine-made products, for he was still surrounded by the most elegant examples of the great days of eighteenth-century craftsmanship. Across the Channel, the French, ever since Napoleon's day, had inaugurated institutions to give advice on manufacturing. Their most important industrial plants even arranged for schools to train designers; for the French realized that taste was not only a matter of tradition but decidedly of training. For all this, the English, with superb insularity, believed—when they thought about it at all—that taste, knowledge, and skill were inborn; that to train designers was so much Continental fiddle-faddle. Moreover, the upper classes frowned on a Prince Consort who interested himself, not in the usual occupations of the wealthy, but in such unaristocratic concerns as the method of glass-blowing and the designing of flats with bathrooms for workmen—a conception then undreamed of.

As Albert worked seriously and unselfishly in every

84

field of endeavor for the general welfare, all the learned societies in Great Britain recognized him as their most valuable ally. In 1847, the Society of Arts, a body founded in 1753, made him its president and the Queen gave the Society a Royal charter. Hitherto inactive, the group planned, under the new president, to hold occasional exhibitions of choice specimens of contemporary industrial production in order to arouse interest in what were then designated as "art manufactures." As a trial balloon, they launched their first exhibition that same year. This idea was in itself so unusual that it might have failed had it not been for the energetic efforts of one of the Society's council. This gentleman was actually forced to beg a few of the great manufacturers to submit, as a personal favor, enough of their selected wares to make at least some kind of showing.

Much to the surprise of the industrialists, the public found this new type of exhibition of great interest, and when the attendance at the second attempt tripled that of the first, the manufacturers needed no further coaxing to send specimens of their products. After several of these exhibitions had been assembled, the cosmopolitan-minded Prince resolved to find a way to educate his adopted country along sounder artistic lines. A practical man as well as an idealist, Albert realized that the days of the craftsman were gone forever. If the quality of British design were to be bettered, improvement must take place in the mind of the designer—the servant of that ruthless master, the power-driven machine. Unlike the old-time craftsman who was in complete control of his product, the designer was bound tightly by the limitations of the stamp, the die, the mold, and the press. Even within these restrictions, however, there was, as the Prince had learned through his close observation of manufacturing processes, an enormous opportunity for improvement. As England was at least a century ahead of continental Europe both in government and in public conduct, the Prince considered his adopted country the rightful place to start a movement for "the diffusion of civilization and the attainment of liberty." The altruistic idea was already germinating. One of his fellow members of the Society of Arts, having just returned from the Paris Exposition of 1849, felt that British manufacturing might be considerably improved if it had a chance to see the best of what was produced elsewhere. As this coincided with his own thinking, the Prince willingly sponsored the idea and the world's first International Exhibition got under way. Private subscriptions were raised, manufacturers canvassed. De-

spite enormous opposition from the press, from the politicians, from church extremists and from the Tory-minded who viewed an international exhibition only as a gathering place for radicals and foreigners, the great idea continued to grow.

Inconceivable difficulties had to be surmounted. Only three weeks were given to the architects of the world in which to prepare ideas. None of them was found acceptable. The building committee was forced to contrive a plan of its own, an improbable monstrosity of brick topped with a hideous iron dome. Even the Hyde Park site selected by the Prince was the subject of a fearful hullabaloo. Though eminently suitable for such a purpose, as it was almost bare of trees, it still held a few large elms which suddenly found a passionate group of defenders. Ludicrous as this opposition was, it forced the novel solution which added enormously to the charm of the Exhibition. Three great controversial elms were allowed to remain, and survived to become a memorable feature of the gigantic glass-house which literally surrounded and engulfed them.

Paxton, whose nimble mind saved these arboreal primadonnas, was a man of countless affairs and wide abilities. Strongly objecting to the approved plans for the building, he suggested to a member of the building committee that he had some ideas of his own on the subject. In nine days he was ready to submit them. Fully aware of the political importance of the trees, the noted engineer conceived the idea of surrounding them with the semicircular roof and magnificent transept of a glass and iron building—a novel use of familiar materials. His idea, visionary though it seemed to the very vocal opposition, appealed at once to the Prince.

Paxton's design was published in the *Illustrated London News* and the public took it at once to their hearts. Having already seen the earlier plans, they were attracted at once by this delightful winter-garden idea, this fantastic palace which was to be conjured up for their delectation with magician-like speed. And indeed they stood about gaping as it was being put together, for it actually was completed in the bare seven months allotted to its construction.

No one will ever be able to estimate the effect of the Exhibition on the millions who saw it, nor can one guess how many, many thousands were ever after dissatisfied with the honest lines of their sturdy, old-fashioned possessions, once they had examined the fantastically elaborate creations of the endless displays. In the clear daylight of the Crystal Palace, not one line or detail

Many examples of the rustic, used as a decorative treatment, were shown in the Crystal Palace. Among the most deplorable was furniture, carved in *imitation* of rough-surfaced branches.

was obscured. Every level of society saw the wonders spread out in the vast conservatory; not only the well-to-do, to whom the entrance fee was a small matter, but even the poorest of country folk and farm laborers, who moved about in flocks, shepherded by rural clergymen. The clergy, having collected money from their more substantial parishioners for these mass jaunts of the humble, were earnestly determined to give their open-mouthed charges the benefits of culture as manifested in eleven miles of tables and displays. When their smocked and hobnailed parishioners were satiated by an overwhelming amount of "art manufactures," the clergymen led them toward less abstruse fields: the latest in agricultural implements. There they could rest themselves while they scowled at these new-fangled inventions. On the other hand, those fascinated by machinery—and this included the greater part of the Victorian public—stood entranced before the latest in locomotives, and all the other steel and iron wonders which steam had made possible within the short lifetime of their Queen—who had been only six years old when the world's first train ran in her own England.

In the seemingly endless line of exhibits no one could fail to find something of interest. Strange carved furniture from Burma, textiles and pottery from Tunis,

flowers made of beetle wings and of feathers of rare Brazilian birds, table tops of Florentine mosaic, silver coffee services from the Turkish bazaars — all these objects conveyed their lessons of patient craftsmanship to a public enchanted by their beauty and novelty. The smart set of society could take delight in the exquisite lines of pleasure carriages, and the plain artisan's wife be absorbed in British ribbons, French dress-goods and sparkling jewelry. The antiquarian could ruminate over a rustic oaken chair carved from logs supposed to have been immersed in a river for over twenty centuries.

In truth, it might be said that only one thing was missing in the entire display—one thing which no manufacturer, no Victorian anywhere, could bear to face. This was the straight line, honest and unadorned. In revolt against a century of ornamental excess we have turned again to the straight line and simple contour. Because of this reaction we can never again experience the naïve pleasure which average citizens of the early industrial age experienced at the sight of sheer elaboration. The very prodigality of its arabesques gave them a sense of civilized elegance.

This addiction to the highly embellished has been crystallized in the term "Victorianism"—a loosely used synonym for overdone elaborateness. We flatter ourselves that we have entirely discarded this quality; nevertheless it still permeates our environment everywhere. For no matter how we vaunt our "functionalism," we shall, in all likelihood, continue to live in surroundings in which some extraneous ornament is present, since there probably always will be persons born in the world who prefer the elaborate to the austere, the naturalistic to the stylized, the permanent wave to nature's chaste smoothness. That ornament fulfils an inner sensory need is unarguable: quickly bored with simplicity, the eye craves novelty and seeks out detail. At the present time, when taste is against ornamenting the object, we nevertheless soften the starkness of functionalism with ornamental textures, and offset simplicity with the curving lines and patterns provided by the shapes of natural foliage. Used as a foil or an embellishment to modern interiors, the plant is, after all, a kind of ornamentation, or, in the last analysis, certainly the admission of the need for it. The difference is one of degree. The Victorians were gluttons for decoration: today we diet.

The Victorians felt that they inherited the earth; to them everything was new, stimulating, exciting. Each strove for his portion of the endless stream of goods the new machines were turning out, and if the sum total of their decorative achievements was a tasteless mélange, they could hardly have avoided it, for no consideration whatever was given by the manufacturer to the tout ensemble. It is this concentration on the part, rather than on the whole, which has brought such particular criticism on the period. But at that time it could hardly have been otherwise. Today industry has learned to correct some of its earlier errors. Through many agencies working in common, the present-day manufacturer produces articles which can be harmoniously combined with articles produced by others, even by those whose taste is far from educated. By such methods, the home decorator has been taught to look at the whole instead of the part—and this much is progress.

When the Crystal Palace Exhibition burst in its iridescent glory on the world, everything displayed was considered marvellous; to question the good taste of any of the objects on show required genuine courage. But it is pleasant to reflect that even then there were persons of excellent judgment, and that they were especially invited, and by the Exhibition Committee itself, to exercise their critical faculties for the benefit of the British manufacturer. Though in general the age paid little heed to the pronouncements of these critics, it is only fair to note that the opinions they expressed, based on the timeless values of form, proportion, and restraint, were such that the principles involved are not open to question even today.

It is a pity that the suggestions then offered were not generally accepted, for sound guidance was never more needed than in the first powerful surge of the Industrial Age. Manufacturers were without precedents for their ventures, as the world in which they lived found itself for the first time without a characteristic style. To remedy this lack, it turned for inspiration to the great past and unblushingly evolved its own style—an eclectic mixture based on the nine great style sources which had influenced European civilization. Designers who stood in awe of tradition dipped indiscriminately into all of them: they filched from the Egyptian, the Greek and Roman. They borrowed from the Byzantine, the Saracenic, and the Gothic, and appropriated wholeheartedly from the Renaissance, in particular from their favorite periods — the Cinque-cento and the Louis Quatorze. When taste governed their adaptations of motifs of former days, the results, while not aesthetically stimulating, were at least acceptable. When, however, they evolved a jumble of several totally unrelated styles —adapting the ornament of one style to an object con-

structed along the lines of an entirely different style (for no other purpose than that of adding embellishment)—the result was one of those deplorable hybrids which brought down both contemporary and present-day criticism upon the hapless designers' heads.

While the Victorian traditionalists were putting together their historical hodgepodges, another set of designers, intent on freeing themselves of all artistic precedents, developed a new decorative style. This style, which might well be called the "natural" or "imitative" style, turned to Nature for all its forms and concentrated on the most conscientious reproduction possible of her growths and textures. Innumerable examples of curious novelties which resulted from the uncontrolled application of this new idea bloomed in every corner of the Crystal Palace. Sponsors of this new trend visualized—and indeed carried out—a heartwarming marriage between romantic imagination and the machine. "We would have everything in the house touched by the divining rod of the poet. An inkstand . . . instead of being a literal glass bottle, or a fine piece of bronze, might be fashioned to represent a fountain with a muse inspiring its flow . . . our goblets might bubble over amongst hop-leaves or the stems of blossoms. . . ."

If half of this deluge of naturalistic ornament had

Flowers of glass springing from clusters of metal foliage were of the utmost realism in conception and modelling. They were used as chandeliers, gas brackets and centrepieces.

The Coalbrook Dale Dome, a towering rustic garden house, demonstrated the ornamental possibilities of cast iron.

did not feel that their taste needed perfecting. Having been shown drinking glasses shaped like tulips, gas-burners in the form of arum lilies, glitter and shimmer, pattern upon pattern, the opulence of articles made for the wealthy, they liked everything they saw and determined to have their share in these benefits of progress, in no matter how feeble or tawdry an imitation. For this was indeed the common man's exhibition; from now on all the substances used in industrial productions, all iron, wood, paper, glass, ceramics, textiles, metals, would be shaped to appeal to his, rather than to princely, tastes.

Some of the most important industrial art-products of the period were the ornamental articles of cast iron. These made their first notable appearance at the Crystal Palace. Sanguine admirers of cast iron perceived no limits to the uses to which it could be adapted. The mass production of ornamental iron was geared at once to the popular level, for the manufacturers recognized that their market lay in a field which desired a great show of luxury at low cost. Cast iron offered broad scope to both schools of designers. The traditional —as was to be expected—turned for inspiration to the delicate floriations of the ductile wrought iron. This precedent, an apparently sound one, nevertheless betrayed them, for cast iron could never produce anything but a clumsy replica of the sharp and graceful contours of wrought iron. Led astray by the facility with which cast iron reproduced any form for which a mold could be prepared, the manufacturers attempted to imitate, not only wrought iron, but also objects and sculptural forms conceived originally in such different mediums as stone, wood, plaster, and marble.

This very ease of manufacture seduced the followers of the naturalistic school of design into using it for floral and arboreal motifs; these are really the earmark of the period. Impelled by a touching sense of poetic fitness they transformed the evanescent morning-glory into a gigantic iron monstrosity which twined its rigid way up iron trelliage. Or they happily twisted iron grape-studded vines into the most foliated of garden settees, fencing, or verandahs.

Various types of iron fountains, naturalistic and sentimental in conception, made their debut in the great glass edifice. As a fountain was one of the absolutely necessary appointments of every park, square, or garden making any pretensions whatsoever, the offspring of the Crystal Palace examples eventually covered the earth. Many have survived to this day, exhaling an air

been dispensed with, said the Exhibition's more thoughtful critics, such restraint would have resulted not only in better and cheaper articles but might have wrought some improvement in the taste of the multitude. But they railed to no purpose, for the multitude of rusty melancholy as they drip their slow way toward corrosion and crumbling decay.

Here also were shown many examples of the cast iron garden vases which were soon to become one of the class symbols of gentility. Garden vases caught the public fancy at once, both for their likeness in form to the too costly marble urns, and for their genuine usefulness. An iron vase could be set in the merest handkerchief of a grass plot before a city house—for even in these tiny areas the use of an urn permitted the introduction of a bit of floral color. Many of these garden urns still exist in corners modernity has passed by. Each year their pseudo-classic ornaments become less definite after they receive their annual coat of paint: a bright green, a startling black, or even a certain distressing chocolate, so dearly adhered to for this purpose by their original property-respecting owners.

In the 1840's the ornamental cast iron industry began to move forward with enormous strides. As Pennsylvania was then the centre of iron production, it is not surprising that a Philadelphia firm, Wood and Perot, should have been the first to employ iron for decorative purposes. From their plant began to issue the many types of iron work used on houses and gardens all over the country. Nothing was considered more elegant in the 1850's than a cast iron balcony or porch, fastened, like a lace trimming, to the front of a city house. Already a filigree, the verandah's lines were further enriched with a scrollery of nature's own making, for clematis, roses, or honeysuckle were encouraged to clamber up from the small garden plots to overlay the iron lace in an enchanting surfeit. In the North, such verandahs and galleries, once common, have for the most part disintegrated and have been done away with. But in the South, thanks to a more fortunate climate, they still persist and their lacy patterns add a fabulous amount of old-time charm to cities like New Orleans, Natchez, and Charleston.

For their day Wood and Perot's products were excellent artistic conceptions. By 1853, the concern had three thousand or more patterns to draw upon. In 1845 as an evidence of the progressiveness of their firm, they issued "gratuitously" a large folio engraved catalog. Such liberality was, in itself, then so unusual an idea that it provoked much comment. The hundreds of patterns pictured by the catalog undoubtedly furnished lesser foundries with many models which they did not hesitate to adapt to their purposes, for pirating of design occurred in this as in every other field of supposed crea-

In the mid-nineteenth century the cast iron fountain was as necessary an adjunct to a house as a garage is today. Drawing proudly illustrates an American example of casting. 1856.

tiveness. In fairness, it must be noted that at that time no American manufacturer saw any reason for inventing his own designs when there were European talents devoting themselves wholly to creating ideas for express use in the ornamental industries, and—what is more—in seeing that they were published. Every steamer brought over new designs, and publications such as the London *Art Journal,* which paid great attention to industrial design, had an immense circulation on this side of the ocean.

Cast iron was also employed for all kinds of exterior architectural construction, such as shop fronts—and with dismal results. Not content with taking over the entire field of garden and outdoor furnishing, cast iron invaded the house in the form of foliated hatracks and umbrella stands. Even very elaborate beds were essayed in this material—never a satisfactory one because of its intrinsic weight and brittleness.

For inexpensive statuary, in addition to the familiar

French Bronze Merchant's Display. 1860. When bronze statuettes were indispensable
decorations, entire establishments were given over to them.

stag and dog, the Victorian could purchase cast iron busts of political celebrities. In the field of iron sculptures, he could also obtain all kinds of classic and even playful pieces of statuary: Apollo and Hermes, the dainty Hebe, the useful, brightly painted "Sambo" and "Jockey" hitching posts, as well as a myriad of aquatic or sentimental figures. Frequently they were mingled without regard for a harmonious ensemble. The Victorian garden scene, therefore, had its amusing aspects.

For indoor use, metal sculpture was executed in bronze instead of iron. So high did "French art-bronzes" rank in Victorian estimate that to possess a bronze piece was the aim of even modest householders. During their greatest vogue — from the 1840's to the 1870's — extravagant sums were spent on them, for, as "works of art," their possession was viewed as a mark of culture. Around 1855, as the result of an invention which deposited on a zinc casting a thin coating of bronze, an effective article (bronze to the eye if not to the metallurgist) was made available at much lower cost. Since many more people could now afford the pieces, the ownership of a French bronze set of ornaments no longer carried any special distinction; after 1870 they were mantel or pedestal decorations in every substantial

home — these dull-hued maidens, knights, cavaliers.

Revelling in brilliant and coruscating color and devotedly attached to scrolls and arabesques, the Victorian eye found its supreme gratification in a type of decoration used on furniture and small related objects. This most gorgeous of all manufactures, brought to perfection in Birmingham and Wolverhampton, England, was known as papier-mâché. In Victorian papier-mâché was embodied everything the average imagination of the period might desire; nothing could surpass its exquisite bad taste, its irresistible charm for those chilled by austerity of line and chasteness of surface. Its lacquered blackness scintillated with gold and metallic colors; it shimmered with mother-of-pearl. Glittering appointments of papier-mâché were equally fit for the fairy-tale palaces of the imagination or for the residences of Oriental potentates. Although papier-mâché was basically an oriental art, the Pashas and the Rajahs liked the gaudier occidental interpretation better than their own product, and England, after it lost its domestic markets, shipped to them her out-of-date pieces.

Papier-mâché was made from cuttings of waste paper boiled and beaten to a pulp; size and glue were added and the resultant stiff paste formed into various articles

90

by driving it with powerful pressure into oiled molds of the desired shape. When dried, the objects in process of manufacture were coated with lamp-black, varnished, and treated to a series of bakings. The process created an article light in weight but hard and durable. A better quality was made with sheets of a special porous paper saturated with paste and pressed into molds.

Though papier-mâché was fabricated by the French in the early eighteenth century, the employment of mother-of-pearl (which characterizes the Victorian type) was not thought of until shortly after Victoria's birth. In 1825, Jennens and Bettridge of Birmingham, the largest manufacturers of papier-mâché, patented an effective method for its practical use. Later, having evolved a style which would add even more magnificence and glitter, this firm took out a patent in 1847 for this new method—one in which glass beads and jewels were inlaid before the piece received its customary bedizening.

No inch of a papier-mâché piece ever went undecorated. Architectural scenes were the specialty of certain firms, and well-known paintings were frequently copied as decorations. Pearl was also used freely for illustrative purposes; shaped into rivers, moons, and ruined castles, its iridescence added to the sentimental charm of these pictorial subjects. Later on, this imaginative playfulness was carried to such a degree and executed so poorly that articles decorated with this material could find admirers only in those utterly lacking in artistic discrimination.

But at the time of the Great Exhibition, the public beheld the papier-mâché industry's displays when they had reached their greatest splendor. Many manufacturers exhibited, some even attempting large pieces of furniture. After the industrial production of such articles was discontinued, the ornamentation of papier-mâché pieces descended to a ladylike household art. In the 1870's women who aspired to add papier-mâché's rococo to their already over-embellished parlors could take lessons in the technique, for undecorated pieces were obtainable for such amateur projects.

Another notable feature of the taste for magnificence was the widespread use of marble. Hitherto a material associated in imagination with the palaces of princes, marble became, through the magic of steam-driven machinery, a commonplace of nineteenth-century living. When marble first became popular, to own anything made of it gave one a social cachet. Vestibules floored

and panelled with white marble ornamented with delicately worked moldings impressed one's visitors; so did white marble mantels which surrounded the Victorian hearth or the ornamental hot-air register which supplanted the open grate. Marble panelled the bathrooms, and gracefully shaped slabs of this chilly substance topped every article of furniture to which it could be appropriately fitted.

Many varieties of marble used for decorative purposes were imported; much entered the United States as a commercial exchange in transportation. Ships left such ports as New Orleans loaded with cotton for Italy and returned with a ballast of unworked marble or with a shipment of beautifully carved mantels or mausoleums which had been ordered for the wealthy. By 1850, one of the largest "steam marble works" in the country offered the prospective home-builder a choice of one hundred and thirty different designs in mantels alone. This display was a matter of great pride, for then a showroom was a genuine novelty. This firm stood ready to furnish "Cabinet Makers and others with Slabs for Tables, Bureaus and Work-stands" made from a wide range of imported marbles; manufacturers had a choice of three kinds of Carrara, or they could employ "Egyptian, Sienna, Levante, Brocatelle, Pyrenees, Bardilla, or Lisbon" marbles to finish their black walnut pieces.

Pier-console tables topped with white marble, with the back filled in from table-top to floor with mirrors, permitted the fashionables of the 1830's a glimpse of their delicately slippered toes. Surmounted by regal gold-framed mirrors stretching ceilingward, the console tables were ordinarily set between the twin windows of city drawing rooms. As fashions in furniture became more elaborate, the mirrored panel disappeared from this piece, but the pier-table itself maintained its position —flanked by the richest of draperies—as long as "the parlor" itself endured.

Like everything else, Victorian furniture reflected the elaboration made possible by the coming of steam. Such sensible considerations as comfort, good material, and sound workmanship were set aside for a vast splurge of ornament. To gratify the tastes of the wealthy, the most impractical pieces were conceived: cabinets which held hardly anything, but which were so impressive that one side of a room had to be allotted to them; chairs so assertive and bedecorated that comfort was completely overlooked; beds so lofty and commanding that they resembled walnut catafalques. With machines making possible inexpensive replicas of regal furnishings, fresh aesthetic ideas now entered middle-class levels. Strange exciting words, such as *Louis Quatorze,* were frequently on the lips of women who had learned to pronounce them only on acquiring a new "French parlor suite," patterned—even if but remotely—on the style set by palaces. In walnut or in gilt, such suites embodied every middle-class ideal of elegance.

But there were other types of furniture which, of necessity, catered to other facets of Victorian taste. For sober library or earnest dining room, all ideas of fragility were cast aside. Dining room pieces, in particular, were inconceivably ponderous monuments to stability. They were covered with as much machine-carved ornament as could be glued on, in imitation either of the eighteenth-century lavishness of Grinling Gibbons' carvings, or of the voluptuous scrollings of the court of Louis Quinze. The straight line never appeared anywhere, since it was always possible to cover it up with such ornament or transform it into a curve—the only line of beauty the cabinet makers acknowledged. To obtain this curving effect in the legs of Victorian furniture required a great sacrifice of strength; however, this distressed no one except a few artistic purists, persons who were made uneasy by the sight of a series of connected scrolls substituting as supports for an honest sturdy upright.

Less than two years later, decorative influences set in motion by the Great Exhibition swept across the ocean. By 1853, the United States was ready with its own exhibition of "art manufactures," named, in pretty compliment, *The New York Crystal Palace.*

Those Americans who had visited the London Crystal Palace were put out of countenance by the sparseness of the American display. American possibilities in "art manufactures" had barely been represented; those aware of their country's productions in this field were not consoled for their absence by the sight of a 16,000-pound piece of zinc ore or a collection of wooden buckets. Nor did they feel that their country was justly represented by the sight of a printing press, no matter how fast it moved, or by some agricultural products, an organ or so, or even by Hiram Powers' scornful "Greek Slave," though this marble young person, placed in a red velvet niche on a revolving pedestal, caught the flagging attention of all the top-hatted gentlemen and the tired, shawled and bonneted ladies. The "Greek Slave" was indeed the most important "art" object in the display. If one ignored an eye-catching gigantic rubber boot as a piece of blatant advertising,

there was nothing of the least aesthetic interest except a few patchwork quilts, a trifling amount of fancywork, and an herbarium of pressed flowers.

"Try again and do better," suggested the *Illustrated London News.* And the United States was ready to do better—in fact, in 1850 while the Great Exhibition of Prince Albert's was still a dream on paper, a group of American private citizens had already united to back an American exhibition of industry with the idea of wiping out the embarrassing impression which they knew would be created in 1851 in London because of a total lack of any governmental machinery for American participation in such affairs.

This first international venture—this "Association for the Exhibition of Industry," as it was called—was an ill-starred one. The building in which the exhibition was housed—the New York Crystal Palace—was the largest edifice attempted in this country up to that time, although it was only one-fifth the size of its English prototype. Before it was five years old, it was completely destroyed by fire, but during its short existence European manufacturers nevertheless sent to it much that was in the best taste of the day. So prevalent, however, was the idea that ostentation was the chief purpose of this type of display that, in pieces exhibited by American industry, practicality was ignored quite as much as it had been in London. Everyone was enamoured of the idea of "showiness," and therefore such exhibits were not characteristic of what was actually in general use. Rather, they represented the "master piece" — a holdover from the days when every apprentice had to demonstrate his capabilities before he was certified a master craftsman.

Though it had been hinted abroad that the United States had not exerted itself to send examples of its best "art manufactures" to London, the truth was that much that was of fine quality in American manufacture came from small plants employing but few workmen. And at this time these establishments still operated under old traditions, despite the aid they were receiving from machinery. In the 1850's, no such establishment would have dreamed of shipping anything overseas for display purposes alone. But on their own soil the more progressive houses were induced to exhibit examples of their work. Visitors could view both the beautiful pieces of European craftsmanship and the native product side by side—the latter proudly inviting the comparison. Among these representative showings one could examine the work of furniture manufacturers, marble workers, cut glass establishments, and the sumptuous mirrors from the shops of carvers and gilders. Silverware and pianos were also exhibited, to say nothing of beautiful carriages and chandeliers. The two latter articles were the product of industries which, for their time, were outstandingly progressive, for they had actually shipped examples of their best work to London, and by such enterprise had mitigated, at least to a slight degree, the general impression that the United States was given over almost wholly to agriculture and the production of raw materials.

Domestic furniture manufacturers followed all the caprices of European fashion, depending on imported woods for their most elegant examples, but in addition substituting the native American walnut for rosewood and mahogany in less costly pieces. All through the Victorian era black walnut—that really splendid native timber—dominated the American scene; it was used in every room of the house, both as woodwork and as furniture, from the front door itself to the towering wardrobe in the bedroom. By 1840, it was already in high good taste, and its use was then characterized by John F. Watson, in his *Annals of Philadelphia,* as "A modern freak of fashion . . . just because it is getting scarce and dearer, and withall so like Rose wood—But in former days Walnut was the common furniture wood —as being second to Mahogany—As men got more wealthy it was discarded—it became cheaper and cheaper, and was sold as common fuel in my time—But now, it is again a wood of luxury . . ."

Black walnut (the black was stressed to distinguish it from another member of the tree's family, the *white* walnut or *butternut*) endeared itself to the Victorians for many reasons. Not only did it offer a fine frame for the bright colors then coming into fashion and lent itself easily to any amount of carving, but it also attracted the practical buyer, for it showed the effects of wear less than any other wood. To make way for its weighty effectiveness, other quite serviceable native woods were displaced. After walnut came in, pleasant curly maple and birch were considered suitable for only the most modest of country dining rooms and bedrooms. These woods, in the opinion of the day, lacked the "richness" essential for the parlor. And pine and cherry were viewed frankly as rustic timber, fit only for the workbench of the country artisan. In fact, so generally was it conceded that walnut was the only wood appropriate for middle-class gentility that, by 1876, a critic of aesthetics, oppressed by what might be called "the dark

age of house decoration," injected a minor heresy in bourgeois thinking when he questioned "whether the goodness and cheapness of black walnut has not led us into making our rooms too sombre and heavy for a cheerful life."

At the time of the Great Exhibition, glass was a material just coming into prominence in English industry. Until 1845, it had been so heavily taxed that it had not been possible for English manufacturers to compete with fine Continental productions. But after the excise tax was removed the business speedily got under way. By 1851 English plants were producing fine examples—the most astounding being the great "Glass Fountain" of the Crystal Palace which occupied the central position in the enormous edifice. It was a magnificent conception of jewelled brilliance, twenty-seven feet high, supported by bars of iron invisibly embedded in its crystalline columns. From its great height this fairy-like fountain dispensed its shimmering sprays of water from a graduated series of cut glass canopies.

At that time cut glass chandeliers and candelabra were still in high fashion, for the new illuminant—gas— did not exclude this type of lighting fixture. Gigantic examples of these really beautiful objects also caught the sunlight at various points in the Crystal Palace, the most spectacular – again a British product – being twenty-four feet of prismatic glory. The chandelier of cut glass was one object on which endless detail could be showered and still not expose it to criticism for over-ornamentation. For no matter how gorgeous it became, it still fulfilled its initial purpose, which was that of refracting light.

Since English flint glass could not be surpassed in brilliance, British production in this field eclipsed all others. But in the manufacture of colored glassware for which the era showed so pronounced a taste, England could not compete in price with an already firmly established product—the well-known glass of Bohemia. Bohemian glass was considered primarily as ornament and tended to be over-decorated. It glittered with gold and enamelling applied to highly colored grounds which were further enhanced with cutting. Although the best taste of the day regarded much Bohemian glass as gaudy and inelegant, the average homemaker admired her pieces for the very qualities decried by the aesthetes.

While the United States undoubtedly lagged behind in the early manufacture of well designed articles, by 1850 it was considerably advanced in the manufacture of glass. To the Great Exhibition the industry sent

Parian Statuettes so closely resembled marble that they captivated the Victorian world.

Parian "Dorothea," by J. Bell.

By 1855, an American importer advertises four hundred varieties of Parian for sale.

a display of American cut glass which indicated that some genuine consideration had been given to artistic values; even the English conceded that its line and form were excellent. It is evident that the business had progressed from the time in 1828 when Mrs. Trollope, travelling across the country, stopped to see an early glass factory in Wheeling, West Virginia. "We were told by the workmen that the articles finished there were equal to any in the world; but my eyes refused their assent. The cutting was very good, though by no means equal to what we see in daily use in London; but the chief inferiority is in the material, which is never altogether free from colour. I had observed this also in the glass of the Pittsburgh manufactory, the labour bestowed on it always appearing greater than the glass deserved. They told us also, that they were rapidly improving in the art, and I have no doubt that this was true."

By 1851 English table ware had already reached a high standard; now English potteries were ready to compete with their Continental neighbors in certain other ceramics. Great improvements in production had made it possible to enter the field of ceramic "ornaments," those objects which had so fatal an attraction for the Victorian eye. All through the Queen's lifetime it was the fashion to fill every available inch of space on whatnot, vitrine, and china cupboard with these useless bits of pottery, conceived invariably from a sentimental or trivial viewpoint. As more and more persons acquired the above-mentioned pieces of furniture, the demand for "ornaments" increased proportionately. As a result, the "ornaments" finally became so tasteless

that eventually they—together with the pieces of furniture which held them—were swept from the places where they had been so long and so firmly entrenched.

Nevertheless, some really delightful Victorian ornaments were those of "Parian ware," an interesting material first made in England in 1842. Parian ware, sometimes referred to as "statuary ware," was a hard white biscuit porcelain which permitted the reproduction of very fine details. Objects produced in this ware had all the charm of marble—its translucency, its fine granular texture, and its inimitable whiteness. In Parian a material had been discovered which would reproduce the sculptor's art accurately and inexpensively. This fidelity to their original conception encouraged artists to produce their best, and in England the modelling of the human figure greatly improved. Because of the wide demand, all the great potteries produced Parian. Whether they were reproductions of famous pieces or outright imitations of Chelsea or Derby, the Parian shepherds and shepherdesses, courtiers, rollicking cupids, and staid animals were in themselves enchanting bits of toy sculpture. These won their way into Victorian hearts and homes, welcome not only on cottage mantel and in farmhouse parlor, but also on the fancy shelvings of the most costly whatnot.

As the manufacture of Parian constituted an important branch of English ceramics, it was to be expected that Great Britain would send over a fine exhibition of it to the New York Crystal Palace. In the 1850's the manufacture of Parian was undertaken at Bennington, Vermont, under the supervision of an English potter, John Harrison. American Parian was noted for its beautifully modelled flowers and foliage, with particular stress laid on daintily executed grapes and vine leaves. Though an excellent product, the American Parian never quite equalled the English in its elegance of conception, and for the larger examples—the garden ornaments and flower stands—the United States still turned to imported pieces.

English china had early gained its reputation as a well-designed product which displayed a happy union of beauty with usefulness. And while the British potter could never compete in the very highest fields of the ceramic arts with such government-supported manufactories as Sèvres or Dresden, the articles produced for general trade by such establishments as Copeland and Minton and others were nevertheless able to hold their own in the particular fields in which they strove for trade. English "Queen's ware" and other earthenware products of the English potteries were in ordinary use in the United States up until the 1840's. Then a fashion sprang up for white French china in daily use, one which held sway for several generations, for the French china was indeed attractive. So pretty and practical were its forms, so fine and shining its surfaces that it made the heretofore favored blue Canton ware (long the choice of the elect) look coarse and dull. The latter went into hiding in cellar or attic, and for their very "best," the modish turned to highly decorated and much gilded Worcester and Coalport. Handsome though rather bizarre tea-sets of Worcester called "harlequin" were provocative subjects of tea-table conversation, as each cup and saucer was different in color and pattern. Victoria herself owned one of these sets. Plain sprigged china fancied by their simpler predecessors was frowned upon by the luxury-loving Americans of the 1840's as a pattern which was too suggestive of calico—a textile which many of them were eager to relegate to the past.

As yet all this to-do about china and one's best dishes was the concern of only the wealthy. The middle and lower classes knew but one ware and to it they were wedded—or so it seemed—for all eternity. This was the blue—sometimes red or gold—*Willow pattern* earthenware. For the use of this great class of buyers nothing else was ever submitted. And this might never have changed had it not been for Prince Albert. The middle and lower classes should be particularly grateful to him,

for it was he who persuaded a great English manufacturer of ceramics that it might be profitable to bring out some new shapes and patterns in the low-priced field. Reluctantly, the manufacturer consented. So instantaneous was their success that it caused a revolution in the china closets of the day. Indeed, by 1870, a writer on home furnishings in *Good Words,* England's popular monthly, could happily remark that "England and the provinces were giving up a century of hideous predilection for Willow pattern earthenware."

When the flat stylized embellishments of willow-ware gave way, they were succeeded by an invasion of naturalistic forms. This trend (one in which a whole world of modest flowers—both garden and wild— insects, birds, and grasses, was to sprawl languorously over the ceramics of the next generation or two) was already in evidence in London's Crystal Palace. Here one could note that the great porcelain manufactory at Sèvres was showing vases decorated in the Chinese manner with the most naturalistic of storks and grasses. Worcester was ready with teacups featuring butterflies and lilies-of-the-valley, and innumerable other examples definitely foretold visitors that they could now look forward to something other than the solidly packed medallions or sprays of formal blossoms which had hitherto characterized their best Dresden and Sèvres. At once those who could never resist the latest thing made room in their cupboards for the new china bursting with realistic floral delineation.

As the demand for china increased, so did the demand for decorators. To find them—and the necessary skills did not exist in the ranks of the uneducated—the Big Bad Wolf of Industry concealed his jowls with dainty blossoms and wreathed his head with flowery garlands. Thus bedizened, he was able to entice THE LADY from the snugness of her parlor into his den, where he persuaded her to turn her skills at "flower painting" to his and her immediate profit. Afterwards, when the fad passed on to something else, Industry occasionally tried to rid itself of her sex, and to do so, dropped the flowery mask to reveal its natural ugliness. But woman, long since familiar with all his aspects, can now no longer be frightened into returning to the padded nest from which her Victorian predecessor was lured so long ago with the offer to turn her pretty "accomplishments" to profit.

95

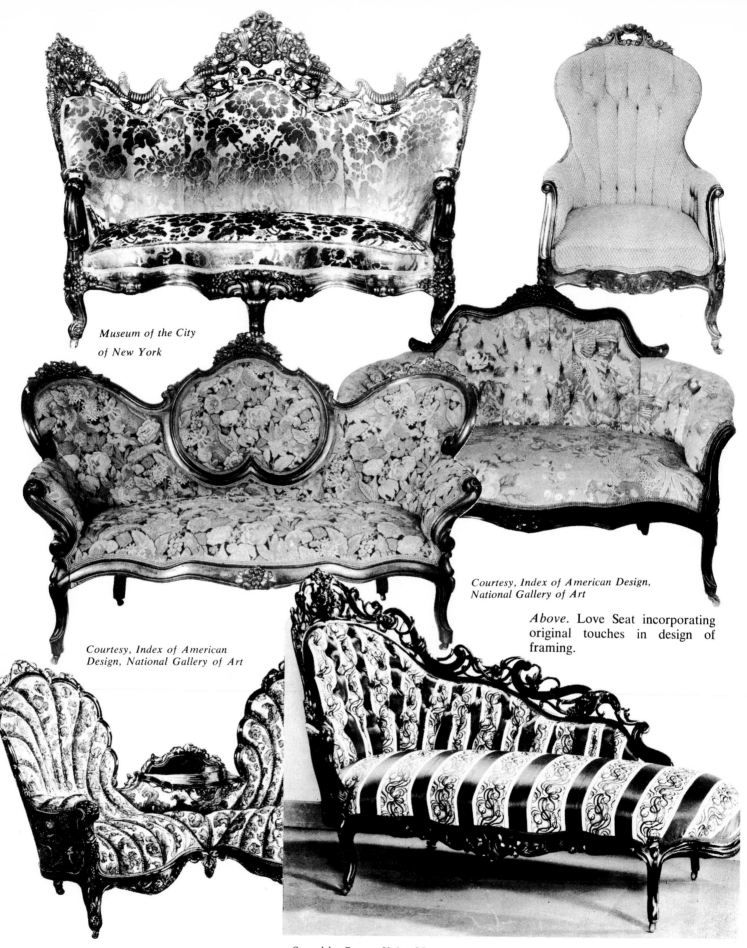

*Museum of the City
of New York*

*Courtesy, Index of American
Design, National Gallery of Art*

*Courtesy, Index of American Design,
National Gallery of Art*

Above. Love Seat incorporating original touches in design of framing.

Owned by Cooper Union Museum

Settee. 1850. Common to this decade was twin-lobed back with bracket at junction of lobes.

The contours of the best Victorian Sofas were defined by gracious curves which stemmed from the rococo. These flowed on in a continuous scrolling line except where interrupted by accents of carved fruit or flowers. Most frequently these were roses or grapes.

Advertisement of "Chair Warehouse," 1858. A collection showing practical pieces as well as
modest versions of the fancy.

Index of American Design

*Owned by Cooper
Union Museum*

*Chester Co. Historical
Society, Pa.*

Above. Extreme left and right.
Berlin-work was the approved
covering for this type of fancy
chair.

Left. Rosewood Chair, made in
Baltimore around 1850 by Robert
Renwick. Probably part of a suite.

*Courtesy, Index of American Design,
National Gallery of Art*

The Formal Chair carried as much ornament as its structure could support. Some chairs were
sheer filigrees of intricately worked curves. Only the wealthy could afford such craftsmanship; the
middle class made its selections from a far soberer assortment, such as is shown at top of page.

Console Table. French. Shown at Great Exhibition. Used with mirror.

Museum of the City of New York

Above. Table by John Henry Belter, cabinet maker working in New York between 1844 and 1867. If splendor was one's aim, Belter provided it to overflowing.

Right. Suites of furniture always included a centre table. In addition, a sofa—sometimes in pairs—two arm chairs and several side chairs went to the furnishing of the long rectangle which was the Victorian parlor.

Courtesy, Philadelphia Museum of Art

Below. "Plain Bureau." The rare person who preferred the unadorned could order furniture planned on as simple lines as the example shown, which appeared in 1868 in a cabinet maker's portfolio of sketches. The descriptive "plain bureau," however, discloses the period's disapproval of anything so forthright.

Victorian taste delighted in "Louis Quatorze," that richly curving style. After machines made the style's costly detailing more widely available, its graceful lines were degraded to just curves, any curves. The pier and centre tables of the wealthy were veritable bouquets of curves, carved from rosewood or ebony. Their marble tops were supported, in defiance of all construction principles, by a tumbling sequence of C or S shapes which accumulated naturalistic motifs in their descent.

Above. The less-well-to-do trailed fashion with tables made of the far cheaper walnut. These, too, had their marble tops, their knots of meagre carving and stylishly scrolled supports, even though their starved curves offered but the weakest hint of the elegance they aped. This type of table was once ubiquitous.

98

Courtesy, Index of American Design,
National Gallery of Art

Courtesy, The Valentine Museum, Richmond, Va.

The stability of Victorian life was reflected in the massiveness and immovability of the larger pieces of furniture. They were built to last and to stay where installed. To add elegance to their bulk, they were often loaded with ornament.

Above and right. Courtesy, Index of American Design,
National Gallery of Art

Piano, made in Philadelphia by Loud and Brothers. *C.* 1840. Mahogany, enhanced with rosewood, brass, gilt, and ebony.

Courtesy, Chester Co. Historical Society, West Chester, Pa.

Fire Screen. Frame of Louis XV scrolls encircling panel. The latter was a favorite spot to display one's needlework.

Below. Desk at left. A substantial masculine piece in which utility is the first consideration.

Right. Lady's Desk of carved walnut. An engaging oddity of the period 1840–1850. Then it won admiration for the very reasons which today draw criticism—its hybrid details and the various treatments given the wood.

Courtesy, Index of American Design, National Gallery of Art

Courtesy, Art Institute of Chicago

Chester Co. Historical Society, West Chester, Pa.

Courtesy, Philadelphia Museum of Art

Around 1850, American manufacturers began to turn out simple suites of bedroom furniture for use in cottage or country place—then a new craze. Made of native woods enamelled in pale blue, or in lilac, drab, gray, or black, a set of eight pieces decorated only with banding sold for less than $40. Floral decorations increased the cost a trifle— but what a pretty gaiety these pieces added to a simple bedroom! *Above.* Cottage Furniture. Made in Philadelphia around 1850 by Hart, Ware and Co.

Wicker Garden Chair. Exhibited in London in 1851 by a New York manufacturer. Wicker furniture, then a "tasteful novelty," was later to become a tasteless plague.

Courtesy, Index of American Design

Bureau, 1878. Sacramento, Cal. Pine, painted yellow with brown incised line decoration. Ornaments of turned walnut.

Courtesy, Victoria and Albert Museum

Papier-mâché's delicate sentimentalities and iridescent shimmerings brought delight to the wearers of crinolines.

Below. Workstand which displays, in addition to the usual decoration, a pearl-and-jewel-decorated top.

Courtesy, Victoria and Albert Museum

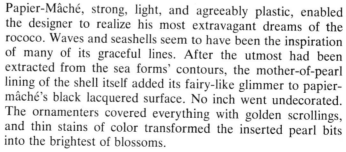

Papier-Mâché, strong, light, and agreeably plastic, enabled the designer to realize his most extravagant dreams of the rococo. Waves and seashells seem to have been the inspiration of many of its graceful lines. After the utmost had been extracted from the sea forms' contours, the mother-of-pearl lining of the shell itself added its fairy-like glimmer to papier-mâché's black lacquered surface. No inch went undecorated. The ornamenters covered everything with golden scrollings, and thin stains of color transformed the inserted pearl bits into the brightest of blossoms.

Courtesy, Mrs. Roland de Hellebranth, Ventnor, N. J.

GORGEOUS WAS THE WORD
FOR
PAPIER-MACHE

Papier-mâché articles were designed expressly to catch the feminine eye; the intent was frankly to dazzle. Papier-mâché was produced in a great variety of accessory pieces. When its bright frivolities—such as workstands, stationery cabinets, glittering tables and fancy chairs—were introduced into the parlor's solid pomp, they added an unquenchable note of gaiety.

Centre. Music Canterbury. *C.* 1860. Ornamented with the graceful devices typical of papier-mâché's intricately worked surfaces.

Courtesy, Victoria and Albert Museum

Left. Tilt-top Tables. The romantic landscape, bedizened with pearl, never lacked admirers. They were not, however, those who boasted a "severe taste."

Below. Tea Tray. 1850. The most familiar of articles.

*Courtesy, Philadelphia
Museum of Art*

CAST IRON, INDOORS AND OUT

When cast iron verandahs were thought to contribute the ultimate touch of elegance to a residence, builders in the 1840's were apt to make their selections from the comprehensive catalogue of Robert Wood (later Wood & Perot) of Philadelphia. Through the medium of this catalogue—itself a unique venture—the firm's designs "for railings, settees, chairs, tables and other ornamental and architectural iron work" were installed all over the States. Other foundries soon copied their models.

Above and below. Details from verandahs, Baltimore, Md. Variations in design were easily produced by rearrangements of the same molds.

Both, Courtesy, Index of American Design, National Gallery of Art

Above, left. Gorham's produced this Mirror Frame in silver plate. Foundrymen at once adopted the idea, producing cast iron replicas, identical except for blunted contours and loss of detail unavoidable in the process of casting iron.

Above, right. Though popularly known as the "Jenny Lind," the design of this Cast Iron Mirror suggests rather that it was planned as a Civil War memento, for study of its detail discloses flag, war trophies, and monument.

RAILING, 1856

Upper left. Woodcut, advertising the latest in step railings. The identical pattern can still be found, mounting the white marble steps of the city house.

Photo by Oscar May

Temple-fronted mid-Victorian mansion, Baltimore. Flounced in crinoline fashion with a double row of black iron-lace porches.

Below, left and right. Umbrella Stand and Footscraper were indispensable adjuncts to tidiness.

Photographs, Courtesy, Index of American Design, National Gallery of Art

Photo by Hans Burkhard

Verandah in Philadelphia, 1949, frames the vista of today in the iron vineries of a century ago. In 1851, the Veiled Vestal made an indelible impression on millions. See p. 44.

Horticultural Hall, Philadelphia, 1949. This Moorish structure, bursting with statuary and tropical verdure, was erected for the Centennial in 1876. There the Blind Girl of Pompeii presented a touching contrast to sportive fountain babies.

Courtesy, Metropolitan Museum of Art

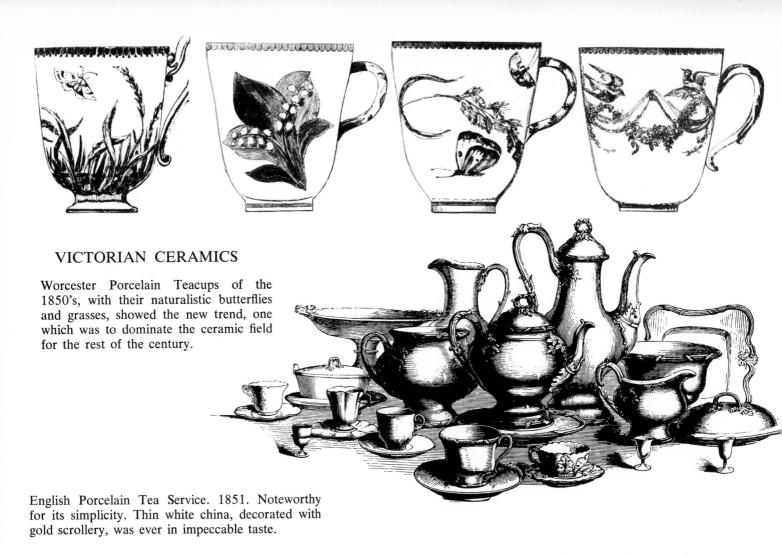

VICTORIAN CERAMICS

Worcester Porcelain Teacups of the 1850's, with their naturalistic butterflies and grasses, showed the new trend, one which was to dominate the ceramic field for the rest of the century.

English Porcelain Tea Service. 1851. Noteworthy for its simplicity. Thin white china, decorated with gold scrollery, was ever in impeccable taste.

Below, right and left. Courtesy, Museum of the City of New York

Mantel Vases, used in pairs, fell into two groups: the white cottage type, and those which were showpieces of ceramic art. The period's love of exuberance in decoration is shown in these vases, where scrolls of lusty gilt foliage form but the background for the figures of "Uncle Tom, Little Eva and Eliza." Most vases were less dramatic.

The Statuette of imitation bronze or iron was put to work to support gas jets.

Electroplating of metal, patented in 1836, permitted endless elaboration. A characteristic example was the Epergne, an essential decoration of the formal dinner table. That this glittering bush of metal and glass was devoid of any feeling of structure disturbed the public not at all. Vastly preferred was the opulence it typified—an opulence accentuated by the rich mounds of fruit and flowers with which each compartment was heaped.

Below. A silver Swing-pitcher (for ice water) graced the American sideboard.
Below, next. The coal-scuttle was transformed by "art-manufacturers" into the "Coal-vase"—a silly elegancy.
Below, right. Epergne, made in Boston, praised at the Great Exhibition.

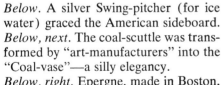
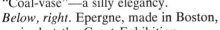

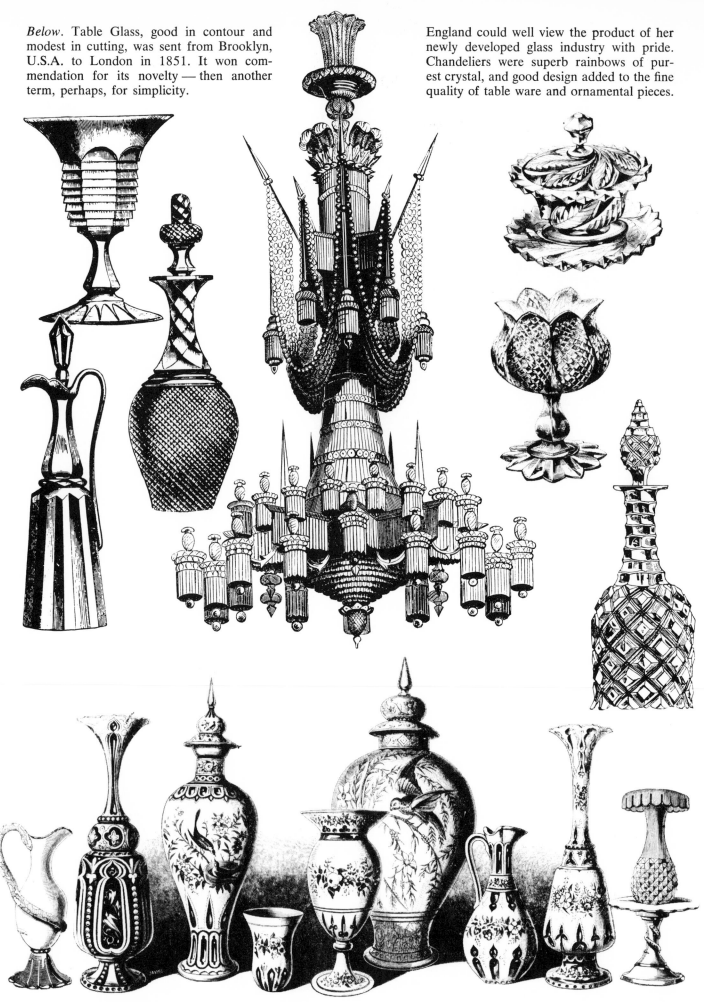

Below. Table Glass, good in contour and modest in cutting, was sent from Brooklyn, U.S.A. to London in 1851. It won commendation for its novelty — then another term, perhaps, for simplicity.

England could well view the product of her newly developed glass industry with pride. Chandeliers were superb rainbows of purest crystal, and good design added to the fine quality of table ware and ornamental pieces.

Bohemian Glass. Prague, 1851. Primarily used for ornament, Bohemian glass tended to over-elaboration. It was rich in color, gold, workmanship, but often poor in form. Despite this, it was viewed as the acme of elegance and ranked as unsurpassed decoration for bureau, sideboard, whatnot.

ALBUM 7

Of How to Mount the Ladder
Of Niceness and Gentility
Of the Royal Family, the Camera, &
The Truth-telling Daguerreotype
Of Etiquette Books and Snobbishness &
Of Godey's Lady's Book
The Sacred Word of Genteel Womanhood
Of the Sewing Machine &
Of Felling, Stitching, Hemming, Tucking
Of Binding, Cording, Quilting, Braiding
Of Fancywork and Embroidery
Homespun and Hundred-dollar Handkerchiefs
Of Fashions and Fripperies &
The Embellishment of
The Victorian Male

ALBUM SEVEN

✎❋✎

THE WORLD OF
REFINED ASPIRATIONS

"It is a lovely sight to see
A maiden in the privacy
Of her own chamber—where the day
In gentle studies glides away:
Her spirit breathes through all things round—
The dainty volumes that abound;
The silken broidery in its frame,

That might e'en Flora's labour shame:
The easel, where no critic's eye
A meretricious taste could spy:
The harp, on which she loves to play,
Singing the while some sweet old lay;
Here gay and placid speed the hours
Among her music, books and flowers . . ."

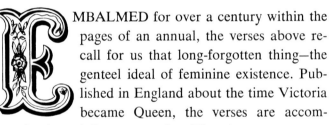 MBALMED for over a century within the pages of an annual, the verses above recall for us that long-forgotten thing—the genteel ideal of feminine existence. Published in England about the time Victoria became Queen, the verses are accompanied by a delicate engraving. That the young person it depicts is of flawless refinement cannot be doubted, for the engraving shows her marked with refinement's very insignia—black silk "mits." In thus covering her hands with these fashionable articles (even when absorbed in painting or sewing) she labels herself unmistakably as above the classes who need bare hands to perform the world's necessary toil. In 1843 the print appeared on this side of the Atlantic in America's most fashionable periodical, *Godey's Lady's Book*. Undoubtedly the engraving made an impression on the magazine's readers, bent on becoming ladies as soon as possible. If wearing "mits" or "mitaines" at the most inconvenient times stamped one as a lady, they, too, would wear mits. And wear them they did, even at breakfast.

At that time, every picture and any advice were earnestly pondered. For a remarkable thing had been happening on this side of the ocean. Here, in America, for the first time in the world's history, the common man

and woman could envision a future comprising at least some small degree of comfort and education. Now everyone so minded could aspire to be "ladies" and "gentlemen." Had they not seen others rise to the highest rungs on fortune's ladder—persons who started with no greater advantages than they themselves possessed? Did not this demonstrate that advancement seemed possible without family background or inherited means, that wealth could be acquired by one's own efforts? Was it not already in the hands of sons and daughters of poor mechanics and in the families of California miners?

This vision-filled people was the raw material from which, at least in great part, the fabric of American Victorian life was to be woven. Behind them was a powerful drive. Behind all the pushing, the striving, the social competitiveness which furnished endless subject matter for the literary and pictorial satirists of the period was a touching motive. Everyone wanted to be considered "nice"—to be thought better than one had been before.

With the first signs of improved financial conditions began the struggle to advance oneself. The upward climb was not only hard but frequently pathetic, as a helping hand to guide one's first steps was sometimes difficult to find. To be sure, it was glibly suggested that one observe and then emulate one's betters, but often

113

the most eager aspirants to culture were situated in locales devoid of examples to copy. But the publishers soon came to the help of those craving instruction in all phases of living and brought out many books to fill this need of the socially perplexed. In these studies, the amenities took first place. Decorum and intense respectability became the preoccupation of all who looked on Victoria as an example. To the average woman bent on self-improvement the pictured aspect of England's Queen offered encouragement. Here was no pampered royal beauty shrouded in romantic tradition, but a person quite as bourgeoise, both in contour and in feature, as herself. That such scrutiny was possible was striking evidence that the world had undergone a change: something had happened which stripped—and for all time— every vestige of undeserved glamour from the occupants of thrones. This something was the coming of the camera, invented by one of the Queen's own subjects, Fox Talbot. The Royal family, in its everyday wholesomeness, was now photographed for all the world to see. The Queen, not in her jewels, velvets, and ermine of Court functions, but as a plain little hoop skirted woman topped with a pork-pie hat. Her children clad in equally simple fashion surround her, all solemnly holding the pose before the camera in the manner then necessitated by the primitive equipment.

Whatever may have been the effect of engravings of Winterhalter's idealized paintings of the Victorian court, (they have done so much today to establish the pictorial charm of that era) that effect was cancelled by the camera's truths. The public kept on acquiring pretty pictures of the Royal Family which they bought to satisfy their love of romance: the noble father and mother posed with magnificent dignity in the background, the foreground filled with little girls and boys balanced on ottomans, their exquisite frocks outspread like butterflywings. But purchasers of the prints now knew them for the graceful fictions they were, and were forced, even if unwillingly, to accept the photographs as facts, for many of them had themselves submitted to the daguerreotype and to its hard, unpleasant revealings.

Though the socially aspiring could learn to face the camera with carriage and demeanor patterned on a study of the stateliest models (clad in gowns ordered from the dressmaker in greatest vogue), the uneasiness ever present in those ambitious to rise was not so easily concealed. Therefore, the manual of deportment was the ever present mentor. The early etiquette books (planned to awaken their fair readers—and with none

too delicate an approach—"to the consciousness of a few habitual misbehavements") dealt with matters differing considerably from those taken up by our present-day arbiters. Then the very essentials of manners had to be imparted, the necessary foundation laid.

The Emily Post of the day, Eliza Leslie, brought out her *Behaviour Book* in 1853. At that time, she found it obligatory to tell her countrywomen not to listen at doorcracks; "not to rock, as it was ungenteel;" not to intrude into the "spare room" through "over-solicitousness for your household goods." This latter admonition —curious as it seems today—was necessary, for socially uninformed hostesses had a habit of peeping into their guestrooms to see if the visitor of the moment had done anything amiss, such as pulling up the shade to permit the entry of a ray of sunshine—a most heinous act. But there were also hints for the thoughtless guest. The latter was warned never to make her hostess fidgety by choosing, from among all the assembled furniture, her best needleworked piece to sit upon. "We have known ladies who were always uneasy when their visiters sat down on a sofa or ottoman, and could not forbear inviting them to change their seats and take chairs." So evident is it that right was solidly ranged on the side of property that Miss Leslie never hints that the hostess herself might also need advice on social composure.

The word "gentility" is linked inseparably with Victorian days. Innocuous and old fashioned as it appears today, the term nevertheless created much perturbation in every stratum of social life. Suddenly, girls in average families became infected with the idea that the first step toward "gentility" was a contempt for household affairs, and in this, unfortunately, they were aided by their hardworking mothers. The latter, finding themselves suddenly transferred, after years of drudgery, to more affluent circumstances, made up their minds that their daughters would lead easier lives. To such women the hallmark of "gentility" was a servant, and in order to back up their professions to "ladyhood," they often "put up" with "help" of appalling incompetence. So quickly did this false standard take hold of the one-step-removed-from-the-backwoods public, that, even as early as the 1840's, thoughtful observers began to call attention to the silliness of this "genteel" posing, for it was obvious that too many little maidens seemed to have "got above themselves," in the phrase of the day. Young girls whose assistance about the house was actually needed, devoted themselves instead to aping—in so far as their varied conditions permitted—the ideal of graceful idleness set forth in the verses written by that exceedingly worldly woman, the Countess of Blessington, quoted earlier in this chapter. Therefore, it is not surprising that serious writers, concerned as to the effect of such propaganda for uselessness on the youth of the United States, made frontal attacks on the most popular delusion of the day—namely, that an interest in practical matters was *vulgar*—a word then used quite as frequently and as glibly as *genteel*. Special children's books were prepared, juvenile literature being then regarded as the most fertile soil in which to plant the choicest moralistic seeds. One such little American story-book is called *The Useful and the Beautiful*. Its masculine—probably clerical—author is bent on showing "the possibility of blending with intellectual pursuits matters of business which are indispensable in every well-regulated house." None of his happy young maidens has time available for the decorative pursuits of Lady Blessington's verses; they are too busily engaged in acquiring a knowledge of chemistry while being shown how to make bread, of exercise through sweeping and dusting, of charity by visiting the needy, and of gardening by taking care of the window plants.

Despite the flood of uplifting *books,* the greatest vehicle of them all for diffusing the cultural and moral ideas of the period was *Godey's Lady's Book*—the monthly publication which for so long stayed in the vanguard of that new type of periodical, the ladies' magazine. For all of forty years, from 1937 to 1877, "Godey's," as it was affectionately known, was edited by Mrs. Sarah Josepha Hale. A Victorian lady to the core, "Godey's" editor was also a remarkable woman with many ideas far in advance of her time. But as she was most tactful in advocating them, her "gentility" went unquestioned, and, to her vast public, "Mrs. Hale" and "lady" were synonyms. To all its readers, "Godey's" represented the ultimate authority in matters of culture and taste.

Today, when magazines are commonplace and their price a trifling item in a budget, it is difficult to comprehend the powerful influence exerted by "Godey's" and one or two other competing periodicals, at a time when money circulated far less freely. Those who could afford a new trinket but who chose instead to spend the money on a magazine subscription were regarded by their neighbors as beings set apart—marked, as it were, by a superior degree of culture. To understand the importance of magazines, simply put yourself in the place of a village girl of the period. You might be consumed

The home of the solid citizen was furnished in sober style.

with a burning desire to have things "nice"—and yet never be able to lay your hands on the small sum needed to subscribe to the journal which set forth all the means by which you could attain your ideal. If, however, there was in the tiny village in which you lived even one subscriber, you were quite within your rights in regarding her copy as one on which you had a partial claim, and you never hesitated to borrow it. Indeed, you were even justified in accusing the owner of *unneighborliness* if she showed any tendency to withhold it. And at a time when Americans were still dependent on their neighbors for all kinds of help, no one liked to be marked with this stigma.

Magazines thus borrowed enabled the earnest student of their pages to ponder on the most recent whims of fashion, mull over and probably reject the latest ideas in housekeeping (for women were apt to be conservatives in this field), and, most important of all, glean up-to-the-minute information on the newest in embroidery and fancywork. Equipped by the ladies' papers with the latest word on the subject, even the backwoods girl could achieve some wisp of homemade elegance (though she had to install it in surroundings incongruous in the extreme). Thanks to the reservoir of skills and inventiveness built up by her pioneer forebears and

115

ever ready to be tapped, she knew she could copy whatever was there pictured and contrive a working substitute for the missing material, for no Victorian woman was ever deterred from undertaking a project because a minor constituent was lacking. As an example of this pioneering ingenuity, let us consider the subject of tracing paper. Today we buy it. In that day if a piece were needed, a woman was most likely to prepare it herself with oil and paper, for her sex had not forgotten (they had heard the tale too many times) how oiled paper served their mothers and grandmothers as windowpanes in ruder days. To have a piece of paper when needed, at a time when it was not only expensive but difficult in rural districts to obtain, the early Victorian saved every scrap, particularly all old letters. These she turned to amazingly good account in mending, in making quilt patterns, and for use as tracing paper—reserving the blank areas for this last purpose. With the help of a little oil, some form of which was always at hand, the paper was rendered transparent, and she could proceed to "take off" the idea shown in the magazine. Spots of grease on many an old magazine are witness to this ingenious practice.

Marietta Holley, who produced her works hidden in true Victorian modesty behind the name of "Josiah Allen's Wife," holds forth in 1869 in "Godey's" chief competitor, *Peterson's Magazine,* about the vicissitudes of publications which fully served a community as carriers of culture. "I who set such store by my magazines and was just as careful to keep them whole and clean, as I was my Sunday Bonnet have got back a lot of books so dirty that to discern the reading the strongest spectacles are powerless in spots. . . . Old men have burnt them, by holding them too near the light—old women have peppered them with snuff. Young men have sowed them with tobacco. Young women have greased them for patterns. Children have stuck the leaves together with molasses and pried them open with their tongues. They have been cut with shears, gnawed by babies, and worried by pups . . . blackened with candle snuff and whitened with tallow."

Through the medium of the ladies' magazines the desire for "gentility" and all its outward symbols permeated quickly and effectively the farthest reaches of the country because a great portion of the public sincerely believed that the spiritual values of culture and refinement were actually to be obtained from contact with material things. Thus the more intensely one toiled to adorn one's home, on the lines of the models given, the more rapidly one's family acquired the polish which such elegant surroundings demanded. In other words, the more fancywork, the better the manners! And in pursuit of its readers' decorative ambitions, their "blessed Godey's" always stood ready to help; for although, as editor, Mrs. Hale disapproved of snobbish imitation, she personally sympathized with her public's craving to make their surroundings "nice." To assist its more remote subscribers, the journal conducted a shopping service. If its readers could not find the raw materials of the arts at the cross-roads country store where they traded, "Godey's" willingly forwarded patterns and materials.

Since often the only means by which a woman could vaunt her superiorities was through the products of her needle, her achievements with that slender tool frequently stirred the social waters to a degree which women today cannot in the least comprehend. So completely have women relinquished their once important talents to the machine that they are unable to enter imaginatively into the ambition to excel, ambition which once kept the fingers of their feminine ancestors in active competition with their sisters.

Although up-to-the-minute women prided themselves on always knowing the newest thing in fancywork, the conservatives stuck to their long-preferred form of display, the elaborate quilt. Unquestionably, quilt-making offered an emotional outlet to many a woman striving in rural isolation for something beyond the crudeness of her daily life, for some channel for her inarticulate love of beauty. As long as the homemade quilt was a necessity of life, women were somewhat restrained by lack of time from producing the more elaborate forms. But after the Jacquard machines began turning out spreads and coverlets, quilts made in the United States (particularly in the expansive decade between 1840 and 1850), were articles produced simply to display their makers' skills. They then reached their highest standard of beauty and excellence.

After the coming of the Jacquard machine, another product of the industrial age conferred an even greater boon on American womanhood, in fact, on all women. With the arrival of the sewing machine in the 1850's, women beheld a lovely vision: emancipation from long slavery to the needle. Prior to the invention of the sewing machine, almost every woman was perpetually engaged in practical sewing. Like everything else in Victorian life, hand-sewing was an occupation governed by set conventions, rigidly observed. The most restricting of

these was the ruling that all useful work—and this included plain sewing—was to be completed before midday dinner. (It was a matter of common politeness to ignore the fact that in understaffed households even "refined" women of "nice" families were occasionally forced to lend a hand to the hard-worked maid.)

In theory, "nice" women seated themselves every afternoon in their parlors and applied themselves to genteel afternoon avocations: they twiddled with their accomplishments or worked on elegant trifles or entertained visitors at tea. In reality, however, the ladies kept their fingers busy with plain sewing—the always-needed gentleman's shirt or piece of feminine underclothing. If a male visitor appeared, an amusing scurrying-about took place, for Mrs. Grundy decreed that no *gentleman* must ever observe a *lady* in the act of sewing on her undergarments. This would be the height of impropriety.

At the first signal of a visitor, all those engaged on white work hurriedly thrust their chemises or pantalettes under the nearest pillow or crammed them into their work-baskets. The stage for the pretty scene, "Victorian Ladies at Home," was now set, and the actresses in the playlet—one by which no one was deceived—scattered to play their respective parts. One of the favorite "props" of polite gentility was the gaily decorated painting box, placed conspicuously on the

centre table. The artist of the family made a bee-line for this article in order to present to the entering guest the picture of a cultivated young person deeply absorbed in putting a particularly careful touch to an incompleted painting, although the most cursory examination would disclose that the painting had been under way for a long time—its surface being far from fresh. Indeed, there was no especial need to push toward its completion, for it was useful even in its unfinished state; its sepia tones were valued as an ornamental addition to the centre-table display. The middle-class Victorian relished these little tableaux of elegant leisure which she created for her audiences, and diversified them from time to time by changing the props. One of the most common was the embroidery frame. This article, always useful but frequently very decorative as well, was made in several styles. The table and standing wooden frames were the most popular.

To the early Victorian eye—especially the masculine eye—nothing presented a more appealing picture than a lady working at her embroidery frame. This was an occupation which set off, not only the fashions of the day, but its most admired feminine characteristics as well. Every astute maiden knew how to swing her dark or flaxen curls in a fascinating manner as she concentrated on an exacting bit. And as she applied herself

117

to her task, with what modest grace she spread out her wide skirts to accentuate the wasp-like delicacy of her waist and with what knowingness she allowed her long lashes to sweep against the transparent pallor of her cheeks! Giddy young ladies were never in too great haste to complete their needlework pieces unless they were planned for a pressing need. Some girls kept their frames filled with half-finished projects all through their maiden years, not only as irrefutable proof to the critical of their industry, but also with the keenest sensing of the embroidery frame's value as an important adjunct—especially in those well-chaperoned days—to their matrimonial schemings.

As long as sewing was a process carried on entirely by hand, time and patience set the limit to the amount of elaboration possible. But after machine production made cloth much cheaper, and the sewing machine turned out clothing so much faster, every one could attempt to be "stylish." Even those who had gone about in homespun—certainly a material whose long-wearing qualities precluded much interest in changing styles—could now purchase pleasing fabrics at less than they could weave them, for American cottons and woolens were brought within the range of the most modest pocketbooks. No longer need one sigh for the unattainable, once symbolized by a length of expensive English print or calico. By 1863 American mills at Lowell were producing calicoes to perfection "in the most approved shades," which that year were quiet tones of "stone, drab, mode, cuir, and pale green, covered with tiny figures in brilliant and good colors."

The new materials together with the new sewing machine stirred up the whole feminine world. For the first time in history, the average woman's costume could display the intricacy of detailing formerly the prerogative only of the wealthy, if its maker chose to apply her skills and patience to that rather frivolous end. Women went to extremes over clothes and fashionable whimsies in dress. Textiles were covered with needlework patterns of the utmost delicacy, for the nineteenth century admired fineness of execution above everything else. All arts were judged by this arbitrary standard. To achieve it in sculpture, painting, drawing, engraving, and even handwriting—for the latter was still practiced as an art—required manual dexterity of the highest order. And to establish it as the ideal in needlework demanded not only a finicking patience, but a marvellous delicacy of touch and the best of eyesight as well.

Fashion changed its focus of interest with great fre-quency; at one time it concentrated on but one article of luxury, the possession of which marked its owner as highly elegant; then, without warning, it switched to another. About the time of Victoria's accession, costly imported embroidered handkerchiefs were one of the distinguishing tokens of the lady of fashion and the lady of refinement. Since these articles were solely for display, they were held by the gloved tips of the fingers. The nouveaux riches were apparently at first insensible to the subtle charms of these exquisite bits of workmanship. Eliza Leslie, commenting acidly on the fashionable sillinesses of the 1830's, says: "Parvenues can seldom bring their minds to give much for pocket handkerchiefs [she notes that at Stewart's in New York they cost $60 and $80 apiece] but prefer laying out their money in things that make a great show." And one of her flighty heroines exclaims: "Do not call these divine handkerchiefs gew-gaws! Only look at this, examine the work and see how exquisite it is—like a delicate bas-relief sculptured by the fingers of a fairy." But it was not long before even the "parvenues" learned to appreciate these refined touches to costume, and by the 1850's the desire for fragile embroidered articles was general. The finest of collars and the most transparent of undersleeves held the centre of the fashionable stage, and to fill the constant demand they were now executed not only on the Continent, but also in Ireland. There, after the famine of 1846-1847, children in Irish convents and schools were taught how to embroider in order to aid that impoverished country towards recovery. Within a few years, what had been set up primarily as a philanthropic enterprise became a successful commercial one, giving employment, it was estimated, to more than half a million persons.

Among other aspects of Victorian dress, fabrics in particular were of great elegance and often extremely expensive. But neither quality nor price were absolute guides for the aspirant to gentility; indeed, they but concealed the many pitfalls in the path of the most earnest seeker. Judging by the frequent strictures on the excessive use of color written by those who felt it their duty to instruct their sisters in "correct taste," the dress of that period must have reached heights of gaudiness never since even approximated. Still, women would have had to be superhuman to resist the allurements which industry spread before them: the novelties of texture and design and color. The new aniline dyes suffused fabrics with such brilliant and intense colors that no uneducated eye could withstand their fascination. Women had to be told not to wear the entire rainbow at once; two colors were enough for any costume. Furthermore, to wear certain hues was actually to endanger one's social status. If, in the 1850's, you ventured forth in reddish lilac, reddish purple, or even reddish brown, this unfortunate choice marked you not only as lacking in discrimination, but also as being "ungenteel"—that most devastating of all social judgments.

Moreover, if you aspired to be a lady, no matter what fashion's caprice might be, you were careful of the scale of pattern you chose. Not for you were white grounds covered with large red flowers and green leaves! Even if this type of design were selected in the most costly of brocades, "it had," in the eyes of Miss Leslie, "the look of calico." And ladies, even the most impeccable, were perennially on their guard to see that nothing they wore suggested that humble fabric, with its connotations of plain folk who could afford nothing more expensive. But let no lady think that even her flawless gentility would permit her the social error of appearing in a public place—at luncheon in a resort hotel, for instance—in figured mousseline de laine, then a popular material. "What is it," again says the authoritative Miss Leslie, nose visibly tip-tilted, "but *woolen* calico, and gives an unladylike look to even the most decided lady." They who strove most earnestly to do the correct thing found it difficult to maintain balance on this arbitrary tightrope; they erred if they leaned to the side of simplicity or individuality, but it was equally fatal to tilt the other way and to discover that they had then committed the most reprehensible error of being overdressed for the occasion.

Both the sewing machine and the crinoline burst on the world at about the same time; a fortunate coincidence, since nothing was better devised to display all the mechanical possibilities of the recent invention than the great bell of the hoopskirt. With one accord, women fell in love with the new marvel which could "fell, stitch, hem, tuck, quilt, cord, bind and braid, as well as embroider." Instead of accepting the leisure made possible by this labor-saving device, they preferred to experiment with its enchanting possibilities; because of its facilities, no type of trimming was now too elaborate to attempt.

Trimmings began to rank almost as works of decorative art and were often quite as tedious to produce. Sometimes they resembled sculpture in their plasticity; again they seemed inspired by geometry, and most certainly mathematics was needed to forward their con-

struction. Occasionally it seemed that the treatment accorded decorative details of the great crinoline was appropriated directly from architecture—then a not surprising circumstance, since the conception of the hoopskirt was so frankly a structural one. Women strove to outdo each other in the adornment of their dresses. Each month the magazines brought out detailed patterns for dress embellishments, totally unconcerned about the length of time which might be consumed in executing these ideas. But prospects of infinite labor never deterred women in their desire to be stylish. Each month they waited impatiently for the latest hints on how to contort some innocuous material into the arabesques which fashion dictated. The making of these decorations really partook of the nature of the finest of craft work; to execute any of them precisely required such deftness and accuracy that they could only have been worked out by persons to whom the tradition of fine handwork had descended in a line as yet unbroken.

Sometimes the less gifted, sadly disappointed with the results of all their earnest toil to attain the refinement symbolized by some dress gadget, would complain to the magazines about the lack of detail in the instructions. But, as good workmanship was then still taken for granted, fashion editors displayed slight sympathy with the unskilled. "Godey's" editor answered one such complainant with what today seems amazing tartness: "We give the pattern," she says, "and the design. Every good workwoman can work from them, and bad ones would be no better off, no matter how long and particular the description."

As the Victorian era developed, ornamentation and beauty became synonymous terms—a criterion which women unanimously adopted. Therefore, no young lady ever looked with scorn upon the gift of a "volume of erudite patterns for lace, bead and other work." In fact, such a pattern book was viewed as a most acceptable offering for a gentleman to give to a lady. Instead of resenting its practical aspect, the feminine recipient lost herself in its contents and, having chosen something she considered suitable for her purpose, planned to work it out as a return gift to the donor, this Victorian male who, not yet far removed from the Georgian, still continued to display some of the eighteenth-century taste for elaboration in dress. Today, though the male has been persuaded to add to his conventional dull garments certain colorful touches—and he will wear, at least for relaxation or for sports, garments made of pseudo-batiks inspired by the South Seas, or sweaters

Men's Carriage Robes were crocheted from bright wools with horse and gigantic flowers worked out in gaudy Berlin-wool cross-stitch.

whose ornamentation is of European peasant origin— he is no longer willing to sport any of the elaborate embroidered accessories showered on his great-grand-fathers: vests, every inch of which was masked with Berlin-work, and braces or suspenders covered with needlepoint flowers. No man was then abashed to display a tobacco pouch of crocheted and decorated silk, nor did he ever hesitate to pull from his breast-pocket a cigar-case stiffly brilliant with finely executed bead-work. Neither was he fearful of being seen in domestic circles with his head topped with a smoking cap embroidered with braiding or flowers on the richest of velvet, its elegant texture further heightened with touches of gold and a handsome swinging tassel. In men's trouser-pockets lurked long, limp, silk purses, dark in hue and patterned with the silver of cut-steel beading. When a man went hunting, he might sally forth with a game-bag ornamented with devices appro-priate for the sport. It is worth noting that, as the period advanced, patterns selected for the decoration of men's accessories became more robust, perhaps in delicate awareness of the fact that men were about to slough off all remaining traces of Georgian dandyism. The flowers are replaced by more masculine motifs, such as hunting caps and whips, imps and devils, fighting cats, or fox heads, all appropriate devices for the toes of slippers, articles which, when worked by feminine hands, ever headed the list of gifts for the Victorian male. Whether of embroidered silk or soft kid, woolworked canvas or velvet, a pair of slippers was, together with braces, always regarded as a signal token of affection. Happy indeed was the maiden, who, after making such a present, received a letter such as this written in 1855: "If I tell you I valued it more highly than a letter, it is not solely on account of its greater intrinsic value nor because I wanted what you sent but because it is another proof of your consideration and regard. To me it is acceptable because of the labor and trouble it has cost you and the satisfaction I shall feel in wearing them—a voluntary offering from my best friend bearing evidence of her handiwork and industry."

Women, almost mystically compelled to put a design on everything, invaded other masculine areas of living to give them a touch of "refinement." Behind excellent horses, Victorian men, in all their bewhiskered dignity, drove out with knees covered by highly ornamented carriage robes or woolen afghans. Sometimes brilliant, sometimes restrained in hue, the knitted or crocheted species of this useful adjunct was frequently constructed of wide bands of contrasting colors—a definitely Oriental idea. On these bands were worked curious conventional designs which the era dubbed "Turkish." This comparative severity in patterning was obviously a concession to sterner masculine tastes.

Since the disappearance of the horse-drawn vehicle, the world has settled down to a much greater democracy in demeanor than was possible in Victoria's time. Then the possession of a pleasure carriage was an unarguable demonstration of social position and wealth—one which, moreover, carried infinitely greater significance than does the possession of an automobile in these times. In Victorian days, the leisurely pace of the open carriage presented an irresistible invitation to exhibit one's taste by one's dress, one's wealth by the degree of elegance of one's conveyance, and one's love of elegance by the richness of its appointments.

During the Queen's reign, social conventions demanded a rigorous formality in deportment. But it was almost impossible to be anything less than dignified, for the stately costumes then favored permitted only the most restrained of bodily movements. This formal bearing was reflected in the ritual of social intercourse. Custom demanded that every lady when calling should have in her gloved hand—her too tightly gloved hand, it usually happened to be—a card-case, for calling cards

were an essential part of the polite ceremony of visiting. These cases were frequently beautiful examples of the jeweler's or craftsman's art—delicate filigrees of silver or gold, of mother-of-pearl, ivory, or tortoise shell, carved and inlaid in ingenious fashion. It is apparent that by 1856 such trinkets were already an accepted fashionable appointment, even in the supposedly cruder American life, for "Godey's" carries an advertisement for them in that year. Not only card-cases but the cards themselves furnished a vehicle for snobbish exhibition. At a time when visitors were far rarer than today, these souvenirs of social contacts used to be placed in card-racks—pieces of feminine handwork made of flower-decorated bits of bone, paper, wire, and gilt. Hung beside the mantel mirror, they were planned as an ornamental feature of overmantel decoration. When the mantel shelf began to be considered as an area for formal display rather than as a spot on which one deposited curiosities, the calling-card racks were removed from their traditional place and the cards themselves piled up in fancywork trays on the hall table. Here they were quite as available to the inquisitive who went through them, one by one—the direct if ingenuous method by which the Victorians used to gauge the social status of one another's visitors.

So prominently did love of display bulk in the American woman's life that, by 1869, more thoughtful writers of the period were moved to protest. When household ornaments, furniture, equipages, rich and showy food, and elegant garments took first place, and hygiene, cleanliness, sanitation, and well-cooked plain food were ignored, no less a person than Harriet Beecher Stowe suggested that our false standards needed overhauling. "Of what use," she says, "were brick houses whose fronts were plated with brown stone, whose entrance doors were expensively trimmed with carving, fine metal work and engraved glass panels when such showy houses sometimes lacked even a bathroom and food was prepared in an unpainted gloomy kitchen?"

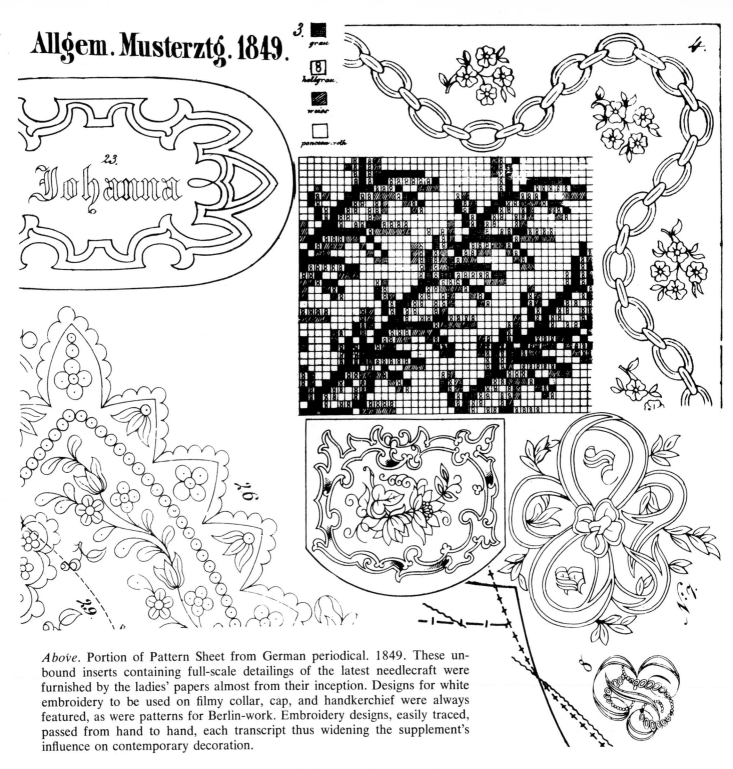

Above. Portion of Pattern Sheet from German periodical. 1849. These un-bound inserts containing full-scale detailings of the latest needlecraft were furnished by the ladies' papers almost from their inception. Designs for white embroidery to be used on filmy collar, cap, and handkerchief were always featured, as were patterns for Berlin-work. Embroidery designs, easily traced, passed from hand to hand, each transcript thus widening the supplement's influence on contemporary decoration.

Border for Crocheted Wool Afghan. Carriage Robes featuring bands of giant cross-stitched flowers covered the knees of the Victorian male when driving.

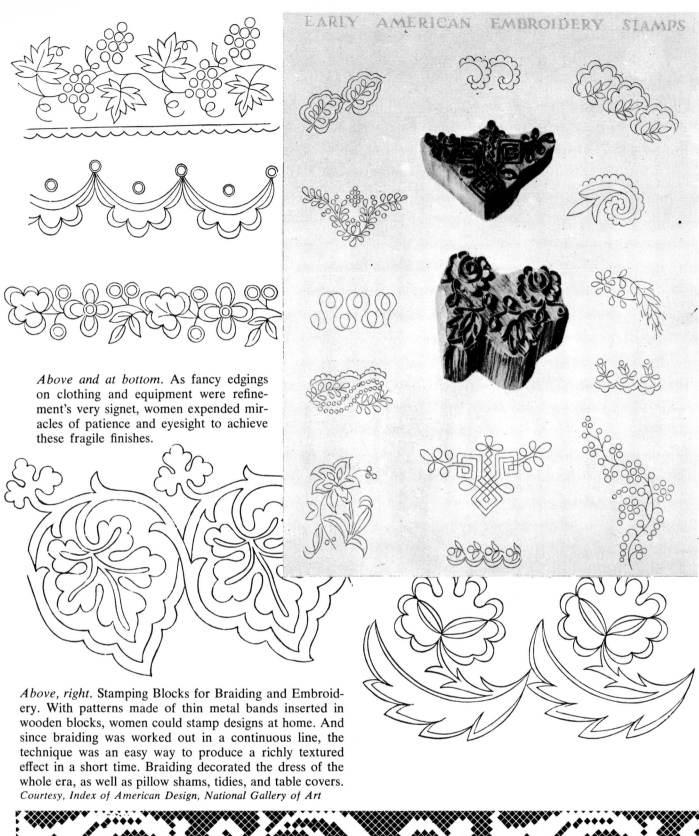

Above and at bottom. As fancy edgings on clothing and equipment were refinement's very signet, women expended miracles of patience and eyesight to achieve these fragile finishes.

Above, right. Stamping Blocks for Braiding and Embroidery. With patterns made of thin metal bands inserted in wooden blocks, women could stamp designs at home. And since braiding was worked out in a continuous line, the technique was an easy way to produce a richly textured effect in a short time. Braiding decorated the dress of the whole era, as well as pillow shams, tidies, and table covers.
Courtesy, Index of American Design, National Gallery of Art

123

Refined touches gilded masculine apparel. *Left.* Embroidered Braces. *Above.* Detail of embroidery on shoulder strap of Game Bag (*below*).

Embroidered Cigar Case.

Ladies lavished embroidered gifts on the males of their circle. As a change from slippers, a ladies' paper of high authority came forth with patterns for decorated hunting accessories. Shown here are Game Bag and Shooting Muff of gray linen. Following are crocheted Tobacco Pouch and silk Purse—standard masculine gear.

Above. Floral fantasia on linen damask.
1851.

Above. Ladies' Color Box. 1851. To prevent their clash-
ing with neighboring elegancies, these utilitarian articles
which held painting materials were disguised as ornamental caskets.

Ladies carried their music to parties in highly decorated
Portfolios. *Above.* Wreath embroidered in fuzzy chenille
on Music Portfolio transformed it into a properly elegant
appointment.

Nothing provided a more refined touch to household and personal linens than one's initial, almost lost in a decorative web of white embroidery. Pillow Shams flaunted the most gigantic examples.

TWO-LINE SMALL PICA ORNAMENTED, No. 2.

PHILADELPHIA 1849.

TWO-LINE SMALL PICA ORNAMENTED, No. 3.

WASHINGTON PA.

TWO-LINE SMALL PICA GOTHIC CONDENSED SHADED.

STRAYED OR STOLEN &C

TWO-LINE SMALL PICA TUSCAN.

G WASHINTON.

TWO-LINE LONG PRIMER ITALIAN SHADED.

CHRIST'S CHUR-

TWO-LINE LONG PRIMER ANTIQUE SHADED.

ABRIDGMENT, E&

TWO-LINE LONG PRIMER GOTHIC DOUBLE SHADED.

THE CONSTITUTION.

TWO-LINE LONG PRIMER ORNAMENTED, No. 1.

NORTH AMERICAN

LEWIS PELOUZE,   PHILADELPHIA.

TWO-LINE ENGLISH ANTIQUE CONDENSED OPEN.

APPRENTICE. &

TWO-LINE ENGLISH TUSCAN SHADED.

HUMOROUS

TWO-LINE PICA CONDENSED ORNAMENTED. No. 1.

PENNSYLVANIA RAIL-RO

TWO-LINE PICA TUSCAN ORNAMENTED.

B. FRANKLIN

TWO-LINE PICA ORNAMENTED. No. 1.

VIRTUE MODESTY.

TWO-LINE PICA ORNAMENTED. No. 2.

CORNUCOPIA 21

TWO-LINE PICA ORNAMENTED. No. 3.

IMAGINATION.

LEWIS PELOUZE.   PHILADELPHIA.

The printed page would have appeared undressed without its quota of embellishments. Of these the most usual was the Ornamental Initial. Its design reflected every variety of the romantic trend. *Above.* Specimens of Fancy Printing Types. Louis Pelouze, Philadelphia. 1849. *Courtesy, Free Library of Philadelphia*

Free Library of Philadelphia

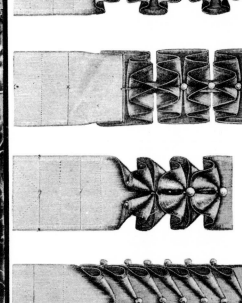

If lack of funds forced women who followed the styles to curtail expenditure, there was no curb put to the energy wasted on dress embellishment. "Samantha Allen" comments: "I should judge there was from half a bushel to three pecks of ruffles and knife pleatin's that lay round her sewin' machine . . . she said she must stitch 'em, and pucker 'em all that day, and her face looked so care-worn and haggard that I almost pitied her. . . . 'What makes you lay so to ruffles, Mahala, it is a wearin' on you and I can see it is.' 'Oh,' says she, 'I do it because the folks do. They wear ruffles a sight now.'"

Above. Section of Poster. Thread advertisement. *C.* 1880.
When fashion was based on the elaboration of material, and demanded that Ribbons be quilled (*upper right*), or Overdresses (*above*) be quilted on every inch of a rich fabric, the thread industry was a prominent advertiser, as its products were essential to the ornamental result.
Right. French Work Box. Mother-of-pearl and carving contributed glamour and refinement to the prosaic tools of needlework.

Courtesy, The Art Institute of Chicago

ALBUM 8

Of Pleasure in Wealth &
New-found Furnishings
Of Gold-stamped Muslins &
Wool-worked Footstools &
Magentas and Crimsons and Bismarck Browns
Of Merino and Brussels Lace
Lambrequins and Flower-strewn Wiltons
Plum-pudding Wallpapers &
Black Marble Mantels
Of Plump Padding and Ottomans
Plush and Pincushions
Of Unpleasant Haircloth
Funereal but Practical

ALBUM EIGHT

≈❋≈

THE WORLD
OF THE
OTTOMAN AND LAMBREQUIN

HE year was 1840. England had a young queen, and in America the house which for fifty years had remained unchanged had a new young mistress.

Round the walls a dozen mahogany chairs made their prim accustomed border, and above the sedate wooden mantel the stately gold mirror presided as always. The young lady scrutinizing the parlor found it impossible to decide what the original color of the panelled wainscot had been, for it had faded through the years to something for which there was no name. No matter—she would have it removed in any case, and the mantelpiece with it.

As on the day of its installation, the grandfather's clock in the corner ticked its quiet measure. In its glass-panelled door were reflected the slender pencillings of light which filtered greenly through the Venetian blinds. "How woefully old-fashioned it all is!" she sighed. On the mantelpiece were the too familiar brass candlesticks and a huddle of shabby ornaments which, because of sentiment, had never been discarded. On the other hand, sentiment and care had kept gold splinters of light twinkling attractively on the brass-tipped feet of the round mahogany centre-table for the past half-century. It was now summer and the fireplace opening was filled in with the customary wallpapered chimney-board. "What an unsightly picture of a fat man and a giraffe," thought the establishment's new mistress. "I shall certainly remove His Majesty George IV and his cameleopard the first thing. Such a subject no longer bears contemplation in a proper American household! And neither does this shabby carpet, Turkish

though it be. I shall select an elegant Brussels the next time I drive out."

Given carte-blanche to refurnish, this indulged young person had already expended much thought on transforming the house into something which her fashionable circle would approve. With one sweep she would consign all the mahogany to the attic, for she planned to replace it with the smarter rosewood. On the walls she would hang one of the new figured wallpapers from floor to cornice. To top it off, she had selected a deep bordering which pictured a group of ladies and gentlemen pacing through a veritable forest of gray traceried columns. This would provide a far more elegant effect than the previous uninteresting painted surface. And how pleased she was that she could get rid of the austere Venetian blinds! Soon the windows would be crowned with magnificent gilt cornices and massive curtain rods of heavy brass. These would support the best of worsted damask curtains to loop gracefully and trail on the floor in the extravagant manner of the pattern books she had so recently leafed through at the upholsterer's. Heavy gold lilies would serve to hold back the rich folds and permit one to glimpse the glass curtains. These were not to be the usual embroidered or lace-edged examples, but—if she could find them in the local shops —the prettiest of gold-stamped muslins.

To supplant the wooden mantelpiece, she had ordered one of white marble, in which she planned to install one of the new coal grates. The opening of the marble fireplace would be topped with a pleasing curve—and who would not agree that this was more attractive than the uncompromising rectangularity of the wooden aperture! For the mantel garniture she had chosen a

131

French ormolu clock, and to replace the brass candle-sticks and the dusty visiting-card racks—those tiresome cardboard harps with their eternally loose strings—she would herself confect a pair of shell bouquets whose pastel fragilities would be housed in narrow glass domes.

In her mind's eye she could see the gay screen she planned to set before the fireplace: a bright parrot and roses in Berlin-work. And since wool-worked footstools were in high favor, she would work a set to place before the sofa and the armchairs. On either side of the fire-place would stand her new chairs of carved rosewood which she had ordered long since for these precise spots. These were to be upholstered in the most flowery of damasks which would be stretched without a wrinkle over the hardest of foundations.

She looked forward to selecting the carpet to add the last touch of elegance. As her tastes inclined to the lavish, she would probably choose the largest bouquets of the brightest blossoms she could find, so that the parlor floor would be spotted from wall to wall with these luxurious floral islands, sprawling exuberantly beneath the feet of all the new furniture. "How for-tunate that the parlor faces the north," she thought. Like a scene in a play, the eloquent richness of her drawing room could be on view whenever she chose to show it; and not, as in the houses of so many of her friends, be kept shrouded in eternal gloom to exclude the dreaded sunlight—for there was nothing more feared by all Victorian housekeepers.

To the parlor's rich crimsons, purples and golds, she would add one—and only one—touch of black and white. This would be provided by the newest in steel engrav-ings, to take the place of the dingy old portraits that for so long had scowled alike on family and on guest. When the parlor was complete, she would have achieved the current Victorian ideal of richness and "genteelness" in furnishings.

These were the standards which were to replace the qualities of austerity and dignity, refinement and ele-gance of line which characterized the Georgian and Colonial furniture. Owing to the fact that great masses of the public, suddenly become rich, demanded goods and furnishings which would satisfy their cravings for luxurious appointments, a general lowering of aesthetic standards was occurring. The tastes of this new flood of buyers altered even the character of color schemes. Up to this time, pale grays, stone, and drab were used on woodwork and walls—sober tones quite in harmony with the neo-Classic styles for which they had served

as background. But by the time the Queen built her home at Osborne, the colors chosen for this royal residence reflected the taste for brighter hues: the royal sitting room was tinted pale apple-green, the bedroom salmon-pink, and the drawing room pale blue.

As Victoria's reign progressed and furniture became more elaborately confused in line, the colors used to set it off became progressively richer and darker, almost as if the owners feared to view their elegant monstrosi-ties in too sharp silhouette. The later color schemes of the Victorian interior seem based not on practical con-siderations of sunlight or its lack, but on some obscure reasoning which connected color with the function for which a room was planned. Thus, dining rooms were to be decorated in "warm, rich substantial hues," terms equally applicable to the food then served in these handsomely furnished chambers set apart for the serious ceremonies of breakfast, dinner, and supper. Libraries were to be papered in grave or severe tones, halls and stairways in cool, impersonal colors, but parlors and drawing rooms could be as gay as they pleased. Only the bedrooms were allotted colors both light and cheerful.

The standard of taste as applied to color varies greatly from generation to generation. Most Victorian color alliances, at least in the materials and proportions in which they were presented, are to us unacceptable juxtapositions. Many of their curious combinations were the direct result of the discovery of aniline dye in 1856. The public was enchanted by the splendor of the re-sulting rainbow hues. If women then used them in a manner which we frown upon, there was considerable reason, for fashion did its share to add to the total confusion. In the 1850's, this imperious arbiter decreed that contrast in color was not enough: there must also be contrast in tone. Therefore, two light colors should never be combined nor should two dark ones be juxta-posed. Today, unless used with the greatest discrimina-tion, we would never consider edging a rich crimson with an "extremely light and beautiful blue" nor would we regard a golden brown trimmed with a deep pink as the last word in refinement. Moreover, present-day taste would not agree that deep green trimmed with light lilac, or rich purple with orange, were color schemes which presented—as was then thought—"a mag-nificent effect." However, the greatest trouble-makers in the Victorian color scheme were the then new "ma-genta" and "solferino." These brilliant purple-pinks, named after two battles in the Austro-Italian war of

Window Draperies and their treatment were the subject of attention. Curtains were hung from gilded "Window Galleries."

1859, clash with everything except the non-combatant neutrals—black, gray, and white. Even though nature is generous with flowers of these hues, no conservative gardener will encourage them, and present-day taste in interior furnishing will have none of them except where a startling theatrical effect is desired. Not so the Victorians. They embraced them in all their eye-shattering purity and used them not only in dress but for many decorative purposes as well. Magenta and solferino queened it on patchwork quilts, and dominated the blossoms in wool-work. And, though it is hard to believe, textiles dyed in these violent hues were employed as draperies and furniture coverings. Other equally potent anilines were introduced, some named in honor of the Queen. Thus we have Victoria blue, Victoria orange, Victoria green.

For several generations, the well-dressed window wore as many draperies as did the ladies themselves. As the early Victorians were blissfully unconscious of the baleful effect of germs and dust, they indulged themselves in all the fabrics their well-filled purses could afford, and kept out—as a matter of principle—as much

health-giving sunlight as the rich stuffs would exclude. In the houses of the well-to-do, windows were literally coated with layers of curtains. Those of Brussels lace displayed, as if price-ticketed, their value to the envious passer-by. In the very highest circles of fashion, there were two sets of these elegant tissues—the one nearest the street drawn back so that a glimpse of the second set, which veiled the interior from view, was nevertheless visible. Over these went swathings and loopings of fine fabrics, crossing and smothering each other. These draperies were voluminous, lined affairs of silk or worsted damask, figured satins or merino cloth, hung with large rings from heavy—sometimes grotesquely heavy—brass curtain rods. The latter also supported decoratively shaped valances, be-fringed and be-corded. Elaborate gilt cornices and florid metal tie-backs topped off these Niagaras of textiles.

In the first years of Victoria's reign, glass curtains were simple muslin affairs, plain or dotted with embroidery, and edged with white or colored ball fringe. They were always white, as anything else in curtains (or in feminine underwear) would have been unthinkable. But though these articles were one as to color, they were unlike in the quality of material, for Victorian underwear was as opaque as possible and the curtains as sheer. One's refinement was judged by the condition in which one's curtains were kept, as the popular literary cliché "immaculate muslin curtains" testifies. Poverty was no excuse for one's windows not presenting a shining muslin face to the world. Muslin curtains continued to be used by those who could not afford expensive lace replacements, but many a genteel heart, restricted to the sheerest and whitest of tissues, nevertheless sighed for something more costly, more modish.

In Victorian days, the ornamental heading to window drapery which decorators term a "valance" was known as a "lambrequin." This latter term, now forgotten, was later used to describe every shaped pendant of cloth, whether it hung from a mantel, edged a table, or swung from a shelf. As lambrequins furnished an easy way to gild the Victorian lily, they became the most ubiquitous of decorative touches. In the less educated but no less aspiring circles of the American middle class, the "high-falutin" foreign word quickly became "lamberkin" and was soon sprinkled through the conversation of every woman given to fancywork.

The present-day fondness for Venetian blinds is but a revival of the esteem given an accessory which was already in high fashion in the eighteenth century. In 1767, Venetian blinds were advertised by their Philadelphia importer as "the greatest preserver of furniture of anything of the kind ever invented." Though their vogue was a long one, it commenced to wear off by 1840, when they began to be thought of as "rather ordinary." At that time, green, their usual color, was going out of fashion, and was replaced by pale tints or white, touched up with gold. But this change in color marked the end of the vogue, and it was not long before the blinds, with their prettily pierced and carved valances, went completely out of style. This should occasion no surprise, for it is obvious that their use would have precluded the full display of costly lace curtains.

If it was felt that the exterior of a house was a little severe, or that the interior could stand a bit more furbishing, window shades painted with flowers or landscapes were added. As early as 1827, painted blinds were in high favor. Decorated in full color, such translucent blinds were frequently hung in parlor or on staircase windows of town houses, in which positions they were considered to "awaken a sentiment of nature in the midst of brick walls." By 1850 they had so degenerated in artistic quality that the discriminating considered them tawdry and vulgar. But as the less cultivated continued to like these brightly colored panels, they could be found—executed more and more poorly—up to the very end of the nineteenth century.

Sketch for decoration of "Transparent Window Shade." 1827. Painting was done by professional decorators on sized muslin.

Preferred subjects were the romantic landscape or rural scene. *Courtesy, Chester County Historical Society, West Chester, Pa.*

Next to elaborate window draperies, the possession of fully carpeted floors was an indisputable index of one's financial position. Since rugs have been a commonplace of existence for several generations, today one assumes that every woman who has been running an establishment has acquired some kind of floor covering. Therefore, no woman who now buys a new carpet as easily as she does a wrap can have any conception of the burning desire for a Brussels or Wilton floor covering that used to fill the hearts of her carpetless forebears.

Before the machine began to turn out floor coverings, carpets were a rare article indeed in middle-class homes. Women made their own floor coverings, or at least if they did not weave them themselves, they accumulated and prepared the material out of which were fabricated their strong, but to Victorian eyes, just too-too "folksy" rag carpets. Aware of the toil and economizing which went into the making of rag carpets, it is easier to project oneself into the mind of a woman who craved a "boughten" one to replace all those yards of homemade stuff. That the longing was both widespread and intense is shown by the frequency with which popular writers of fiction used it as a theme. Even though a woman who was unable to afford a carpet might summon up the moral courage to refrain from entering the carpet warehouse, she still had to confront temptation outdoors, for certain shops, in order to catch her eye, used to flaunt lengths of their wares from the upper stories of their buildings as compelling advertisement of their merchandise. As soon as the family budget permitted, the carpet was invariably purchased and it was the best her means could afford. Her husband might tease her about her pride in the new possession, but in the early days a carpet was such an accepted sign of social importance that women who lacked a factory-made specimen suffered from inferiority complexes. One of the early Ohio settlers, a Mrs. S., who was engaged in developing a home in the 1840's, commented that a neighbor, also a pioneer, feared to call on her because she had *heard* that Mrs. S. owned a Brussels carpet! And although Mrs. S. admitted to the ownership of an article which stamped her with such prestige, she felt that it was not a matter which should have prevented a friendly interchange between neighbors for it was never on view. In fact, it had never even been unrolled, for life in a new village was too harsh and she would not subject her precious carpet to such rigors.

In the 1840's the very best carpets used in the United States were known as Saxony, Tournai, and Brussels. Slightly inferior but equally desirable (at least to the hitherto carpetless) were the Imperial, Wilton, Kidderminster or Ingrain, Venetian, and Scotch varieties. The latter were the lowest in price and the poorest in quality.

Previous to this influx of floor coverings, none but the aristocracy owned carpets. These, of room size, were what we today call "Oriental rugs," though when they were in fashion they were known as "Turkey carpets." To the nouveaux riches their quiet conventional designs appeared awkward and unpleasant when contrasted with the new flowered yardages. If any Turkey carpets, however, managed to survive the ravages of time up to Victoria's day, their well-born owners continued to use them even if they were threadbare—as a quiet protest against current parvenu standards in taste. For party purposes, rugs were vastly more convenient. Unlike the tacked-down breadths of Brussels, a Turkey carpet was easily removed. The floor, however, was not left unadorned, for fashion demanded that it be ornamented, even with the most transient of decorations, in order that it be attractive. "Our carpets were taken up on these occasions," says the Philadelphian, Elizabeth Duane Gillespie, in her *A Book of Remembrance,* "and a man came to chalk the floor. I remember one huge, stiff-looking basket which was chalked on the floor of our parlor: the man took half a day to do it, and I felt sorry when the flowers were scraped away in a few minutes by the feet of the dancers." Later in the 1850's, when the fragile embroidered satin slippers of the ladies were the subject of even greater concern than the appearance of the floor, this decorative custom, being certain to soil the slippers, was discontinued.

The most fastidious care was given to carpets. As floors were apt to be rough, machine-made carpets were laid over a foundation of "China matting"—a cheap imported material woven of grass. Matting also served as a summer floor covering after carpets were taken up, but persons in genteel circles who could not afford a real carpet made shift with this grass substitute all year round. It was not very long-wearing, it exhaled a curious odor when damp, but it was not unattractive and was in use all through the nineteenth century. But padding was only one of the problems which the possession of a new carpet entailed. After protecting its underside from the roughness of the floor, the meticulous housekeeper was equally concerned with keeping its surface immaculate. In the dining room for this purpose she used a large piece of wool or linen cloth, which was

Courtesy, Valentine Museum, Richmond, Va.

Drawing Room of 1850's typifies Victorian elegance. Wickham-Valentine House, Richmond, Va.

spread out under table and chairs to catch fragments of food. This cover, called a "drugget" or "crumb cloth," was used in cottage and in castle alike: Queen Victoria, good bourgeoise housekeeper, thus protected her plaid carpets at Balmoral from crumbs dropped by her royal offspring. It was necessary to sweep or shake out the drugget after every meal, a task which was only one of the many which kept housemaids and housekeepers busy in those days when the respect for, and the preservation of, one's worldly goods was a concern of primary importance to everyone.

All newly constructed Victorian houses bore a close resemblance to each other. Every city parlor in conventional circles boasted a tall gold-framed pier-glass between the two front windows (there were usually only two), accompanied by matching elaborate window cornices. Sometimes for nice balance the opposite end of the room was decorated in identical fashion. In front of the pier-glass was a stand which held either a pair of Sèvres vases or a clump of wax flowers under a glass dome. Over the large mantelpiece was placed the cham-

ber's real showpiece—the inevitable mirror or "looking glass," as it was then called. To a present-day observer it would seem that these houses could not have avoided a close resemblance, for they and their appointments were purchased in the market of the time. But by the 1850's their very sameness brought down upon them a flood of criticism, directed, it must be stated, by those who had enjoyed the opportunity to observe the decorative trends of more established cultures. With amazing bluntness N. P. Willis, a widely travelled American, aims his critical gun at the American nouveaux riches. Unquestionably an Anglophile, Mr. Willis makes his comparisons: "The feature most carefully avoided in an English house [incomes of $2,000 to $10,000] is any general look of newness—the raw aspect of new furniture being repulsively associated in their minds, with people of low origin, to whom no belongings of a home have descended and who have suddenly become rich." Mr. Willis also suggests that an Englishman of taste, if compelled to furnish a house in the States, would select his furniture from a second-hand dealer who

Courtesy, Metropolitan Museum of Art

The Back Parlor was the setting for family life. "The Fiedler Family."

specialized in "all things old, odd, and rococo, [there is evidence that in 1855 the business of dealing in antiques is a new one] rather than buy new pieces from the warehouses of the day."

In making this suggestion the writer is showing up a curious bit of snobbery which was developing in this country. For, parallel with the trend of the nouveaux riches to greater expenditure for more and more grandeur, ran this odd and little-mentioned current in taste, one to which can be credited the very beginnings of the American interest in antique collecting. Since about the only things that newly-come-by money could not purchase were the traditions and appurtenances of long-standing family background, those of gentle birth began to lay stress on their inherited possessions. By 1856, a note in Watson's *Annals of Philadelphia* indicates that the taste for antiques was already spreading beyond the classes which started the vogue. Furthermore, the Philadelphia antiquarian states that his home city was not the source of the fashion. "A modern freak of fashion—begun at Boston and brought here, has been the revival of old furniture, found in garrets and lofts:—

by the art of *varnishing,* they have been brought out with display—the gathering of such, came in time, to such a demand, as to call for much new-making of chairs, &c., exactly in imitation."

The diaries of little girls innocently reveal the emphasis which was even then being given to background and family possessions. A New York City child carefully lists the household antiques: their age [a mere 25 to 40 years], their cost, and even the names of the cabinet makers who had made them. And in the diary of a New York State village girl* of the same period we read: "I think if Grandmother is proud of anything besides being a Bostonian, it is that everything in the house is forty years old. The shovel and tongs and andirons and fender and the haircloth sofa and the haircloth rocking chair and the flag bottomed chairs painted dark green . . ."

t this pride of well-established Easterners in their antique furnishings was of slight interest to those who were busy exchanging the simple forms and dull hues of their pioneering days for all the new elaborations pouring from the factories. Those whose wealth steadily

* Caroline Cowles Richards—*Village Life in America. (1852-1872).*

137

Courtesy, Valentine Museum, Richmond, Va.

White marble Mantelpieces, of wedding-cake elaborateness, were surmounted by gold framed Mirrors topped with waterfalls of carved gilt scrollery spangled with flowers and birds.

Black marble Mantelpieces, supplanting those of white, were gloomy affairs, suggestive of mausoleums. No amount of gilt, in fender or ornaments, lightened their hopeless sombreness.

increased refurnished frequently—an American custom which, from the European point of view, showed a shockingly flippant attitude toward one's possessions. Nevertheless the American woman blithely proceeded to keep up with fashion, happily discarding her white marble mantel in the 1870's for one constructed of funereal slabs of chocolate or mottled black marbles, even though the change-over was no improvement. And, with the same lightness she would remove her once-cherished wax flowers from the mantel to supplant them with the approved garniture of the day—the black or bronze clock with its pair of matching urns or storytelling statuettes. These sombre mid-Victorian mantels were set off by wallpapers whose heavy luscious tones conveyed the suggestion of plum-pudding fruitiness then thought highly desirable. When walls were not covered with gilt rococo scrollings or with highly naturalistic representations of flowers and fruit, the housekeeper was apt to choose a conventional design in self-color, the texture of which bore a close resemblance

to the skin of a peach. These designs were silhouetted against plain or satin backgrounds and were known as "flock" papers. In high style by the 1850's, their vogue was an extended one. To those craving an elegant effect, these textured papers offered an adequate visual substitute for damask or cut velvets, for at a little distance they bore a close resemblance to these fabrics.

Flock paper was made by dusting an adhesive surface with finely powdered fibers of silk, cotton, or wool. As the ornament, because of the way it was produced, was of necessity unshaded, the flock papers—although they were unpleasant to touch—were aesthetically unobjectionable. For conservative tastes, reluctant to accept surroundings colored in other than the long-familiar light hues of their painted walls, wallpapers were brought out in tones which approximated the earlier fashion. In the 1840's and 1850's self-toned rococo, floral, or landscape designs in neutral colors—grays and stone and pearl—were in the best of style. To give a finish to these quiet hues one could purchase hand-

138

Courtesy, Fort Hunter Museum, Harrisburg, Pa.

Country-house Living Room with original furnishings. The casually-draped Lambrequins are natural linen trimmed with red and blue wool bands. Note the low "Easy Chair," trimmed with wide band of woolwork, a textile used also on Ottomans, Pillow and Gothic piece. Wallpaper is dark blue and white, Mantel is dark gray marble. Portrait is that of a boy.

blocked borderings, the predominant coloring of which was selected to harmonize with the draperies. Favorite border motifs were festoons of drapery, richly fringed and caught at intervals with clusters of flowers. Although one of the points stressed by salesmen was the number of colors used on a hand-blocked wallpaper, the arbiters of good taste advised one to shun papers which had too great a variety of hues or too large and showy motifs, as well as those which playfully simulated architectural constructions. Such pseudo-mural decorations were "but gaudy shams and false magnificences," now completely out of place in the genteel home (though they might still be tolerated in such public places as cafés, taverns, or theatres). As a result of these latter dicta, these last remnants of eighteenth-century taste, together with such once-favored tints as "new milk" and all the delicate blossom tones, must make way for the upstarts—the maroons and rich crimsons, sage-greens and gold-shot browns—the only colors strong enough to furnish the background for the heavily carved

walnut on which fashion now beamed.

A great deal of this Victorian furniture, as has been noted, was exceedingly uncomfortable. If one leaned back, its scrollings and carvings turned a chair into a minor instrument of torture. Because of this distressing characteristic of the wood-framed Victorian piece (especially if it had been constructed for sheer display), other types were devised for use. In their way, however, these were quite as showy as were the carved formal examples. On the pieces planned for comfort, no trace of wood was visible; upholstery, and that of the richest, covered every bit of the frame. These overstuffed pieces were salient examples of one of the important facets of Victorian taste: that which gave unstinting admiration to the smooth, unbroken, generous curve. "Cushioned chairs," as they were called, were not only comfortable but were also not as expensive as those on which much carving and high polish were lavished. In the construction of an overstuffed piece, only a rough wooden frame was necessary. Even carved feet could be dispensed

139

The "Ottoman" or *Causeuse* was the hub of the luxurious drawing room. The padded central feature which formed the backrest supported a vase of flowers, palm, or marble statuette.

with, since they would be hidden behind elaborate fringes, thickened and enriched to please the taste of the day. Often the trimmings which finished the bottoms of these plump armchairs and sofas were far more costly than the elegant stuffs they embellished.

Silk plush—that luxurious exaggeration of velvet— was one of the favorite mid-Victorian textiles for furniture covering. So great was the appeal of plush that it was used, in utter disregard of serviceability, even as shelf-linings. And by 1868, mirrors covered with scarlet plush bordered with gilt and ebony were the last word in oppressive magnificence.

After being frowned on for quite some decades, the clumsy overstuffed Victorian piece is with us again, fringe and all. But certain favorites in padded furniture, once considered extremely smart, have gone completely out of fashion. Such a piece is the Victorian "ottoman" or "divan" (the terms seem interchangeable in early days). While the name "ottoman" still persists in the

nomenclature of furniture, it is used at present to describe an oversized footstool. In the 1830's an "ottoman" (the Turkish origin of which is obvious) was a low cushioned seat for three or four persons, placed in a recess. Romanticism inspired by Byron's works was probably responsible for the introduction of this oriental piece of furnishing into the Victorian interior. Byron's lady admirers, neatly braided and coiffured and stiffly erect in their chairs, read Don Juan (surreptitiously, we may be sure) and dreamily speculated about his heroine, who could lounge voluptuously and whose hair

> "Fell in long tresses like the weeping willow
> Sweeping the marble underneath her chair,
> Or rather sofa (for it was all pillow,
> A low soft ottoman . . .)"

All during the romantic literary movement—roughly speaking, from 1820 to 1850—the ottoman stayed in high fashion, but examples could still be found even in the 1870's and 1880's. This later Victorian ottoman was a square, hexagonal, or circular seat, luxuriously padded and upholstered, placed in the centre of the room. Though impressive ottomans of this type have long since disappeared from the domestic interior, specimens can still be encountered, unaltered in character, in an occasional art gallery. And ottomans on the classic model, but constructed starkly of bentwood, were once popular seats in railway stations.

The term "tabouret" used to be applied to a high square stool on which a grown person could sit. Through Victoria's reign, the importance of the piece diminished and "tabouret" came finally to mean a small low table or stand to hold plants or knickknacks. The earliest tabourets and ottoman-footstools were choice spots on which to display one's masterpieces of Berlin-work. These were ruthlessly stretched over a compact filling so that each stitch in each brilliant flower would be displayed in its perfection.

Haircloth-covered furniture is an article whose slipperiness and unpleasant texture will never be forgotten by anyone who ever sat on the disagreeable stuff. For some decades its hard, smoothly rounded surfaces were admired, but by the 1870's it was beginning to be thought old-fashioned. Because haircloth was indestructible, it was the favorite selection of those with limited means—persons who, when they chose furniture, intended it to last a lifetime. In order to mitigate its sombreness, haircloth was sometimes woven in self-toned allover patterns or in shadowy floral wreaths which glimmered on the black walnut chairs and sofas with which it is forever linked. Though such pieces were brightened with trimmings of brass nails, and were referred to during all the time they were fashionable by the flattering term of "black satin hair," they were never anything but lugubrious in appearance. In fact, to many still living, the sight of haircloth-covered suites can never be wholly divorced from funerals. Shut away in the rarely-used "best room," the sleek black furniture was visible only on the solemn occasions when that ceremonial chamber was opened for death's melancholy rites, or for that equally solemn nineteenth-century event—the visit of a relative from distant parts.

As Victorian exuberance doted on curves, it is to be expected that this luxuriating in rounded forms would not be restricted to furniture, but would be manifested elsewhere, wherever possible. Cushions—today quite unimportant decorative features—reached their ornamental apotheosis in mid-Victorian days and were conceived in shapes and types which are no longer regarded either as desirable or as possessing any elements of beauty. Fancy ran riot on these accessories to comfort.

The prevailing craze for obese upholstery affected even the pincushion. As we have seen, the pincushions of Victoria's girlhood were trifling things. From those playful objects they developed through the years into heavy, thickly stuffed cushions covered solidly with bead-work of crystal and metal, edged with cascades and fringes of additional bead-work. During the long period when women aspired to appear as smoothly and as firmly packed inside their garments and as free from wrinkles as were their well stuffed pincushions, many pins were necessary to attain a flawless contour. Therefore pincushions were important trappings in Victorian life. Their portly forms commanded the central position on all bureaus and dressing tables between the cut glass bottles, and bristled in porcupine fashion with jewelled stickpins and hatpins. Furthermore, Victorian women, in order to have a pin always handy, never moved without small pincushions hidden in pockets concealed in the folds of their full skirts.

Ornamental "bachelor's pincushions" found their way into men's pockets and supplied the pin needed daily to fasten a fresh flower in one's buttonhole, for the boutonnière was then an indispensable part of masculine attire.

In the 1890's the first few touches of negligence and comfort were introduced into feminine dress, and they came as startling novelties to women long inured to the discomfort entailed by their restrictive garb. But their advent was welcomed by the younger generation, who were beginning to strip away many other formalities of Victorian behavior. And eventually this new freedom in dress spelled the doom of that most familiar of Victorian accessories, the pompous Victorian pincushion.

THE STUFFED PIECE

Ottoman for a Recess. 1827. Forerunner of the davenport.

All through the Queen's lifetime, elaborately worked textiles formed the keystone of decoration. Upholstery became an art, its medium the tightest of stuffing, cording, buttoning, tufting, and draping.

The Stuffed Piece, which was developed along reasonable lines during the Second Empire (see *above*), began, by the 1890's, to hint of the elephantine, both in contour and howdah-like trappings. (See *right*.)

Right. Of English manufacture, this "sumptuous lounge chair" was covered with sea-green satin, dressed up with pink festoons.

Above, centre. The "conversation chair," a French introduction, accommodated its occupants *vis-a-vis*.

Below. Miniature Furniture, 1850–1860. Made by upholsterer at Buckingham Palace.

Courtesy, Victoria and Albert Museum

The "Spanish"
Easy Chair

Reaction against stuffiness set in.
By 1876, those who valued simplicity did over their drawing
rooms in chintz and light paint.
Ottoman is the feature.

The "Jersey"
Easy Chair

The "Persian Divan"

Above. Three Easy Chairs of the 1870's and 1880's.

Fashions for femininity and for furniture took on the
same stance, same tight contours, same flounced edges.

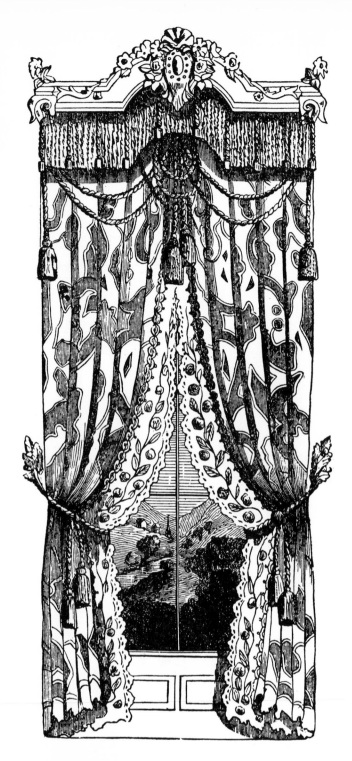

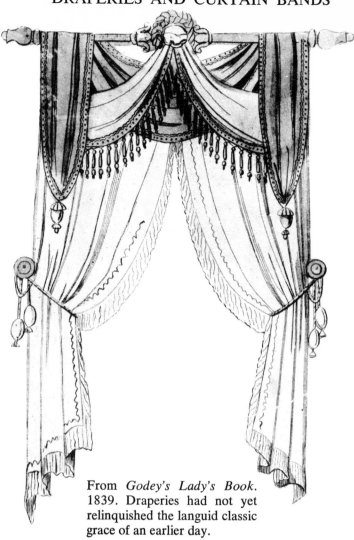

From *Godey's Lady's Book.*
1839. Draperies had not yet
relinquished the languid classic
grace of an earlier day.

Lavish outlay on window draperies was a particular stamp
of worldly success. *Left.* Contemporary Sketch for Cur-
taining. 1853. A combination which provided "richness
with neatness." The cornice was known as a "semi-oval
type." Deep bullion fringe takes the place of a lambrequin.

Below. Curtain Bands or Tie-backs were used to loop up
curtains gracefully during the day; in the evening curtains
were drawn together for warmth and privacy. The world
of fashion used Curtain Bands of stamped gilt. The
showiest were studded with Bohemian Glass flowers.

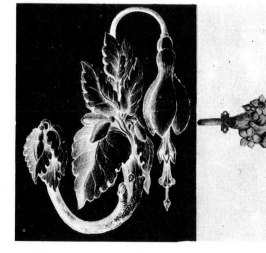

144

Courtesy, Museum of the City of New York

The top of the lofty Pier-glass was joined to the heavy carved gilt Cornice Boards to form a splendid heading from which the handsome but weighty Draperies could be suspended. This unit, of more or less elegance, was standard equipment in the Victorian parlor.

Tassels. German. *C.* 1870. Magnificence in draperies demanded impressiveness in the cords and tassels which accompanied them.

LAMBREQUIN AND ANTIMACASSAR

To knot fine ecru twine into the pillow lace known as macramé was an occupation to which the artistic devoted themselves in the 1870's. The work was hard on delicate hands, but women persevered until they had made a fringed lambrequin for mantelshelf or edging for corner bracket.

Left. Macramé Lambrequin and Crocheted Antimacassar.

Courtesy, Valentine Museum, Richmond, Va.

Above. Lambrequins of "Application" Embroidery and beaded Berlinwork. The lambrequin's sole purpose seems to have been to spare the public the sight of a structural edge. To take away "that naked look," lambrequins were swung from everything that could support them. They were made of plush, velvet, damask, felt, beads, woolwork, leather and many other materials. From 1870 to 1890, they were a decorative "must," one which every woman achieved, using anything for the purpose, even pressed autumn leaves pasted on thin muslin.

The Antimacassar, a small auxiliary covering for chair or sofa, was evolved to protect upholstery from soil. The earliest examples were of starched white crochet. Time passed, color replaced white, the antimacassar became the "tidy." There were tidies of cretonne, lace, velvet, wool, and even crazy-quilt work.

Left. Tidy-making became a mania, one which caught the attention of *Punch.*

146

CUSHION AND PINCUSHION

Right. Pincushions were magnificent affairs. Velvet embroidered with chenille and pearls.
Courtesy, Museum of the City of New York

Visitors to Niagara Falls brought home souvenirs — star-shaped Pincushions of beaded magenta velvet.
Courtesy, Miss Florence Cannon,
Philadelphia

Cushions, strewn about, were thought to make a room look less stiff. Sofas had their quota of elaborate plump fantasies in needlework, and tall-backed chairs were fitted out with Chair Bolsters —tightly stuffed sausages swung from cords.

Right. Lambrequin. *Harper's Bazar,* 1873. German ideas for needlework set forth in American periodicals affected taste for the worse.

From the collection of the Cooper Union Museum

Fireboards, which filled in grate openings in summer, were covered with hand-blocked wallpaper panels, in later days with Currier and Ives lithographs.

From the author's collection

Window Shade in full color. European. *C.* 1840. Tracery and vase printed from woodblocks. Flowers hand-painted. Impudent union of the Gothic and the sentimental.

Right. Flock Paper from boudoir. *C.* 1840. *Courtesy, Victoria and Albert Museum*

Courtesy, Index of American Design

Festoons of drapery, richly fringed and caught at intervals with flowers, long held a position of honor as borderings. French. Hand-blocked. First half of nineteenth century.

Right. 1851. Cylinder printing united low cost with elaboration.

148

CARPETS

Victorian taste preferred naturalism to conventional design,
multi-color to monotone. *Right*. Ferns in greens on black
were unusually simple. *Below*. Palms, cacti, plus Louis XV
scrolls, were a novelty.

Before the days of kerosene, oil-burning lamps were of various types. Their bases were of bronze, marble and ormolu, their shades of ground glass decorated with cutting. *Left.* Sinumbra Lamp, *C.* 1849. *Centre.* Argand Lamp. English. *Right.* Mantel Lamp. *Courtesy, Index of American Design, National Gallery of Art*

Carved gilt Mirror Frame (background), made in Philadelphia, won first prize in its class at New York's Crystal Palace. *Courtesy, Historical Society of Pennsylvania*

ALBUM 9

Of Bouquet-making as an Art &
Of Horticulture as a Virtue
Of Calceolarias and Coxcombs
Geraniums and Dahlias
Of the Pouting Moss-rose Bud
The Pensive Ear-drop &
The Adored Camellia
Of Sentiments and Sentiment
Of the Shaping of Blossoms
In Wax or with Paint-brush
On Velvet or Paper
Of Foliage Pressed in Books
Or Disciplined in Carpet-bedding
Of Wardian Cases
Ivied Parlor Walls &
Of Gardening Victorian Virgins

THE WORLD

OF

FLORAL BEAUTY

TO make a Victorian bouquet, first promenade through your garden with basket and shears, and collect your best blossoms lavishly. You will defeat your purpose if you let even a trace of niggardliness enter your mind, for it will prevent you from attaining your end—the solidly packed effect which swallows up an amazing number of blossoms.

Consider your color schemes as you cut. After having gathered your choicest specimens, select the largest dark red rose or pale immaculate lily for the central feature. With coarse thread, fasten this to a small stick. Then, holding this support in the left hand, lash to it a series of flower circles, each blossomy round a contrast in color to the preceding one. Occasionally, as you carry on your pretty task—tying tightly as you go—you may wish to insert a few sprigs of fine grasses to lighten the floral mass.

When you have attained the size desired, set off the bouquet with a ruffle of small or feathery scented leaves: smilax, rose-geranium, southernwood or myrtle are the choice of the really fastidious. If you desire a rustic effect, you will prefer, rather, to edge it with the leaves used by country folk, who always grow a plant of striped ribbon grass, "dusty miller," and variegated foliage for this precise purpose. If you wish to add a final elegant touch to the creation, paste a handsome butterfly or two on one of the largest leaves in the green frill—and your bouquet is all that a Victorian bouquet should be.

Before the nineteenth century, the average man displayed little interest in floriculture. In fact, so busily engrossed was he in maintaining himself and his family that there was practically no time left for any such non-productive pursuit. Any aesthetic interest in flowers was then limited to those who were not themselves obliged to labor over the actual cultivation thereof. Freed from worry over the finicky inhabitants of his garden or greenhouse, the eighteenth-century fancier of rare blooms could shower unstinted praise on his gardener's prize specimens—the black auriculas and tulips, the drab ranunculuses and puce-colored hollyhocks for which the Georgians had so curious a fondness.

None but the gentry, however, succumbed to the appeal of these dingy blossoms. When the average British cottager found time to stick a few plants in his tiny garden plot, he remained content with the annual rainbow display provided by softly colored polyanthus and crocus, lilac and laburnum, the deep pink of honesty, the cerulean of forget-me-not, the gold of wallflower, and the reseda of mignonette. Since Great Britain's climate is conducive to luxuriant growth and perfect blossom, it is not surprising that the English have always loved flowers. Emigration to America did not eradicate that love. But in this country a general indulgence in the taste had to be postponed until the busy settlers themselves should first have taken root in the new soil and until they could find time to devote to such sheerly decorative pursuits. Until that day came these hard-working folk, if they craved any flowers, were obliged to depend on such self-sustaining specimens as lilac, mock-orange, or snowball set by the doorstep.

After it became less difficult to earn one's daily bread, the urge to beautify one's surroundings began to put forth its first modest shoots. About the time Victoria

Victorian Garden Design. 1843.
Flower-filled urns, neat paths, and clipped grass plots kept gardeners busy.

mounted the throne, a new type of publication devoted wholly to gardening appeared in the United States to foster the transplanted English love of horticulture. Since we of today have benefited so greatly by the spade work done by these initial promoters, it is interesting to review the suggestions then brought forth—suggestions which were to develop not only into our present general adoption of gardening as a worthwhile occupation, but which, in a short time, converted even the hesitant of the period to universal acceptance of the idea.

In 1837 one of these periodicals diffidently points out to the city dweller that "a city flower garden would be a comfort of the first order." And the same article puts the question to those arch conservatives, the country folk: Might they, too, not now devote a little space around their houses to the development of a lawn and a few flowers, instead of planting corn and potatoes right up to their doorsteps?

Radical ideas such as these, however, were never presented in the expectation that they would be received on their own merits. Invariably they were bedecked with moral preachments, for in the early days of the young Queen's reign, accent was laid almost entirely upon the uplifting aspects of horticulture. The entire clergy was behind the movement, passionately eager to convince working folk of the benefits to be derived from gardening. That this was disguised propaganda—at least in England—for the status quo may not be evident to present-day readers, but in those days every member of

the humbler classes understood clearly what ideas lurked behind the term, "Moral Rectitude," when used in gardening discourses; at once he recognized this term as the cloak for one of the great reform crusades of the day —Temperance—no matter how skillfully the speaker tried to gloss over his intent. Drinking, then about the only indulgence possible to the average laborer, was all too prevalent. Armed with the knowledge that a man encouraged to garden was a man discouraged from frequenting the tavern by at least the amount of time he spent in innocent horticulture, those most vocal in their advocacy of gardening projects pretended that they had quite another purpose in view than the advancement of sobriety. As they handed out prizes of money and gardening books, as well as copies of "Watts' Hymns" to the children, they hinted (and this appears to be aimed at the mercantile classes as well) that "scientific observation might be a profitable asset to a man, even if it could not be assayed in terms of dollars and cents"; that an education could also be extracted from "the accurate and intelligent observation of the floral parts and their beauty", to which was added the palliative: "Everything to please, and nothing to offend, either the morals or the nicest observer, is the true characteristic of the flower garden."

Reassured by the impeccability of this latter sentiment, the "nicest observer" (feminine) very timidly began to set her thinly slippered toe on this unfamiliar territory. After it became the mark of the cultivated to

154

display an interest in botany and gardening, all the socially ambitious pretended to share in it. But in spite of the dabblings and the potterings, it was evident that for a long while the "genteel" middle-class American woman continued to feel that any real interest in outdoor horticultural processes was certainly countrified and somewhat unrefined.

There was no doubt that the Victorian woman loved to promenade in gardens and greenhouses; that she delighted in flowers for their perfume, color, and ornamental possibilities. But in time, this delicate bow to horticulture showed itself for what it really was: only another phase of that mawkish sentimentalism which threaded the whole fabric of Victorian life. Sensing the enervating qualities inherent in these affectations, the ladies' periodicals continually stressed the benefits to health to be derived from actual participation in gardening. Nor did they fail to call their readers' notice to its possibilities as a picturesque, graceful occupation for even that most fragile of beings, the Victorian *lady*.

As the taste for floriculture began to spread, the ladies' magazines, while relaxing their pressure on the moral aspects, continued to dole out such unscientific conclusions as this anonymous bit (and a great favorite it was with a public which felt far happier if it could summon an ethical justification for any of its activities): "Flowers teach the lessons of patient submission, meek endurance, and innocent cheerfulness under the pressure of adverse circumstances. . . . Many are the moral precepts they inculcate, bidding us admire the wisdom of their omnipotent Creator, in their infinite variety of forms and colors, and perfect adaptation to the situations they occupy." It must be noted, in extenuation of this mawkish approach to flowers, that it was only another aspect of the warm emotional wave which washed over the English-speaking world when it found itself fed up with eighteenth-century cynicism. For this alteration in sentiment the world needed a symbol, and flowers, pink, white, and innocent as the young Victoria, were of that symbol the very essence.

Previous to Victoria's time, commercial flower-growing was not an occupation in which persons engaged on any but the most modest scale. After transportation methods improved, businessmen found the commercial growing of plants to be a fresh source of profit. To keep up the new interest in floriculture, they ushered in one novelty after another. It is to these early growers that we owe two outstanding favorites invariably associated with reflections on the period—the fuchsia and the gera-

nium. As the wheel of Victorian horticultural fortune slowly turned, one flower succeeded another. Camellias, dahlias, geraniums, fuchsias, and cacti each had their turn. People specialized in making collections of the fashionable fancy of the moment, each striving to bring these recherché specimens to perfection in order to outdo fellow collectors. By the time the aspirant to horticultural honors was successful in a certain field, the rules of the game changed, some other plant became the vogue, and a start must be made all over again.

The Victorians were immensely partial to flowers which were capable of extensive development along the lines of plumpness and roundness of form—qualities then admired quite as much in floral contours as in feminine ones. A great favorite, now almost forgotten, was the calceolaria—those funny, overblown blossoms resembling little speckled golden balloons. Another plant which typified perfectly the period's love of bulk, rich surfaces and deeply suffused color was the coxcomb, a flower which conveys the impression that its solid form has been the work of a fashionable upholsterer. Generally ignored up to the present except by country folk, this unbelievably overstuffed, be-ruched and beruffled creation was, in itself, the epitome of Victorian fashion. Its thick velvety texture resembling nothing so much as padded magenta plush, its intricate convolutions, the violent contrast presented by its yellow-green foliage with its regal crown taken all together constitute a perfect example of what was then considered worthy of aesthetic admiration. In truth, the more a flower could be made to conform to the social ideals then paramount—formality, order, and symmetry—the more highly it was appreciated. The dahlia, compact of all these excellences, became in its turn a great pet. Introduced in the early nineteenth century, the dahlia was a closely scalloped, solidly built sphere of geometrically arranged petals which bore little resemblance to the huge, frowsy creation admired by the present-day fancier.

The dahlia reigned in the garden, but, until they were supplanted in the 1870's by the tea rose, camellias or "japonicas" queened it in the salon. In truth, they were the darlings of the entire fashionable world, occupying the same position in feminine affection as does the costly orchid today. For many years they were the preferred ornament for ladies' coiffures ("a waxen white camellia nestled in her braids"), even though in the far-off 1840's the price asked for a single blossom was all of a dollar, then a considerable expenditure for but one flower. The very wealthy chose camellias for table decorations. Often these were centrepieces built up of small bouquets piled in pyramids. After the dinner party, the mounds were taken apart and the small bouquets distributed to the ladies. The publicity given in 1852 to Dumas' play *La Dame aux Camélias,* added a touch of wickedness to the appreciation accorded this popular blossom.

The fuchsia was also possessed of many endearing attributes; the lines of its sentimentally curving branches and bell-like blossoms reproduced in precise miniature the swelling lines of the crinoline and the fashionable languorous droop. And never could it have escaped its popular name, "ear-drop," for the blossom swung from its sprays exactly as did the long and lovely earrings then worn by every woman. Growers specialized in introducing new varieties of its tassel-like form, so modest in its carriage, so bold in its color combinations: scarlet and purple, magenta and shell pink, crimson and white.

In 1865 an American seedsman, Peter Henderson,

son, brought out the zinnia, which he had developed from an insignificant Mexican flower into a tightly ordered, many-layered disc of aniline magentas, brazen scarlets, brick reds, and lemon yellows. The trim lines of the zinnia, in harmony with the era's taste for neatness, were admirably suited to form the concentric

circles of color in formalized bouquets—for flowers, whether for personal adornment or for vases, were never arranged in any other manner.

Bouquet-making was considered one of the decorative arts. It was governed by its own tenets, rules which were far more restrictive than those of today's flower arrangements. Bouquet-makers aimed at but one thing—formality and solidity; beauty of line and color played no part in the assembling. Because of the method of its construction, the Victorian bouquet could evolve in but a few shapes: it invariably turned out to be a sphere, a cone, or a mushroom-shaped knob. Bouquets were an essential part of a well-dressed woman's costume at every social function. At one time they were so large that their weight actually became a burden to those who were fashion's slaves.

Occasionally artistic and independent souls rebelled against these hard, artificial bouquets; rather than be saddled with these "French vulgarities," they preferred to utilize their garden flowers to form what they invariably referred to as "old-fashioned English nosegays." Only sweet-scented blossoms were selected for these groupings: clove pinks and spicy carnations, fragrant white lilies and honeysuckle, reseda or mignonette, the flaunting cabbage rose, and the shy but beloved moss-rose bud. The whole odorous collection was edged —not with that abomination, florist's lace-paper—but with the airy spray of artemisia, a perfumed green lace of Nature's own making.

The geranium, today in many regions a humble flower found only in farmhouse windows or in park borderings, was in highest fashion all through the nineteenth century. So easy of culture was it that it was probably closer to the hearts of more people than any other plant. Pelargoniums (Martha Washington geraniums), with their velvet petals of red and purple, commanded much admiration from a public which went limp before this potent color combination. Geraniums were developed to bring out qualities then greatly valued. Great stress was laid on parti-colored foliage, a feature today almost forgotten. Beds of geranium leaves, in fuzzy whites, greens, and reds, resembled gigantic pieces of the fashionable Berlin wool-work. In the 1870's practically all lawns were hemmed with neat borders of scarlet geranium and starred with geometrical beds of it. Set off with the startling blue of lobelia and the gold of calceolaria or marigold, these groupings of primary color then exemplified the best in horticultural taste, for the Victorians looked to the floral world to add pure strong color to their environment. Power and not poetry was what they sought. Therefore, no matter how cerulean blue the hydrangeas were, a border of scarlet geraniums never detracted one whit from the effect, nor was the "substantial beauty" of a brownstone front lessened by the woeful clash provided by window boxes overflowing with pink and purple petunias touched off with ruby geraniums.

Paralleling the lively interest displayed in the actual world of horticulture ran an equally strong interest in its pictorial representation. Every young lady of any standing whatever was taught how to paint flowers. In those days, when flower painting was a diversion only, it is pleasant to find that the work of one young lady, at least, had a "dollar-and-cents" value. Indeed, her accomplishments along this line helped considerably to forward the business of her father, Grant Thorburn, the first large commercial seedsman in the United States. Not only was she the best "flower drawer" in this country, says the successful Scotsman, but her work surpassed even outstanding foreign examples which were sent him in the line of business. When a customer demurred at paying one dollar for a bulb which resembled an ordinary onion, the proud father says: "We turn to the *natural* drawing of the flower, in her book; he throws down his money with more pleasure than he ever did for a play-ticket."

As an innocuous amusement for young girls, flower-painting won general approval. "By the way," says Miss Mitford, "I do not know any accomplishment that I would more earnestly recommend to my young friends than this of flower-painting. It is a most quiet, unpretending, womanly employment. . . . Then it supplies such pretty keepsakes, the uncostly remembrances which are so pleasant to give and to take. . . ."

Much of the drawing master's time was given over to teaching young ladies the rudiments of the art. Techniques were evolved by which even those who were not able to draw accurately could still achieve a presentable piece of work. The most popular of these methods was based on stencils provided by the instructor. Stencils, then called "theorems" or "formulas," also furnished the means by which many early paintings of flowers and fruit on velvet grounds were accomplished, a method then referred to as "Oriental Tinting." Painting on velvet began as a free-hand art. In the earliest days of the nineteenth century it was applied to chair cushions, ottomans, fire screens, bell pulls, reticules, and purses. The pigments used were homemade decoctions prepared

by the master and doled out to his pupils as needed. By the 1830's the art of velvet painting had become so popular that liquid colors could be bought readymade in the American fancy-goods shops and the drawing master was then able to give up his tedious stewing and straining of pigments. Around 1850 the term "Oriental Painting" or "Pearl Painting" was transferred to a totally different technique—one in which flower studies were painted on glass in transparent oil-stains, the background filled in with opaque light tints or with the solidity of lamp-black. Tin foil was crushed, then smoothed out and placed behind the floral forms previously indicated with line and thin colored stain, so that it glittered attractively when viewed from the picture side. Poorly executed specimens of this technique—and there seem to have been many—are called today "American Primitives," a far more attractive name than "Victorian bungle," which describes them with more accuracy.

Few of the lady flower-painters were really creative artists. After they left the seminaries or were no longer under a drawing master, it was necessary for them to copy from flower prints prepared especially for this purpose. The public's constantly mounting craving for all the earmarks of culture created a great demand for colored floral lithographic studies. To profit by this vogue, publishers of books, and periodicals as well, brought out innumerable prints, which ranged from the accurate botanical study to the frankly decorative. These appeared not only in those journals which catered to the ladies, but even in such stately American literary magazines as "Graham's," which was edited for a brief period by Edgar Allan Poe. In addition to this spate of flower studies, publishers supplied their readers with poetic sentiments inspired by a confused contemplation of the innocent floral world. This type of literary gem was so overwhelmingly maudlin that one specimen, pulled dripping from the vast flood of similar inanities, must suffice: " 'Flowers are the Alphabet of the Angels' as some one has prettily said. Scattered over hill and valley they speak what no tongue can express: their beauty and fragrance suggesting a world even more beautiful than this."

This supposedly vocal quality of the floral world was put to good use by both the young and the bashful. A sign manual of the language of flowers was devised, and bouquets—sometimes rather curious ones—were put together, not for aesthetic satisfaction, but to convey messages for the tongue-tied. This fashion furnished an innocent recreation not only for the sender who con-

Hand-colored Engravings (above) were the feature of floral gift books. From *The Poetry of Flowers and the Flowers of Poetry.*

Mignonette-Heliotrope-Pink declare that: "Your qualities surpass your charms; I love you with a pure and devoted love."

cocted these floral billets-doux, but for the recipient who resorted to her code-book for interpretations if she had not previously memorized the significance of each blossom. To cater to this fad for floral occultism, publishers brought out innumerable floral gift books. They were always illustrated—to a varying degree depending on their cost—and the lithographers were kept busy, from the 1840's on, supplying pictorial matter to accompany these floral dictionaries. From these volumes one was able to extract—among hundreds of meanings assigned to specific blossoms—the reassuring knowledge that a moss-rose signified "Pleasure without Alloy." If a tulip flaunted its bright head in one's bouquet, it meant "A Declaration of Love," and a spray of Peruvian heliotrope shyly proclaimed "Trust in Thee." A young lady whose affections were sentimentally engaged dreaded to find a sprig of ivy, for it suggested that only "Friendship" was involved, while a garden anemone reminded a flirt that the sorrowing sender was "Forsaken." For every waxing or waning emotion one could find an appropriate floral symbol.

No modern maiden can ever experience, on receiving a box of flowers delivered by a shop, the intense thrill which her grandmother felt when a bouquet was brought to her by the maker himself. Then, as a messenger for an emotion otherwise unexpressed, it car-

ried a portentous significance. Sometimes, instead of awkwardly assembling the meaningful blossoms himself, a gentleman would make his choice of symbolic flowers at the florist's. The latter would then arrange them tastefully, edge the stiff bouquet with paper lace, and finish it so that it could be carried in an elegant silver or jewelled holder called a *"porte-bouquet."* But even these semi-commercial clusterings were always carefully studied to discover whether they conveyed a sentimental cryptogram.

Flowers which bore a resemblance to the form of the bouquet-holder were pressed into like service; a calla lily filled with a cascade of fuchsias or a waterfall of lily-of-the-valley served as an enchanting gesture of friendship, for at that time flowers were esteemed (far more than they are today) as offerings of sentiment which everyone, from the highest to the lowest, could both tender and receive. Even Queen Victoria used to present bunches of spring wild flowers gathered by herself and her ladies to those whom she wished to honor, and these were viewed as her most valued gifts.

The art of copying flowers and fruits in wax was an outstanding Victorian accomplishment, though by 1880 it was no longer fashionable. Thanks to their domed glass coverings, enough examples have survived

Jasmine-Strawberry-Tulip proclaim: "Your amiability and the excellence of your character compel me to declare my love."

Pansies-Broom carry the modest hope: "My heart would be at ease, if my solitude were blest with your society."

to indicate how prevalent the art once was. Nothing is more truly evocative of the crinoline period than these glass bubbles massed with wax flowers, some of them really beautiful in workmanship and composition. After a vast public saw magnificent examples at the Great Exhibition (a whole section was devoted to wax flowers), the taste for them became widespread. Those who devoted long hours to the fabrication of the waxen blossoms regarded their work not merely as a craft but as an important art form, one that partook not only of the qualities of sculpture and modelling, but of painting as well. The art required deftness, patience, observation, and artistic ability, for only those wax flowers were considered successful which imitated nature so closely that the beholder was actually deceived into thinking them real. She who could also reproduce Nature's accidentals—the bruise on a pear, the bee in the throat of a blossom, the browning edge of a leaf—was credited with displaying not only playful caprice but a high degree of artistry as well.

As the century rolled on, this art, which so far had been purely decorative, began to take on a realistic purpose—that of provoking appetite. Representations of food, rather than of flowers, moved into the spotlight. By the 1870's ironstone epergnes supporting startlingly realistic displays of edibles simulated in wax had become

the newest thing in decoration for the sideboard. These motley aggregations were an embodiment of the unsated Victorian love for profuseness. And what better place to display it than in the Victorian dining room!

But not everyone who desired a wax flower or fruit grouping could afford to make one, for they all represented a certain outlay of money for materials and instruction. When they were beyond her means, a woman occasionally turned to pressed flowers and leaves as a touching substitute for the much desired object. Children on their Sunday walks were now taught what materials to collect, how to arrange and paste them on pieces of cardboard. These, shaped as wreaths and crescents, they hung as ornaments on plain whitewashed walls. Or they fastened them on cardboard frames which then were used to set off that cherished novelty, the photograph of friend or family—allowing it just enough space to peer out solemnly from behind its fragile decorative edging.

Reasons far more compelling than the decorative one inspired pressing of flowers. As passionate collectors of sentimental souvenirs, most of the public could not discard these tender floral messengers of affection and kept them as mementos, flattened between the pages of books. Open any thick volume of the period, open any untouched casket of love letters, and you will disinter the brownish fragments of what were once gay and living flowers. A volume of the favorite woman poet of the era, Mrs. Felicia Hemans, this very day discloses one of these bits of pressed sentiment: three faded, formless blossoms still linked together with a time-stained scrap of thread. The tender feelings which prompted the preservation of these relics may have evaporated even before the color disappeared from the petals, but the flowers survive, as convincing evidence of the romantic sentimentality which inspired the act.

Since the Victorians admired rich textural effects and deep strong colors, and cultivated seemliness and decorum in all things, what was more natural than to strive for these desirable qualities in their gardening schemes? The result of one particular venture in domesticating Nature was known as "carpet-bedding"—a fashion in horticultural planting whose ordered formalities once constituted the ultimate in gardening elegance. Carpet-bedding endeavored to reproduce geometrical patterns or conventional designs with plant material, not as had been done in earlier days, with neatly clipped borders of box and arbitrarily trimmed shrubs, but by a careful combining of plants both for their variety of color and for uniform habit of low growth. About 1870 the whole world gave itself to this gardening absurdity and through several following decades remained infatuated with its vegetal stylizations. Half a century has passed since "carpet-bedding" went out of style. Today it is rarely seen except in certain extremely old-fashioned parks and in the very restricted domain of railway gardening, for the railroads still find it a quaint and charming method of combining advertising with horticulture. After the tedious setting-out of the plants, carpet-bedding required very little attention other than clipping. Every well-conducted place had its immaculate lawns spotted here and there with flower beds—areas shaped like stars and crescents, butterflies and fleurs-de-lis. Victorian gardeners were also fond of "ribbon borders," plot edgings assembled of narrow stripings of low foliage in silvers and golds, purples, reds, and gray-blues.

So attached were the home-loving Victorians to ornamental gardening that they gardened all year round. Long before the snow covered the tidy "carpet beds," even before the fan-leaved palms were wheeled into their winter quarters—leaving the once-brilliant garden to those permanent tenants, the melancholy iron deer and Newfoundland dog—the processes of floriculture were being carried forward once again in a summer atmosphere, for every fashionable house boasted a conserva-

tory. And if this modish setting for horticulture and for romance was lacking, every social aspirant planned to have one annexed to a convenient corner of her residence. However, if her means were too small even to dream of such a prospect, she resigned herself to the immediate creation of a display of fine plants in her windows, set off in the starched lace frame of the parlor curtains.

Like everything else in the period, the Victorian houseplant was subjected to embellishment. Its plain earthen pot was invariably set in some form of container, or the pot was swathed in a cover, the more fantastic the better. As the lack of space in urban communities began to limit gardening activities, sometimes to mere window sills and plant stands, industrial designers produced a wide range of ornamental flowerpot coverings to comply with these conditions. Hanging baskets of terra cotta or wire filigree and window boxes of tile and wood vastly extended the indoor possibilities of floriculture. The foundrymen, too, spilled over with ideas for elaborate plant stands of iron.

The Wardian case, one of the most delightful innovations, permitted the cultivation of delicate ferns and exotics indoors. This case, a diminutive glass-house, made its first bow to the public at the Great Exhibition in 1851. There it was hailed as "one of the great inventions of modern times, called forth by an increasing love for flowering plants and ferns." Wardian cases were often handsome pieces of cabinet-making. By the 1870's, as mentioned before, snobbishness was so interwoven in the mental texture of the day that a writer on floriculture could quite openly stress the comparative costliness of the Wardian case as the strongest recommendation for its adoption. "Hanging baskets," says he, "were in fashion in 1860, but after a year or two they were as common in the tenement of the mechanic as in the palaces on Fifth Avenue. They gave way to the more expensive rustic stand or Wardian case, which being less readily imitated by people of limited means, is likely to continue longer in fashion." For all that, even the exclusive Wardian case could not escape being eventually democratized; the terrarium of the present day is nothing but a revival of the original idea, conceived on a far smaller scale and with little or no consideration given to its original importance as a piece of furnishing.

Not content with vying with each other for lavish perfection in their window gardens, and in caring virtuously for the exigent "lady ferns" of the drawing room, young ladies patiently worked with English ivy indoors to carry further their ideas of tasteful decoration. The present-day fancier of ivy is happy if a small plant will survive a few months under modern conditions, but the Victorians had great tubs of it which lived on from year to year. These lent themselves agreeably to all sorts of decorative conceits. Ivy was used to outline graceful arches over doorways, to cling as a stylized tracery around window trims, to swing in long garlands from brackets. Its hardy foliage could even be trained to form a green curtain for a window, through which bower one could peer at one's neighbors—a popular diversion in a less sophisticated age.

The Germans, who were very much attached to ivy as a house plant, coaxed it into startling effects. They induced it to mount stairways by twining it through the banisters, and the devoted *haus-frau* sometimes even persuaded it to cover the whole side of her parlor, draping it in heavily sentimental fashion around the ponder-ous gilt frames of the family portraits or wreathing the marble statues with its amiable shoots. In America it was used with somewhat more restraint, the better New England homes permitting it only to make a dainty frieze around the sitting room.

These, then, were some of the period's methods of decorative prettifying with ivy which we still cling to, for we try to achieve a similar effect with wallpapers patterned in imitation of its natural growth. But ivy had even further possibilities; quick-growing and docile, it lent itself to being trained into the symbolic forms so dear to Victorian sensibilities. Nothing was more prized as a decoration in the 1870's than one of these living tokens: an evergreen cross and crown, a deep green anchor, or a verdant heart. On the altar of family life these symbols of deepest spiritual significance were ten-derly erected and were kept in emerald perfection by the Victorian vestal virgins entrusted with their care.

Courtesy, Chester Co. Historical Society,
West Chester, Pa.

"Tucker China." American. 1826–1838.

THE MOSS ROSE is hardly known today; yet when Victoria became Queen, there were twenty-four varieties. The rich mossiness which clothed the buds inspired endless picturings and sentimental murmurings. Industry transferred them to china and textiles, and gave them dominion over the scrapbook picture field.

Fuchsia pendant. Gold with ivory-nut flowers in red and green. *Courtesy, Index of American Design, National Gallery of Art*

THE FUCHSIA was given much admiration. The fondness for it undoubtedly coincided with Victorian fashion's taste for the pinks, crimsons, scarlets, and violets embodied in its graceful bells. Its unique form lent much charm to bouquets. And in young ladies' paintings its distinctive droop, no matter how indifferently executed, made identification certain.

THE CAMELLIA was the outstandingly fashionable flower in mid-Victorian days. Florists specialized in white camellias—the choice for weddings and funerals. No wax flower grouping was complete without some facsimiles of its curiously striped roseate varieties, such variegations exercising a peculiar attraction for the Victorian mind. Camellias portrayed in wax were always successful, their texture being an exact parallel of the natural flower's own waxen unreality.

THE PASSION FLOWER was a great favorite, patterning the glass of window or conservatory with a cloud of sky-blue blossoms. The fanciful had long detected a resemblance in its botanical parts to certain symbols of the Crucifixion—hence its name. Moved by these associations, those given to home arts copied its complicated form in wax, leather, or muslin.

VICTORIAN DECORATION
PENNSYLVANIA GERMAN INTERPRETATION

In 1846, when Eliza Geissinger was eleven, she carried home from the Moravian Seminary in Bethlehem, Pa., this quaint result of her labors in painting class. That she found painting difficult can be deduced from her moss rose, its stem almost lost in her struggle to suggest its mossy covering. *From the author's collection*

Above and upper right. The Victorian rose and pansy have supplanted the tulip in these decorations used on salt box. *C.* 1870–1880. *Courtesy, Mrs. Paul Auman, Millheim, Pa.*

Courtesy, Montgomery Co. Historical Society, Norristown, Pa.

The pheasant is a familiar motif in Pennsylvania folk art but the technique—satin stitch on paper—stems from another tradition, the needlework used on eighteenth-century aristocratic costume.

With tall house plants huddled around the parlor sofa, the romantic
maiden in modest circumstances could create for herself the illusion
of a conservatory. By adding movable screens of rooted ivy she
could construct a bower which would foil the most prying chaperon.

Below, left. Wax Flowers provided a focal point of color. Much
artistry went into their fashioning. Flowers of good size were pulled
apart and used as patterns; smaller ones were stamped out with
dies. Dealers furnished foliage, tools, sheet wax, and vases.

Courtesy, The Metropolitan Museum of Art

*Courtesy, Chester Co. Historical
Society, West Chester, Pa.*

Courtesy, Philadelphia Museum of Art

Right. Wax Fruit. In the 1870's women left off making wax flowers for the
parlor and turned instead to decorations for the dining room. Spread out under
glass shades were startling reproductions of fruit, slices of layer cake, jelly in
glasses, homely vegetables (complete with caterpillar), and rugged oyster shells,
open and closed, flanked by cut halves of hard-boiled eggs.

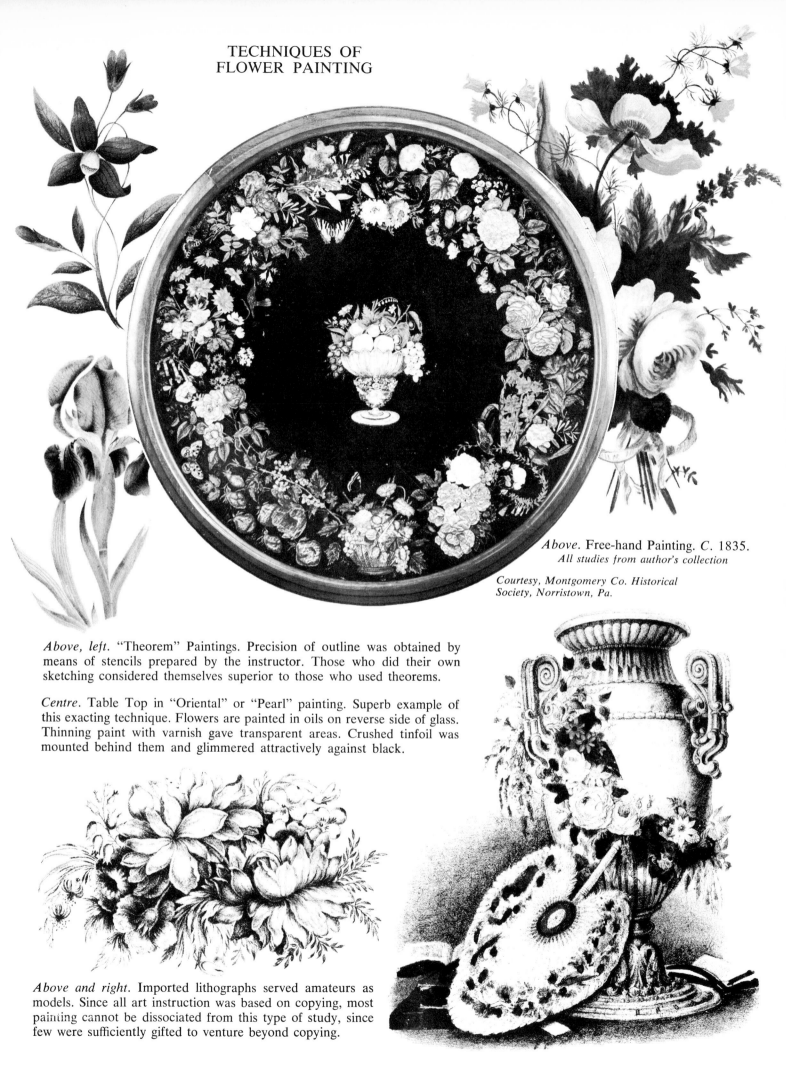

Above. Free-hand Painting. *C.* 1835.
All studies from author's collection

Courtesy, Montgomery Co. Historical Society, Norristown, Pa.

Above, left. "Theorem" Paintings. Precision of outline was obtained by means of stencils prepared by the instructor. Those who did their own sketching considered themselves superior to those who used theorems.

Centre. Table Top in "Oriental" or "Pearl" painting. Superb example of this exacting technique. Flowers are painted in oils on reverse side of glass. Thinning paint with varnish gave transparent areas. Crushed tinfoil was mounted behind them and glimmered attractively against black.

Above and right. Imported lithographs served amateurs as models. Since all art instruction was based on copying, most painting cannot be dissociated from this type of study, since few were sufficiently gifted to venture beyond copying.

165

HANGING BASKETS

GARDEN VASES

FLOWER STANDS

A basket of richly colored plants, hung against the lace-tempered sunlight of the living room, was essential to complete furnishing.

Besides practical examples of terra cotta (*above*), there were fanciful Hanging Baskets of wood, wire, and moss, poetical ones of conch or nautilus, bucolic ones of gourd or coconut shell.

Courtesy, Index of American Design

In gardens planned in the "Grecian" style, stone or composition Vases were used at first "to give a classic and refined aspect to the situation." By 1850 American foundrymen were ready with cast iron examples.

Brimming over with vines and packed with choice flowering and foliage plants, iron Vases punctuated the grass plots of every park, companioned every well-kept place. *Left.* Parian Garden Stand. 1857. *Right.* Plant Stand. 1855.

ALBUM 10

Of Polishing the Rough and Refining the Vulgar
Of Beautifying the Home
With Decorative Felicities
Of Tables Topped with Beadwork &
Portraits Framed in Shells
Of Ornaments, Here, There, and Everywhere
Of Fancywork Manifested
In Seeds, Eggshells, Feathers, Putty
Pine Cones and Leather
Of Potichomanie
Spatter-work &
Of the Crazy-quilt
Of the Omnipresent Dust-collector
The Catch-alls and the Work Stands
Of Bee-like Swarms
Of Ribbon Bows
Ubiquitous

ALBUM TEN

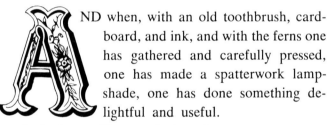

THE WORLD OF
"ELEGANT ORNAMENTS"

"When, out of shreds of old woolens one has fringed and crimped a lamp-mat, from which the globe of flame shall rise as if from a bed of moss, one has done something useful; when one has wrought a vine of the reddened October blackberry wreaths to lay over the tiny corner shelf that was needed to hold vase or bust, but could not be afforded of richer wood than the plain unvarnished pine, one has done something useful; when one has made a rustic frame of twigs and acorns and cones for the print that never could have been hung on the tiresome bare wall if it had waited for the costly frame from the picture dealer, one has done something useful."

HARPER'S BAZAR, MAY 17, 1873

AND when, with an old toothbrush, cardboard, and ink, and with the ferns one has gathered and carefully pressed, one has made a spatterwork lampshade, one has done something delightful and useful.

And when, with a sturdy barrel, a saw, some cornhusks for filling and some material for covering, one has made a luxurious "Sleepy Hollow" chair, one has done something thrifty and useful.

And when, with the flat wire drawn from an old hoopskirt, a cheese-box or two, and with an extravagant outlay of silk, yarns, and infinite patience, one has made a ladies' standing work-basket, one has done something fearful and useful.

And when one has made a small cardboard basket and lined it with merino, and then covered every inch of the exterior with a "tasteful arrangement" of acorns, alder catkins, and the scales of pine cones, to achieve a knitting-basket which will inevitably snag and roughen every ball of yarn placed in it, one has made something provoking and useful.

And when one has emptied the shell of a large egg, covered it with a network of tasseled silk crochet, filled the fragile container with earth (to the immediate detri-

ment of the crochet), and therein planted a tiny sedum, suspending it with silken cords as a hanging-basket which will require the utmost daintiness in handling, one has made a plain Victorian fancywork mess!

Was the outlook from your windows unattractive? If so, it was not necessary to live with it, for it could be obliterated artistically, and for only a few dollars. For this sum you could purchase a translucent colored copy of a famous painting, fasten it to the window glass, and achieve so fine an effect that genuine stained glass was thought coarse and highly colored in comparison with this "elegant" lithographed copy.

And were you concerned about worn surfaces on an old bureau? Nothing was easier than to transform it into a piece which appeared to be of the richest inlay. First, stain it the black of ebony, then glue pressed leaves to it in carefully considered patterns. Cover the whole thing with layers of varnish and you will have changed a shabby something into something "richly elegant."

Never leave a favorite book—your Bible or Mrs. Heman's verses—on the table when you can construct a bracket of wood, wreathe it round with leaves and grapes of muslin dipped in plaster, and with little expense contrive an imitation carved marble support for it.

All these and innumerable objects of the same ilk

were, in the eyes of the women who fabricated them, "ornaments"; they were, moreover, ornaments of unquestioned elegance. Women lived out their lives in a tangled thicket of them. That the material from which such ornaments were contrived might not be worthy of all the labor they expended on it was a matter to which they were quite indifferent. In fact, the more ephemeral and inappropriate the material was, the more it seems to have inspired the devotees of fancywork to incredible flights of imagination. Putty and velveteen, cattails and barrel-hoops, roots, twigs, and alum, cheeseboxes and chopping-bowls, were but a few of the substances which gave impetus to creative abilities. It is the memory of these manifestations which compelled the public to repudiate even the best decorative features of the Queen's long reign. No one who retained any recollection of that mass of beads, crochet and clutter which adhered to all furnishings and to large areas of wall space was capable of evaluating justly anything which the period produced. Critical judgment had to be withheld until this accumulation of misguided handwork disintegrated and disappeared. Today one can find much charm in the best examples of Victorian decoration and even extenuating reasons for the bad—those horrific specimens of "fancywork" referred to derisively by succeeding generations as "dust-collectors." At present the taste for handmade "ornaments" is practically non-existent; or if it survives, it is but a pale shadow of its Victorian self and is easily fobbed off with an article commercially produced. Powerful indeed must have been the urge which impelled the Victorian female to bedeck her milieu with these superfluities. Indeed, she seems driven by a desperate desire to render her home as inviting as possible, as if subconsciously aware of that inevitable day when she could no longer hold her family within its seductively padded walls. So great was the desire for information which would help even the most unpretentious to create something which they believed to be beautiful that innumerable books and articles were published to assist these earnest gropings after the higher "elegancies." The author of a modest volume which appeared in 1859 accents the importance of providing an education in the ornamental arts for the feminine householder "so that she may possess the art of embellishing and beautifying her humble home, making it more attractive and pleasing to her husband, while she refines and purifies the hearts and desires of her household, by surrounding them with things of beauty. . . . Visit a home . . . in which no flowers bloom, no

painting or pictures hang upon the walls, or ornaments, however insignificant, adorn the tables or mantels, and you will find the inmates low and grovelling in their desires. . . . It is the wife that is the presiding genius of home. . . . Let her learn to create those adornments that make her home pleasant and attractive. If she belongs to the humbler walks of life, so much the more need of her understanding how to make the most of a little."

Unlike the British leisured classes, who had inherited a definite pattern of occupations and obligations with which they filled their days, Americans found themselves without an established pattern. Though they adopted many of the accepted social methods for killing time, the American conscience did not rest easily in these practices. As a result there sprang up a curious clash in the American temperament when the citizens of the United States found out that their recently acquired pagan leisure did not lie down peaceably with the puritanic moralizing about industry to which they were accustomed. Had not that mentor of the middle classes, *Godey's Lady's Book,* pronounced authoritatively: "There can be no excellence without industry. The mind of the idle, like the garden of the slothful, will be overgrown with briars and weeds—and indolence, under whatever fashionable name, is a more dangerous enemy to practical goodness and to moral and intellectual improvement than even dissipation."

Lectured in this fashion, and by their favorite periodical, even the most dreamy of the feminine targets of homilies saw to it that their hands were kept busy with fancywork. Although it could not then have been realized, most of the time-killing works to which the era was so zealously given resulted from this conflict—from the social and emotional predicaments in which the Victorian woman floundered. For those who craved a really sound education, there were at first few opportunities. Men did not intend to make it easy for women to compete with them in the cultural, artistic, or economic fields. Woman was constantly urged to be content and happy in the lovely home she had created with funds which her successful husband had supplied. Gail Hamilton, a popular writer of the sixties, suggests to unmarried girls, restless in their fathers' houses, that, rather than seek employment outside in some "rough commercial establishment," they find happiness at home in kindness to "papa." As a career, they might try to "brighten his home . . . medicine his weariness, freshen his ideas . . . pour youth into his age, and keep him mellow, and receptive, and alert. . . . " If a woman grudgingly conceded

any validity to the above ideas, there was little left for her to do while husband or father was at business except to beguile her many tedious hours with fancywork or "novel reading." Indeed, for some decades past, so prevalent a "vice" had "novel reading" become that its practitioners received all the upbraiding and admonitions which cigarette-smoking and drinking evoke in today's moralizing critics. In 1843, when a new ladies' paper, *Miss Leslie's Magazine,* was brought out, its editor felt so strongly on the subject that she published (at considerable expense, she stresses) a mezzotint entitled "Romance and Reality," in order to bring home visually to her readers the evil effects of this lamentable indulgence. The print features a slovenly female, slippered feet on chair, absorbed in a book. So thoroughly has she succumbed to its intoxications that she is beyond paying any attention to her surroundings. The pictures are askew, the slats of the Venetian blinds awry, the bed unmade, and the floor littered with novels already devoured or waiting to be read. Her husband sulks in his chair, her poor, neglected child drinks from the spout of the teapot, the cat retreats beneath the bureau, and the dog, unreproved, gnaws at bones under the table. In

that day when no one was surfeited with pictures, every woman caught the lesson the engraving conveyed.

Under the circumstances, the Victorian preoccupation with useless and often unbeautiful handwork should not be viewed with too great superciliousness by present-day critics. As the occupational therapy of its day, it contributed greatly to the preservation of the emotional balance of innumerable women who, lacking such manual and aesthetic outlets, might have fretted themselves into nervous wrecks through intolerable boredom. On the other hand, it was actually less harmful in its over-all results than the incessant dreamy absorption in trashy novels. No one could set out to make any of these "pretty fancies" (as they liked to think of them) without bringing to its construction the qualities of neatness, deftness, a lovely patience, and a craftsman's intelligence—all praiseworthy attributes.

At the same time, there always were—and still are, for that matter—energetic women who loathed inactivity and who found genuine relaxation in the contriving of some tedious though ultimately quite useless piece of "fancywork." And this habit was frequently part of the makeup of even such hard-working persons as farm servants, who would keep their hands busy while their bodies rested. A New England writer, recalling a New England farm in the 1850's, gives a charming picture of such a maid:

> "Hannah had queer ways. She was given to interior adornments, and the fruits of her needlework were thick in the house. These were not fine, but considering the material from which she wrought them, they were worthy of praise. She pinned black broadcloth cats to the wall, brought out in silhouette upon red flannel . . . She hung novel comb-cases under all the bedroom looking glasses. These were of varied shapes and materials, some of broadcloth, some of straw, and less pretentious ones of covered cardboard, all much stitched with colored silks. The patchwork around the house was endless. Hannah hoarded scraps of silk and cambric, and pieced them into pin-balls, chair-cushions, and coverlets. She glued painted pictures to the inside of wide-mouthed glass jars, which she filled with flour and planted with asparagus, thus simulating quaint vases. She embossed blown egg-shells with the pith of bulrushes, coiled around bits of bright silk, and hung them upon pine boughs in the fireplaces of the front rooms. Homely handiwork, but well-seasoned with the true flavor of rustic life."

Although some of Hannah's occupations undoubtedly displayed a bucolic note, in others, such as gluing pictures to the inner side of glass jars, she was definitely following a type of fancywork once the rage in the boudoirs of French aristocrats. This "art" was known as *potichomanie*. To find this elegant craft practiced by a servant on an American farm is indicative of the levelling process which, in the nineteenth century, overtook all the fancywork arts. None was wholly outmoded before it had been experimented with on each descending rung of the social ladder.

Like most of the other early ornamental "arts," the popularity of *potichomanie* endured for many decades. The "art" offered means of transforming a vase of plain glass into a decorated article which its maker fondly regarded as quite the equal of the Sèvres, Dresden, or Chinese porcelain she set out to imitate. Necessary to the "art" were sheets of paper printed in colors with motifs appropriate to the different styles. These, naturally, could be purchased. A fine scissors, some glue, some oil colors to fill in the interstices between the glued-on pictures (Hannah's use of flour for this purpose *is* a rural touch)—and the vase, unlike many other types of fancywork, could be completed in a comparatively short time. In the 1880's women and even children took to pasting colored figures to the *outside* of common pottery jars, which they called "Dolly Varden" jars. Though they gave the paper surfacing a coat of varnish, it was the destined prey of dust and grime, and the end of the venerable craft could be foreseen in this impractical application of its principles. Before it left the scene entirely, however, it appeared once again at the very end of the century. This time, instead of gaily colored pictures, the gold and colored embossed paper bands with which cigars are encircled were glued to the undersurface of glass trays. The fad for these glittering articles—one which united all the social pleasures of collecting with no greater need for skill than is required by kindergarten craft—was a short but enthusiastic one.

Although the well-to-do purchased their fancywork materials in shops, women in humble circumstances, on decoration bent, were not to be outdone. They, too, would have their own "ornaments" and "elegancies" even though forced to fabricate them of any natural material they had at hand. Hannah's use of bulrush pith and eggshells exemplifies this type of primitive ingenuity. Fancywork addicts found other decorative uses for the pliable, tender pith. One example is a religious conceit, the symbol of the Crucifixion. Pieces of pith were cut to proper size and fastened together quickly with common pins to form the Cross; others formed a perfect little ladder and appropriate symbols. The whole was set against a black velvet ground and surrounded with the deeply boxed frame needed for the display of three-dimensional decorations, since much Victorian handwork for wall decoration was quite as frequently conceived of as a picture in high relief as in the conventional plane surface.

Another of Nature's products was turned to ornamental account in 1861, after the rediscovery of an ancient art, the process of "skeletonizing leaves." These fragile skeletons of verdure were used to form "phantom bouquets." Weird yet charming in their etherealness, they glimmered airily against black velvet from the depths of their recessed frames, or, set in pretty assemblages under glass cases, were featured as decoration on whatnot or pier-table. About 1870 women found additional use for foliage in "spatter-work," the newest fancywork novelty. Spatter-work pictures were common "wall ornaments," but the technique, an extremely popular one, was also applied to screens, curtains, lambrequins, and tidies, as well as to napkin rings, watch-cases, and lampshades. Pressed ferns, leaves, and sometimes even conventional symbols such as crosses and anchors were fastened down with pins in graceful compositions on light-colored material—paper, wood, or fabric. These were then covered with a fine spray of India ink, passed from a toothbrush through a wire sieve. On removing the leaves, etc., a well-defined silhouette on a shaded ground was disclosed, one of such delicacy that it savored of the miraculous to the entranced practitioners.

These are but a few examples of the many ingenious methods the Victorian woman devised to adapt natural materials to decorative ends. Since many Americans were still close to the soil, they discovered ornamental possibilities in what would appear to be the most unpromising material. As earlier stated, all sorts of irrelevancies furnished grist to their fancywork mills, and an amazing amount of ingenuity was called forth to transform mosses and dried leaves, pine cones and beans, rice, twigs and sealing wax, shells and seaweed—to say nothing of textile left-overs—into what were considered attractive home furnishings. From time to time the "aesthetes" raised a sour protest that such "ornaments" were vulgar, tasteless, and clumsy, but for the most part these criticisms were ignored by the women at whose efforts they were directed. And in justice to all the dead-and-gone women who confected these mysterious kickshaws, there *is* something to be added as defense of their particular use of materials and techniques. For, singular as their productions were, many were nevertheless the final —if degenerate—flowering of a very old form of art expression, the art of mosaic making. And mosaic making is nothing but a method of working out a design by means of vari-colored fragments. The assembling of fragments of colored marble into a pattern resulted in the classic mosaic; if of colored and gilt glass bits, it was the Byzantine one; if of shreds and patches of mosses and bark into a landscape, it was a Victorian decorative whimsy. But the impulse to construct mosaics, no matter how varying the results, is in each case the same: a love of assembling valueless fragments into an orderly system or pattern. To induce these refractory materials to conform successfully to the vision in the worker's mind brought enormous satisfaction to the maker, and the completed piece invariably fascinated the beholder who never failed to be impressed by the ingenuity and patient effort which had gone into the task.

In the eighteenth century, when only persons with a certain amount of cultivation devoted themselves to the ornamental arts, there raged a fever for manipulating small and lovely shells into stylized bouquets of many-petalled flowers, a shell forming each petal. Shell-work bouquets were charming—the dainty blossoms bearing a close resemblance to the glossy porcelain variety featured on the famous Meissen china ornaments. At that time even landscapes and figures were worked out with shells in mosaic fashion. Later on, the art became less exclusively aristocratic, and small boxes, vases, and frames were encrusted with shells, decoratively arranged to form flowers and borders, on a wax or putty base. The making of these boxes, which began as an amateur pastime, turned into a commercial project. Shell boxes were the almost invariable souvenir of a seashore visit; placed on bureau or whatnot, they served as permanent memento of the trip.

A favorite diversion at the seashore was to search for shells to use in fancywork schemes. These shells served as the bread-and-butter foundation; unusual kinds, if desired, could be purchased from dealers who specialized in foreign varieties brought in by sailors. Particularly sought after were the "rice shells"—tiny specimens gathered in the West Indies. These were the basis of a very delicate art, one which transformed them into jewelry, floral ornaments for the coiffure, as well as articles for the drawing room such as card-baskets. In the 1850's, fashionable mantel garnitures were made of shell flowers. They were assembled in tall bouquets and set in ornamental vases, the latter completely covered with shell decorations arranged in self-toned patternings. Glass domes preserved them in all their pristine beauty.

Other quaint arts employed the quills of porcupines, straw, or the feathers of birds. All these mosaic aggregations were regarded by the public as "works of art"—a term then catholic enough to embrace the "curious" and the "interesting" as well as the "beautiful." In all genteel circles their practice was generally encouraged, for it was felt that they kept many a girl who had nothing to do "out of mischief."

As long as all such decorations were protected from the corrosive effects of time and dust, the contemporary view that they should be considered as "works of art" can be accepted. But after the new books and ladies' papers began to give information on their techniques to a far wider and often less cultivated public—and even hinted that glass, being costly, could be dispensed with —it signified the advent of that period which spawned the wide variety of objects known as "dust-collectors." This generic term described with terrifying accuracy the dingy articles, assumed to be useful, which were decorated with the mosaic techniques. As they could not be sheltered under glass as were the ornamental pieces, they soon became woefully shabby. Since that time the mosaic techniques—at least in domestic hands—

Bracket of Cone-work. Those with idle hands turned out much useless "fancywork" of this type. Used as decoration on wall.

to the article to be made), and equipped with glue, needle and thread, putty, tacks and hammer, the indispensable awl, together with brushes and varnish, the domestic aspirant after beauty without cost could then demonstrate her abilities at turning everything to artistic account. Even beans, with their varied colors, had decorative values. Among other things, they were useful for *chain-work*. Strands of common white beans alternated with crystal beads were assembled to form a skeleton hanging-basket—that fragile and almost useless object which swung as the ultimate decorative pendant in already elaborately trimmed windows. If the maker could afford it, the bean-work frame enclosed a colorful Bohemian glass finger bowl; otherwise she stuffed the airy holder with moss in which she set a plant or vine.

As American nineteenth-century thinking tended to accent the idea that one person was as good as another, the feminine writer of the day, purveying decorative culture, never failed to suggest to her readers that, even at the level of homemade ornaments, the humblest material was quite the equal of the best. In proffering the design for the basket made of beans, she assured her readers that "it would have every appearance of carved ivory"! Canteloupe seeds offered another easily obtainable material for ornamental work. As the seeds presented no technical difficulties, being easy to pierce, this craft had a longer life than some of the others.

Occasionally someone endowed with sure taste and much ingenuity would collect seeds of many varieties and, using artificial leaves and stamens as accents, would work them into really charming decorations. Though made in 1860, one such piece, a wreath of shining, seed-colored flowers, is still in perfect condition, thanks to its deep frame. The wreath consists of stylized multi-petalled blossoms, each seed constituting a petal. Much of its charm resides in the variation in color and patterning of the seeds. Examination discloses pale rice, the deep ivory of watermelon, of corn and canteloupe, the reds and whites of various beans, the purple of popcorn, the shiny browns of apple and coffee, together with the rough husks of beechnut, the curiously streaked seeds of balsam-apple, many types of acorns, and rosettes of poppy-pods, not to mention a host of unidentified varieties of seeds and pods.

Though it had been practised quietly for several decades, in the 1870's "cone-work" burst out as the newest craze. Any piece of cone-work can stand as a superb example of "dust-collector," for these objects, because of their highly imbricated surfaces, offered innumerable

have acquired an opprobrium from which they probably will never be separated. But at the Centennial Exhibition in 1876, at the World's Fair in 1893, and ever since, particularly at rural exhibitions, the technique, based on the use of grains, has been manipulated to form huge, much admired mural decorations. And we still find the same technique used by backwoods people, and it is now considered a folk art. This is an interesting decline for a type of craft which once engaged the attention of the eighteenth-century lady of fashion.

Assembling the raw materials for any of these "mosaic" crafts furnished part of the fun. Suitable contributions from Nature's warehouse were not always immediately available; one was forced to wait for most of the rustic variety until autumn. Therefore, in order to amass all the kinds of pine cones, acorns, husks, and textured twigs with which she planned to fashion things during the long winter evenings, the American girl, then quite affectedly languid, was forced out into the sunshine and was obliged to take a certain amount of exercise. After the harvest was reaped, one could proceed. Starting with a cardboard or wood foundation (according crannies for dust to lodge in. But cone-work was so attractive in its rich texturefulness that its appeal, especially to the fundless seeker after elegance ("It looks just like carved wood!") was overwhelming.

To decorate an article in cone-work—and it was used on flexible surfaces such as lambrequins as well as on rigid pieces such as waste baskets, wall-pockets, and picture frames—one began with the neatly separated scales that had been pulled from pine cones. These were set in regular patterns in a putty base which had been spread on the wooden object to be decorated. Or they were sewed in overlapping shingle fashion on a pasteboard foundation which had been covered with harmonizing brown silk or paper. After the ground had been veneered with the flattish scales, accents of twigs and tiny cones were superimposed according to the worker's fancy. A bright lining, a coat of varnish—and another "elegant ornament" was ready to add to one's large collection of like decorative trumpery. As a craft, cone-work was held in high esteem by rural folk. Even as late as a few years ago at the county fairs in Pennsylvania, and no doubt elsewhere, premiums were still being offered for exhibits of this long-forgotten handwork, as well as for examples of other fancywork of seeds, shells, and beads—the dusty relics of past generations.

But the bogey of dust was never a deterrent to the fancywork craze while it was all-powerful. Nor did any woman ever refrain from undertaking a project because of the ephemeral nature of the materials which went into its construction. When a piece became shabby, she cheerfully discarded it and put in its place the newest fashionable absurdity. The techniques employed in the making of such frivolities were in themselves subjects which furnished the theme of much chatter in feminine gatherings.

Another Victorian art that increased the burden of dusting was "leather-work," based on modelling forms cut from dampened sheepskin, which stiffened and hardened on drying. Then the flower, fruit, or ornament was stained, sized, varnished, and tacked on to whatever piece the maker wished to decorate. By 1850, leather-work was already in full swing as a fascinating employment for English gentlewomen, and was exploited in commercial ways as well. The suggestion was offered that it could be employed as a practical decoration for such up-to-date affairs as steamboats, since it was not so easily damaged as wood carving. After display at the Great Exhibition, the charms of leather-work were soon heralded on this side of the ocean. Its techniques

Leather-work Brackets were regarded as elegant and durable.

Baskets were wreathed with varnished leather hops and foliage.
Leather roses transformed an old table into a boudoir piece.

175

were easily comprehended by a generation adroit in forming flowers from wax, paper, or feathers, and the very ease with which leather could be shaped into naturalistic forms tempted the deft-fingered to twine walnut- or ebony-hued blossoms and leaves around everything conceivable. The less ambitious limited themselves to ornamenting boxes, caskets, cornice boards, and picture frames—the latter the most popular of all.

Though a vast quantity of Victorian handcraft was turned out, it is not surprising that so small an amount exists today, for the very materials in which these domestic arts were executed invited eventual disintegration. Leather, apparently sturdy, was destined to dry and crumble. Even under glass, flowers of wax softened and sagged and lost their crisp charm. Those made of paper, cotton, or feathers soon faded, losing their original brilliance. Articles wrought from shells not only harbored dust, but the shells gradually slipped from their supporting putty. Needlework, if not washable or protected by glass, was fated to become dingy and be discarded by the fastidious. Thus, only articles substantially constructed and smoothly surfaced had much chance of survival. That is probably why more specimens of Berlin-work and its sister, bead-work, have come down to us than of the other more perishable arts. Their basic materials—beads and canvas—were reasonably tough, and pieces executed in the bead mosaic technique were so tedious to work out that they were treated with the respect accorded such tours-de-force. Bead-work was based on the identical patterns used for Berlin wool-work. The beads, too, came from Germany, which continued to keep a tight monopoly on both businesses—both having expanded enormously in the decade between 1845 and 1855 when bead-work became very fashionable.

Fragile basket-shaped containers formed of Beads were made, not to be used, but solely to be admired. Godey's, 1863.

A great deal of Victorian fancywork was based on a large, rather ugly glass bead (known as "Bohemian") which was supplied in roughly cut cylindrical sections, one-quarter to three-eighths of an inch long. These were employed to form the omnipresent lamp or table mat, as well as vase covers, hanging-baskets, and lambrequins. Though the mosaic technique of bead-work was unobjectionable when protected by glass (elaborate pictures and heraldic decorations were successfully worked out in this manner), nothing hindered its admirers from applying bead-work to the tops of small tables—a place where its surface must have been far from satisfactory. And it was also used for pincushions and sofa cushions, chairs, and lounging slippers. Even the casters which held wine bottles were treated to a sheathing of this ornamental woven bead textile, and it could be found on work-baskets, napkin-rings, towel-racks and key-racks. In a broad way, it can be said that it was fastened on every type of article to which it could be shaped and made to adhere.

For every fancy beaded ornament which still holds together, untold numbers of other decorations once thought so vital to the "elegant" appearance of the Victorian home have disappeared. Gone long since are the fairy-like parlor decorations and whatnot ornaments made of alum crystallizations—the brilliant wire brackets and baskets of crystallized alum sparkling like frost diamonds; the picture frame of crystallized moss and twigs which confined the snow-covered landscape; the dainty bouquets of alum-frosted dried flowers and leaves. Long ago the corners were cleared of their many kinds of bracket—that most memorable knickknack of the 1870's and 1880's. During that time a corner without a bracket would have appeared actually naked. The jigsawed or fretwork type was the commonest. Because the materials were inexpensive and the craft easy to learn, fretwork—introduced in the 1860's—soon became extremely popular with young people of both sexes, for the manipulation of the delicate saws was not beyond the abilities of the more progressive female of the day. In truth, so seductive was the charm of jigsaw work to many members of the frailer sex that girls who were short of pocket money brazenly proclaimed—in a "barter corner" conducted in an English periodical of the time—that they were willing to exchange bits of jewelry —their once cherished onyx brooches and their pearl and turquoise rings—for one of the coveted hand-saws. Publishers of fancywork designs soon issued neat portfolios of patterns which had only to be traced on the wood and the enthusiast could begin to saw out the small wooden article of her choice.

Though the wall-bracket served to hold a trinket or two, it was considered fundamentally a piece of decoration. Another type of wall "ornament," planned theoretically to be useful, cannot be disassociated from the more amusing memories of the period. This was the wall-pocket or "catch-all," as it was most patly named, an omnipresent object that contributed, at least in the opinion of the makers, quite as much to tidy housekeeping as it did to the enrichment of interiors. The simplest "catch-alls" were those of carved wood ornamented with a pocket of bead-work or embroidered cloth. The most elaborate seemed nothing but vehicles for practically every needlework or artistic technique at the maker's command. Such catch-alls were edged with ruchings, laced and accented with yarn cords and tassels, decorated with every imaginable variety of fringe and lambrequin. And what was their purpose? Well, often the most intricately ornamental held nothing more than Grandpa's weekly paper or—and it seems a commentary on Victorian housekeeping—a dust-cloth. From the profusion of these devices, it seems almost as if Victorian housekeeping was based not so much on the ancient adage "a place for everything," etc., as on articles into which one surreptitiously stuffed the many things which were constantly getting out of place. As long as the concealing case was highly decorated, catch-alls for dusters were not viewed—even in the sanctity of the parlor—as incongruities.

If this rash of fancy wall-pockets seems today utterly inexplicable, we must remember that the Victorian house was large, steps were many, and women planned how to save them. Closets were few (in rural houses non-existent), and in addition custom then permitted the display of many objects which today would be hidden in drawers. When the mania for these "elegancies" was at its peak, the storage closet and the family bathroom were far from common, even in cities. Therefore, in every bedroom one found a wash stand, and the wall above the stand was invariably crowded with a veritable army of comb-cases, sponge-holders, splashers, and towel-racks, all elaborately ornamented by hand. When bathrooms became general, the wash stand and its fancy fitments disappeared. Today the long-forgotten pitcher and washbowl appear once again, for they have been disinterred from attics. Promoted themselves to the rank of "ornaments" by a generation which never beheld them presiding in utilitarian fashion on all wash stands,

they occasionally make a startlingly inappropriate appearance in present-day living rooms and sun porches and, most mistakenly, even in dining rooms.

Patchwork, an honest Colonial craft motivated by thrift, was altered under Victorian auspices into something quite different. From being a practical adjunct of daily life, it moved up in the world and was given the status of ornamental textile. The Victorians, however, were not content with patchwork of cotton for their purposes; they scorned it as ordinary, even "vulgar." Nothing would do but patchwork of silk and velvet if it were to enter *their* parlors. In this showroom of elegance, even as early as 1850, this richly surfaced patchwork was used not only as sofa pillows and ottoman covers but also as antimacassars. Mosaic making—for that is all that patchwork is—had again attracted women with its mysterious fascinations; they went to untold trouble to collect, cut up, and rearrange tiny remnants of elegant fabrics into all sorts of decorations, some of great unsuitability — a "mosaic window-blind," for example!

By the 1880's silk patchwork dwindled into that supreme efflorescence of tastelessness, the "crazy-quilt." Here in one article were concentrated all the most deplorable Victorian characteristics—the sentimentality, the lack of decorative restraint, the love of rich encrusted textures. Fundamentally, patchwork is a protest against the shackles of needlework disciplines which making a formal design in the craft entailed, while it still permitted the worker to revel in all the pleasures of collecting the materials from her friends, and in all manner of decorative needlework which she applied to the "crazy-quilt" without restriction. The "crazy patchwork" is nothing but what its name implies—a heterogeneous collection of irregularly shaped pieces of silk, wool, velvet, and ribbon joined together with elaborate stitchery into a restless textile, unified only by its border of plain silk or plush. The Victorians used "crazy-work" on the same type of articles for which they considered the more stylized patchwork suitable, quilts being particularly favored. "Crazy-quilts" were, in effect, a textile scrapbook, one pored over by its examiners with sentimental interest, as the maker related incidents which the sight of many of its fragments evoked: "Here is a piece of Aunt Hettie's travelling dress which she wore on her wedding trip to Niagara Falls; and there is all that is left of the lovely olive foulard which I had specially made when I went with Grandpa to the Centennial." Children adored crazy-quilts, not only for the stories which accompanied their display, but especially for the pictorial needlework with which they were covered. As if the rich conglomeration of fabrics and the joinery stitches were not enough, one of the chief features of a fine example was the wealth of playful silk embroidery which was superimposed on the already luxurious surface—the embroidered kittens and rabbits, the cupids and horseshoes, the fans and the initials, that silk hat of Grandfather's and those spectacles of Grandmother's. Then there were the many kinds of birds, the tea cups and the high boots, the Kate Greenaway children who romped so prettily, and, when one ran out of novelties, the always dependable—if no longer stimulating—flowers and foliage sprays.

The crazy-quilt answered the question of what to do with bits of fine fabrics. What to do with old hoopskirts was a problem which bedevilled the thrifty in the 1870's. But not for long. Those consumed by a desire to produce "grand results from apparent nothings" soon applied themselves to its solution, for they could not resist the temptations offered as craft material by this article so recently discarded. The ingenious used the flexible steel hoops as the basis of all kinds of fancywork gadgets, particularly that master dust-catcher of them all, the standing work-basket. The metal hoops were painted or covered with fabric. Then they were looped and bent into this much admired novelty. The utilitarian parts of the work-baskets were themselves decorated with embroidery or with painting, or were covered with costly textiles. The whole frail, tottery structure was finally held together with as many tassels, as much braid, flutings, and ribbon bows as could be made to stick. Such workstands were considered to bestow an additional gracious touch to the parlor, a room which middle-class women of the 1870's strove to make "a little Eden," according to one of their popular writers, "with this and many other similar little felicities."

At first it did not seem possible that there could ever be too many tassels and rosettes. But those who so easily confected these refined touches (and it was far easier to tie a bow than it was to make many of the earlier types of fancywork decorations) eventually over-reached themselves. When clouds of butterfly bows of ribbon fluttered down on everything, to settle even on the easel that displayed an oil painting or a family crayon portrait, and when every piece of fashionable wicker furniture was threaded with satin strands and touched up with perky bows, there was nothing more that could be added, and the fashion for ornamentation died of its own absurdities.

178

Courtesy, Chester Co. Historical Society, West Chester, Pa.

SHELLS—
THE RAW MATERIAL
OF BEAUTY

Shell Mosaic Valentine. A hinged octagon of wood encases a valentine wrought of small shells. One half features a heart surrounded by a formal design accented with shell roses; the other proclaims—in letters disarranged by time —that its maker was "Truly Thine."

Because of their great variety of form and color, shells lent themselves advantageously to decorative purposes. With delicate artistry they were assembled in flowers and piled up in bouquets. Sometimes all color was excluded to produce the effect of porcelain. Though shell flower-making was an eighteenth-century art, beautiful examples were still being produced in the mid-nineteenth century.

Below, left. Rice-shell Work. A fascinating home craft of the 1840's and 1850's. From tiny shells the gentlewoman made exquisite fragilities for drawing room decoration, ornaments for ball dress and coiffure.

Courtesy, The Art Institute of Chicago   *Courtesy, Philadelphia Museum of Art*   *Courtesy, Victoria and Albert Museum*

179

Left. For a novel framed decoration, the Victorian lady cut ordinary goose feathers in the shape of petals and leaves, dyed and painted some, curled others, and assembled them as flowers.

Centre. Hanging Basket of Cone-work, apparently constructed of brown straw braid. Close scrutiny, however, reveals it to be made of pine cone scales sewed to cardboard in precise overlapping rows. Oval areas are of varnished fabric, centred with clusters of small seedpods. Acorns serve as pendants. Cone-work baskets and similar gimcracks were regarded frankly as decorations. As such they never supported anything weightier than sprays of artificial ivy or a few blossoms.

*Courtesy, Chester Co. Historical
Society, West Chester, Pa.*

*Courtesy, The Art
Institute of Chicago*

Lamp Mat of
crocheted wool
flowers.

*From the author's collection
Photo by Oscar May*

Frame of modelled leather work, a once popular craft. An obvious dust-catcher, its life was limited. Today few examples remain, and the foliage on these survivors, once crisp and perky, is now limp and dejected. For foliage patterns the maker used actual leaves and reproduced their veinings with a blunt tool on the dampened leather. The frame encloses a frail basket filled with pressed ferns.

Spatter-work Wall Decoration.
Above and left. Courtesy, Chester Co. Historical Society, West Chester, Pa.

Jigsawed Towel Rack ornamented with Bead and Berlin-work.
Photo by Oscar May. From author's collection

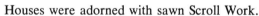

Houses were adorned with sawn Scroll Work.

Above, left and right. In the days before newspapers became daily litter, they were thrust neatly folded into ornamental Wall Pockets for further reading. Frames were carved or jigsawed, bought or homemade. The pocket itself was a sturdy affair of leather, Berlin-work, or of any other form of needlecraft the maker might favor.

"Fretwork," "Sorrento carving," or "Jigsaw work" was a fad which persisted for several decades. A demonstration at the Centennial gave it great impetus. The patterns were commercial productions; with care and patience anyone, from lady to schoolboy, could transform thin wood into openwork brackets, picture frames, towel racks, and small ornaments. The craft's limitations so conditioned the character of its designs that, in general, pieces tended to be closely knit silhouettes of scrollery which, if not inspired in pattern, were unobjectionable.

181

RICH AND BEAUTIFUL
ELEGANCIES

To beautify one's home was a doctrine preached earnestly on on every social level; culture and refinement must inevitably develop from contact with elegant surroundings. Here are Pincushions, Egg-warmer, Standing Work-baskets, Music Portfolio, Wall Pocket, Picture Frame, Wine Caster, Umbrella Stand. Every woman toiled intensely over such hand-worked trifles.

ALBUM 11

Of "God Bless Our Home" &
All the Wool-worked Mottoes
Of "Remember Me" on Bookmarks &
Of Ladies' Morocco Albums
Of Birds Swirled in Flourishes &
Copperplate Penmanship
Of Roses and Violets
Decalcomanias· and the Hand of Friendship
Of Plush-covered Albums &
Of Sentimental Album Quilts
Of Melancholy in Jewelry &
In Wreaths of Hair Flowers

ALBUM ELEVEN

⋝✿⋜

THE WORLD OF
LOFTY SENTIMENT

SHALL we enter the Victorian house by its front or back door? The question is really superfluous, for every wall, every room proclaims generously that it is ever ready to welcome us. If we, as neighbors in a village, go in through the rear in easy village custom, we know we are welcome because a large embroidered motto confronts us at once with that friendly theme. If, on the other hand, we pass through the walnut and cut-glass front door of the city dwelling, ready to pay a formal visit, we are doubly assured of hospitality. Our hostess' greeting is repeated quietly and beautifully by a fancywork "Welcome" of glittering beads and bright wools hung over the doorway in which the lady stands. Following our hostess into the parlor or family sitting room, we pass beneath the pious invocation, "God Bless Our Home." Everywhere we are surrounded by a warm, decorative, emotional glow.

These characteristic decorations, the "Mottoes" or "Door Texts," as they were also known, were so integral a part of Victorian family life that even today the sight of one unfailingly invokes the old-fashioned image of "home": the united family assembled beneath the aureole of the hanging lamp, the child in prayer at its mother's knee, the cat on the mat. The attempt even to visualize the mottoes in contemporary settings carries in itself a touch of sacrilege because their high resolves, the spiritual fragrances they emanate seem to have been set aside in most present-day schemes of life and decoration.

The Victorians were unique in their belief in the beneficent values of pictorialized sentiment. No other generations before or since have placed such touching

faith in embroidered injunctions to hospitality, embellished invocations for heavenly protection, needleworked appeals for family unity. To be sure, other generations had been chidden with preachments from pulpits, but these could be forgotten, or, if enclosed within the covers of a book, conveniently ignored. It remained for Victorians to feature such adjurations to virtue in their daily lives, to magnify them in scale, transform them with color and scrolleries into seductive decorations, and then belabor one another with these high-principled pleadings from every corner of the house. In simple rustic frames or in heavy walnut moldings, the decorative mottoes hung tip-tilted over every doorway, ready to shower the admonitions and blessings they invoked on all who passed beneath.

In working them out so carefully, the makers of embroidered texts undoubtedly derived certain spiritual benefits; she who had labored over an especially elaborate "Welcome" must assuredly have taken to herself an added modicum of social grace as she greeted a guest. Every time she glanced upward at "Home, Sweet Home," her heart must have filled with pleasure, thinking of all the precious values of family life over which the motto ruled. Even the Victorian ceremony of dining was not without its appropriate motto: nothing could have been more moving than the sight of one's family murmuring grace, seated underneath the beautifully worked prayer: "Give us this Day our Daily Bread." Mottoes could be sternly moralistic or graciously benevolent. "Thou, God, Seest Me," no matter how delightfully embellished with beads and bright colors, must have carried many a severe reproof to those not at ease with their consciences. The sinless, however,

The Victorian world succumbed to an army of Mottoes.

To give the Mottoes a touch of individuality, various techniques of ornamentation were employed to bedeck their frames. *Top*. Rustic Frame of spruce. *At bottom*. Border of pine cones.

slept sweetly reassured under the confident embroidered statement, "Thou Only Makest Me Dwell in Safety."

Texts had indeed risen in the world. Earlier, when they were an essential component of sampler design, the discipline their execution entailed was supposed to enrich the ethical and spiritual education of the child. But in the Victorian era, the desire publicly to proclaim one's virtues and sentiments was carried to far greater lengths, and adult needlewomen took over the task of working out ethical beliefs in a decorative manner. As the new public schooling did not deem sampler making necessary to its curriculum, children's samplers now became a perfunctory gesture to tradition. Instead of being worked with silk on linen, they were stitched with the identical wools and canvas used in Berlin wool-work. This substitution of coarser materials was of undoubted benefit to the eyesight of the whole generation, even if the completed articles were not as elegant as earlier ones.

Though the Victorian sampler dispensed with pious sentiments, another method of working, based on the invention of a material known as "perforated card," kept needleworked moralizing alive for a decade or two longer in adult as well as juvenile circles. Perforated cardboard did away with so many needlework problems that its popularity could have been predicted on its appearance. Its appeal, above all, was to those who were discarding the time-honored crafts to follow the seductive ideas offered them by the industrial age. Perforated cardboard was a simple material—a bristol board punctured with minute holes set closely together at regular intervals. Made in varying degrees of fineness, it could be purchased both in sheets and in cards with ornamental borders. It was an enchanting substitute for canvas, since its intrinsic stiffness did away with the necessity for stretching and mounting (always a concern for those engaged with wool-work), yet it permitted the use of wool-work patterns and technique. Already in high favor by the 1850's, it was then employed primarily for book-markers. Expressing sentiments of friendship, religion, or personal affection, these were a universally acceptable gift all through the genteel decades. So easy was the new technique that it enabled even children to share in the prevailing craze for the embroidered sentimental legend, and they took up the fad with enthusiasm. Little Emily could work a marker for Grandfather, for her schoolmaster, and for her best friend as well. Elderly cottagers could offer them with all propriety to any lady, no matter how great, who might have condescended to

186

honor them with a visit. In 1872, Queen Victoria notes in her journal that she spoke with an oldish character "who worked me a book-marker."

After the Civil War, an alert manufacturer conceived the idea of printing the design in colors on the perforated cardboard itself instead of on a separate sheet, as had heretofore been the custom. By this invention, what was already a simple technique was so simplified that anyone who had the ability to stick the needle carrying the colored wool through the correspondingly colored areas in which the card was printed could work a motto or bookmark. Children found this new method so appealing that sometimes even the young Victorian male succumbed to its charms, and worked out, in prettily shaded wools, such admirable masculine sentiments as "Knowledge is Power."

But Victorian parents, though forever intent on the moral guidance of their offspring, by no means placed their entire trust in the sentiments reiterated by bookmark and Door Motto. The very facility with which lettering could be depicted on the perforated card tempted them to provide additional stimuli. Such were the pious texts, one allotted to each day of the week. These were displayed in fancy cases, also executed in this easy fashion. And with firm faith in the molding influences of *beauty,* and with a yet unshaken belief in the guidance values of the injunctions, the conscientious mother worked through all the daily changes, from "Be diligent in well-doing" on Monday to the stern "Remember the Sabbath day to keep it holy."

The field of decorative possibilities for this embroidered cardboard was considerably widened when the material was introduced, around 1870, in gold, silver, and colors. Restless fingers soon discovered further uses for it, based upon the ease with which the perforations could be transformed by means of cuts with a sharp knife into lace-like geometric patterns. Enthusiasts for the new technique employed this fragile material for lampshades and portfolios; they covered boxes with its delicate fretwork and cut out innumerable crosses from the cardboard, which, mounted on bright ribbon, took their place as wall decorations together with other sentimental trifles.

For the fabrication of all the decorative trumpery in which the age delighted, perforated cardboard was the material *par excellence.* One such frivolity was so amazing that it must be described if only to show to what lengths women would go in pursuit of fancywork "elegancies." This object was an embroidered fly-trap made

Cross in Perforated Cardboard Work. Motifs were cut out accurately in a regularly increasing scale of sizes and pasted together in this order to obtain a three-dimensional effect.

of perforated cardboard, dreamed up as a series of cubes, each made of embroidered squares. The fragile fancy was then suspended by ribbons swung from the chandelier. There its constant motion—it was hoped—would drive away the flies from the persons sitting near! A truly Victorian palliative for a problem which the period had made no real attempt to solve. There were only such pretty decoys, covers, darkened rooms, and a patient submission to the pest. Such decorative excesses—and they were legion—were bound eventually to destroy the basic appeal of the material. Except for examples preserved under glass and in books, comparatively little of this "art craft," once so widely practised, has survived.

Victorian young ladies, insatiable gleaners of sentiment that they were, let no wisp of it escape if they could devise a method to capture it. Like the ornamental texts, the Ladies' Album was a method of exhibiting testimonials of feeling and sentimental beliefs, but unlike the texts, the fashion for albums held sway during almost the whole of Queen Victoria's lifetime. So frequently must young ladies have laid themselves open to the charge of being nothing but maudlin collectors of sentimentality that in the album whose pages we shall

187

leaf over, its fair owner protects herself at the outset by stating frankly on its first leaf:

> "This little Book, with all the prose
>   Its varied page imparts,
>   I dedicate to gentle eyes
>   And simpathising hearts.
>   Then all who bring their smile or tear
>   May tearless drop the gem
>   For commonsense shall ne'er come here
>   To praise them or condemn."

This particular volume, as befits the decorative intent of the whole class, is bound in the rich black of papier-mâché which is adorned with the usual opalescent blossoms and gold arabesques. Opening it, on the engraved title page we are confronted with a lacework of elaborate scrollings from which, if we are patient enough, we can disentangle the word ALBUM. As its pages of fine heavy paper slip through our fingers, we come across occasional inserts which are bordered with handsomely embossed designs. Inside these embossed panels are beautifully penned verses especially cherished because they are original contributions, not hackneyed copies of familiar favorites. And, lest the reader have any doubt as to authorship, they are all engagingly designated "original."

Throughout the dainty volume, the chirography is beautiful, almost fairylike, no matter what the subject matter. In addition to the exquisitely written entries, there are occasional delicate watercolors and drawings, smoothly painted in a soft manner then admired as particularly suitable for ladies' albums. The subjects include flowers and shells, and, once in a while, a pencilled landscape. A girlish admirer of Byron decorates the page on which she copies one of his verses with an amateurish drawing of a Greek soldier weeping over the poet's tomb. Various sentimental verses on death take their share of other pages. There is one verse —scarcely perceptible, so faded is the ink—entitled "On a Jessamine that bloomed too early and was Killed by the Frost," and another invocation, "To the Herb Rosemary," which in its day raised neither smile nor shudder. The poet thus addresses that symbolic plant:

> "Come funeral flower! who lovest to dwell
>   With the pale corse in lowly tomb
>   And throw across the desert gloom
>   A sweet decaying smell . . ."

In any case, every girl, whether serious or frivolous (and they all had albums), applied herself to the stimulating diversion of filling the pages with moving fancies written by her friends. Besides furnishing pleasure to its owner, the album provided a perennial source of entertainment to one's guests, who, absorbed in the same hobby, were always eager to scrutinize the tributes collected by others, and to balance the quality of the particular album under examination against their own sentimental treasuries. Young ladies' albums acquired great importance in their owners' eyes, for, as in any form of collecting, the ego is enhanced by pride of ownership. Thus the shyest of girls, album in hand, was always able to summon courage to approach a gentleman for a contribution to her "dearest possession" or to exact an inscription from a person of note. In fact, so bothersome did some young ladies become that an etiquette book of the day warns them against annoying professional authors with their demands for what was, in essentials, the author's stock-in-trade, and to content themselves with a signature.

In the 1820's and 1830's, at the beginning of the fad, the Victorian *lady's album* was no mere aggregation of signatures or flippant verses, as was its latterday successor, the *autograph album.* When albums first appeared in the United States, they were elegantly bound volumes of gold-stamped morocco, often decorated with the owner's name, and filled with blank pages of fine rag paper. The album mirrored the social circle in which its owner moved. If she had artistic pretensions, her album was likely to be filled with paintings delicately brushed in by her boarding-school friends. If she were excessively religious or sentimental, the entries reflected these proclivities. If she assumed an interest in literature, she aspired to fill her pages with selections from the best authors. But no matter what their character, the sentiments in the early albums were always written—at least by all the feminine contributors—in exquisitely fine penmanship. The neatness of every page proclaims that the selection had been carefully practised before being inscribed, so that, even though the spelling frequently might be open to criticism, the penmanship would be flawless. On the other hand, the gentlemen, perhaps irked by too frequent requests, or out of intentional perverseness, were apt to write far less meticulously than was their wont.

For at least three-quarters of the nineteenth century, a beautiful penmanship continued to be expected of everyone making any pretense to culture. People still took great pride in what they referred to as a "copperplate hand," a term derived from the early copy books which were engraved on copper to set the styles for penmanship. In the eighteenth century certain models were especially prepared and "engraved for the particular Practice and Amusement of the Fair Sex." Much practice was necessary in order to learn how to write in "the Italian Hand," the delicate style then considered particularly appropriate for ladies. This penmanship, far more refined than the "clerk's hand," is the one which emanates a faded gentility on every album's time-stained pages.

The craze for ladies' albums flourished both here and in Europe, therefore album pages reflect national tendencies. An Italian example specializes in paintings of classic ruins; an early German nineteenth-century one scorns the commonplaceness of watercolor or pencil decoration; all its pages are embroidered with embellishments executed in finest silk floss, in boastful evidence of the skill of its contributors.

The watercolors in the average album vary in excellence. Those who reached a high degree of perfection in the delicacy they desired for this type of page decoration painted with unbelievable fineness. Obviously executed with the aid of a magnifying glass, such work could have been carried out only with a brush that contained one or two hairs. Today one must in turn resort to the glass in order to appreciate such microscopic perfection. The really talented album painters looked with polite scorn on those who resorted to stencils or "theorems" to provide them with the contours of the flowers they wished to depict. But as stencils enabled the latter to produce a neat even if coarser effect, this mechanical assistance was relied on whenever a contribution was requested.

About the time young maidens were busily trapping contributors for the virgin pages of these early albums, publishers were preparing to bring out the first examples of a new type. The newcomer featured steel engravings of romantic subjects. These inserts added such a note of tonal richness that all previous types of albums, despite their fine paper and elegant morocco covers, seemed pale and uninteresting in comparison. As early as 1826, two albums, known respectively as "Leaves of Affection" and "The Token Album," already adorned with pictorial inserts to catch the public eye appeared on the American market. For this purpose, the publishers, Durrie and Peck of New Haven, used engravings which had already seen service elsewhere in certain annuals. This, however, was common practice, for engravings were costly and publishers aimed to get their money out of them. Eventually, as the Victorian public came across the identical illustrations in book after book, they became rather irritated with this publishing practice. Being amateurs of the steel engraving, they were interested in variety, not replicas.

As the quality improved and the number of the commercial engravings increased, their professional perfection offered a painful contrast to amateur effort and it began to be less esteemed. This resulted in a decline in excellence and, by the 1840's, the vogue for the hand-painted offering of friendship had virtually died out and the steel engraving reigned everywhere in its stead. On the other hand, almost as if to substitute for the loss of the hand-decorated pages, the titles of the albums became more sentimental and the format began to be further enlivened by the introduction of pastel-colored machine-made papers.

For some years deep emotional feeling and even thoughts of death dominated the pages of the average album, but it is interesting to see that around 1840, a touch of worldliness began to penetrate these confines once kept sacred for "the most ennobling thoughts." At first the facetious note was injected only by irrepressible male contributors. By 1839, however, we find a young female who evidently sought for a lighter touch throughout her whole album, for she boldly states her wishes on the title page of her volume: "To poets, Painters, Enigma and Conundrum Makers and all who wish to shine in this our Literary Society: *Wanted* a number of very neat drawings in any style you are most proficient in: to fill up the blank paper in this Album. Also a few good stanzas on different subjects of a sentimental nature. Enigmas, conundrums, etc., will likewise be admitted. P.S. Originals are strongly recommended and dispatch must not be lost sight of. N.B. No charge for admission."

After the introduction of lithography, prices of albums were lowered. It was inevitable that they should then become the fashion in circles not given on the whole to much practice of artistic "accomplishments." The owners of such albums found that those approached for contributions were often not willing to supply much more than their signatures. With these they were forced to be content, and, as a result, the whole character of albums changed for the worse. Other donors who acceded to requests to fill a page were apt now to turn to humorous rather than to emotional or funereal selections. So popular did these frivolous stanzas become that by 1870 the better manuals of etiquette included pages of "Selections for the Autograph Album," so that

Even the Visiting Card was ornamented: first, with beautiful embossing, later, in less fastidious circles, with flourished birds or self-applied decalcomanias or scrap-book bits.

their readers could make a choice. Here were submitted all the traditional sententious and prosy maxims, as well as the affectionate and sentimental. There was also no lack of a new variety—the waggish: "Some write for pleasure, some write for fame, but I write simply to sign my name," or "When on this page you chance to look, Think of me and close the book."

As the ability to execute fine handpainting was becoming steadily rarer among contributors to album pages, German commercial enterprise came forth in the 1860's with a new product, the *decalcomania,* which could be substituted for the same decorative purpose. This novelty entered into competition with another German product, the embossed lithograph scrapbook picture; both were produced for album use, daintily scaled down in size. Those who looked about for ornaments to embellish their contributions never had any difficulty in finding a preferred blossom or inscription in this glossy flood of lithographed images, for in this last flare-up of sentimentality no familiar symbol was overlooked. Never before was one able to have such realistic moss-roses or violets, such naturalistic lilies-of-the-valley or pansies! Pictured in unbelievable perfection of color, they were irresistibly enticing when assembled in a nosegay—a nosegay frequently extended in the "hand of

friendship." This was invariably a dainty feminine hand framed in a cuff of delicately embossed lace. As a symbol, this hand seems to have been outstandingly popular in the latter days of the Victorian era; apart from the plastic ones of Parian or glass, the number one sees pasted in the old albums and scrapbooks is legion.

People were often asked to write in albums prior to going to "foreign parts," a bit of sad prescience on the part of the album owner who thus assured herself of a memento of a traveler who might never return. Many pages in old albums are given over to pathetic appeals for sentimental survival in the memory of others. Girls used to sew a tiny lock of their hair on the pages and write imploringly beneath it: Forget not Maggie,—or Carrie—or Hettie—or whatever other chirpings ending in *ie* they then affected. This fashion for diminutives carried through two generations of Victorians. The Effies and Minnies, Fannies and Lizzies, Jennies and Mamies greatly fancied their fluffy names, acquired, not during school days, but bestowed upon them at birth with all customary solemnity.

After the 1870's, when public education became widespread, and, of necessity, standards of penmanship grew less exacting, the practice of really beautiful chirography was left to professional penmen, itinerants

190

Cartes de visite taken from early albums bring us starched petticoats at their crispest, crinolines at their widest, and infant dowdiness at its most endearing.

who pursued their ancient art in the streets, in parks, and at fairs. For a very small sum they wrote with assured and beautiful scrollings the customer's name on a little package of visiting cards, or demonstrated their bravura technique in a series of sweeping flourishes on elaborate birds and ribbons, swans, quill pens, and eagles. This type of pen decoration was known to its practitioners as "flourishing," and proficiency in it was a prerequisite for any successful instructor in penmanship. Pupils struggling laboriously to acquire the essentials in writing never failed to be entranced by the amazing ornamental effects which could be evolved by the instructor, not only on paper but on the blackboard as well, using only the same free-swinging curves that went into the composition of the favored "Spencerian hand." But few of these penmen now survive. When they vanish, their passing will signalize the disappearance of another art of long standing, for the ornate birds they so skillfully inscribed are not Victorian, as is generally supposed, but are far more venerable, since they were prefigured as early as 1681 in an English copybook in order to demonstrate "the Natural Freedom of the Pen."

A sentimental accessory which allowed one to concentrate at will on the physical aspects of one's dear

friends and relations was the photograph album, a substantial object of padded and ornamented leather or plush, bound and clasped with decoratively treated metal. This pretentious volume which came into favor in the 1860's is inseparably associated with the latter half of Victoria's century. When photographs first appeared, they were small affairs about 2½ inches by 4 inches and were referred to as *cartes de visite*. People began to collect these novel mementos of their contemporaries. Since there was need to keep them together for easy display, the photograph album was the outcome. As a form of social entertainment, this impressive volume shared the honors of the centre table with the daintier autograph album. Today we have reason to be grateful for its massive construction, for it has preserved many likenesses which might otherwise have disappeared. Embedded in the album's thick pages the photographs of Civil War soldiers still survive, along with their hoopskirted relatives and friends—the stylish young ladies leaning stiffly against an ivy-clad rock or steadying themselves against elaborately carved chairs beneath a be-tasseled swoop of drapery.

Another fancy which lent itself both to sentiment and to collecting was the early manifestation of that now commonplace article—the birthday and greeting card.

191

Not content to let these bits of sentiment stand simply as charming examples of the lithographer's art (which by the 1880's had reached a high degree of perfection), the publishers enriched them with silk fringe, tassels, cords, and metal accessories in order to gratify the public's insatiable taste for elaborateness. These tokens, featuring realistic sprays of flowers, holiday symbols, or snow scenes (the latter glittering with ground glass), were an important adjunct to the fashion of making calls on New Year's Day, as custom then demanded that a young man leave a pictorial greeting card for each young lady he visited. Young men bragged of the number of calls they made; young ladies totaled their lithographed trophies, compared them with friends' collections, and then, as permanent evidence of their social prowess, pasted the cards in albums.

As trips to the shore were rare occurrences before the days of railroads, Victorians preserved their marine savor by collecting seaweeds and sea-mosses, which, after pressing, they mounted in albums—a delicate and none-too-easy task. When Victoria was a young girl of fourteen, she made a gift of a seaweed album to her guest, the young Queen of Portugal. For those too indolent to collect the materials, but who yet craved a souvenir, shops in watering places offered "the sweetest wreaths of sea-mosses," prettily arranged to form a border around a verse that pleaded sentimentally: "Call us not weeds! We are flowers of the sea . . ."

In the "Album," "Autograph," or "Friendship Medley" quilt, needlework and sentiment were joined in agreeable union to render service as several types of communal gift. The idea behind these quilts was a simple one: each contributor worked a block of predetermined size with her own materials, and—if it were well planned in advance—was asked to write or embroider her name in the center of the decoration she had devised. As a conclusive demonstration of the regard of one's friends, "album quilts" were highly valued. Sewing circles sometimes presented one to each member who married. And during the Civil War, young ladies whose beaux went off to enlist were given "flag quilts" with their friends' names neatly inscribed on the stars. If a minister was well liked, his wife would be presented with an album quilt on the occasion of his departure to another charge. While most album quilts follow the tradition—that of being appliquéd or pieced in washable cottons—the general passion for Berlin wool-work led a group of enthusiasts in 1850 to use that distinctive technique to ornament an album quilt. This was certainly a most unsuitable choice of a method of ornamentation since it could not be satisfactorily laundered.

The "Friendship Medley" quilt, though indistinguishable in appearance from an album quilt, was not to the same degree a gift of communal affection. To be sure, the blocks of a "Friendship Medley" were the work of a circle of friends, but the quilt was never a surprise to the future owner for she herself had asked each friend for a block. After collecting the individual contributions, she in turn entertained with a quilting party to unite the blocks into a homogeneous article.

All these varieties of sentimental quilts were a popular fad throughout several decades, the height probably being reached in the 1850's and 1860's. As the idea of the album quilt is based on affection, it is not to be expected that it will be as artistic, as unified, as one in which the aesthetic approach dominates. On the other hand, its very scrapbook-like quality (for no two squares were likely to be duplicates) endeared it to its owner. Women liked to pore over their album quilts; frequently they were saddened when, in their examination of the needleworked mementos, they came across the delicately written signature of a friend who had since died. The quilt block was perhaps the only tangible evidence remaining of a precious friendship.

In endowing the human race with hair, Nature unwittingly contributed to the nineteenth century a substance which could not have been improved upon for the intimate expression of sentimental feeling. Though the eighteenth century made use of hair in memorial rings and in medallions (clipping it in infinitesimal fragments and incorporating it in a pigment which they used to depict mournful funerary scenes) these were but modest attempts to preserve tender souvenirs. It remained for the flamboyant Victorian imagination to develop to the full the possibilities of hair as a decorative material. Quite early in the century the French were weaving human hair into delicate chains and experimenting with it in embroidery. But there was nothing in this use of the material to indicate to what extremes the fashion for jewelry and ornaments made of hair was to be carried when business took it over from the lady amateurs and capitalized fully on "the sentimental treasures of the heart."

Because of its lightness, toughness, and pliability, hair could be fashioned into the most intricate of braided and woven devices. When bare necks and arms were the mode, women wore jewelry made of hair, a sombre, odd, but not unpleasing fashion. Necklaces and earrings—dark, airy latticed spheres contrived from the hair of one's dear departed—lay against the pale throats of the fair and much alive. Broad hair bracelets with heavy gold fastenings clasped the feminine wrist, and heavy woven chains of hair supported watches draped across masculine vests. Queen Victoria herself was never separated from a bracelet which contained not only the portrait but also a lock of hair of the perennially mourned Prince Consort.

This attachment to hair trinkets was a sentiment which evolved from acute realization of eternal loss. So well was this understood by the era that the writer of a caption which accompanied an advertisement for hair jewelry could, without ridicule, address the public in this fashion: "Hair is at once the most delicate and lasting of our materials and survives us, like love. It is so light, so gentle, so escaping from the idea of death, that, with a lock of hair belonging to a child or friend, we may almost look up to heaven and compare notes with angelic nature—may almost say: 'I have a piece of thee here, not unworthy of thy being now.' "

The very fineness of the texture of hair had occasionally tempted the worker who delighted in the bizarre to use it elsewhere in the arts. Among other examples shown at the Crystal Palace, the German Exhibit contained a small picture of the Queen, Prince Albert, and the Prince of Wales embroidered with hair in the tiniest of stitches. This technique, notes a chronicler of that famous show, was commendable for its ingenuity even though the likenesses were most unflattering.

Since everyone from highest to lowest viewed the world through a thick haze of emotion, gifts of one's own hair were always appropriate, even on occasions when the most costly of jewels might have been offered. In 1835 on her sixteenth birthday, the Princess Victoria found among her presents a brooch given her by her mother which was woven of that lady's own hair, as well as several bracelets from other donors containing similar personal mementos. The fashion for such sentimental offerings was one which ran on for many years. Meanwhile the time came when the possibilities of hair for ornamental uses were expanded by the introduction of "hair wreaths," bouquets of floral forms intricately fabricated from the combined locks of several members of a family. Set in recessed frames, such wreaths were invariably viewed as handsome household "ornaments." But, if one hankered after something different, one could order a "hair tree" which united, in a simulated arborescent growth, the locks of all the deceased in a family. A delightful concession to genealogical precedence was made in its design: the gray and hoary trunk was woven of the hair of the oldest members of the family group, the branches being tipped with the golden floss of the youngest. These creations were invariably protected by glass shades and were exhibited in the same manner as were wax fruits and flowers.

As commercial productions, hair wreaths and "trees" were in high fashion in the 1860's and 1870's, although several decades earlier domestic circles were already practised in the art of making these mournful trophies. From the amount of hair used in these lugubrious articles, one concludes that the public must have been eternally preoccupied with the thought of collecting and snipping fairly substantial locks from everyone with whom they came in contact; in no other way could they have acquired enough to make these beloved but melancholy garlands.

EVERYBODY'S BEST FRIEND

The Newfoundland dog was the Victorian symbol of protectiveness, of dependability. As the benign guardian of small children he led a busy existence in innumerable pictures of home life. His feminine admirers embroidered his likeness on hearth rugs, and foundries cast his bulk in iron to serve as lawn decorations.

Below. Stereoscope view. *C.* 1865. German. At "The Tea Party," rotund crinolines make room for Bruno.

Below, left. Lithograph of 1834, amusingly amateur in execution. Bulging with ballooning forms and all the approved sentiments: mother love, love of pets, love of landscape (artist sketching in background), and love of noble architecture (Greek temples).

Below, at bottom. Cast Iron Setter with Bird. This city lawn ornament is annually repainted to maintain its antiquarian charm.

Innocence and Roguery

Courtesy, Mr. Edward Austin Walton

Photo by Oscar May

194

PETS-ON-CUSHIONS
ON CUSHIONS

Those who wished to give—rather than receive—attention turned to the Newfoundland's antithesis, the lap dog. The tranquil spaniel and the cat were preferred motifs for embellishment of footstool and sofa pillow. Like the Victorian dogs which sat primly by their mistresses on needleworked cushions (see *right*) the embroidered reproductions were pictured seated also on cushions. These motifs were superimposed on stuffed objects in daily use.

Below. The Tabby, on red-and-gold cushion, meekly confronts the world.

On the other hand, the Tomcat has been glaring "Don't Tread on Me" ever since he was worked out realistically with fur of clipped wool and eyes of glass. While this quasi-fidelity to Nature was entirely outside Art's province, it always appealed to the sentimental and the artistically uneducated.

Mrs. S. C. Hall, 1800–1881, author of *Sketches of Irish Character*.

Pets sat on cushions of fringed and quilted scarlet.

Courtesy, Index of American Design, National Gallery of Art

195

From the author's collection

Perforated Cardboard was a material which lent itself to the expression of sentiments in simple needlework. Easiest to work out were mottoes and legends on bookmarkers. Innumerable examples of the latter were made by children for gifts, and, thanks to the longevity of books, many of these earnestly stitched phrases of moral earnestness have been preserved for us.

Left. Flower Piece, 12″ x 15″, worked in bright shaded wools on perforated Bristol board. A Georgian conception adapted to Victorian materials by a needlewoman gifted with taste and originality.

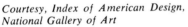

*Courtesy, Index of American Design,
National Gallery of Art*

Courtesy, Free Library of Philadelphia

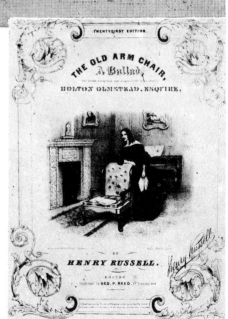

THE OLD ARMCHAIR
I love it, I love it, and who shall dare
To chide me for loving that old armchair.
I've treasured it long as a holy prize
I've bedewed it with tears—and embalmed it with sighs.
'Tis bound by a thousand bands to my heart;
Not a tie will break, not a link will start
Would ye learn the spell—a mother sat there
And a sacred thing is that old armchair.—*Eliza Cook*

After this verse appeared in 1838, "The Old Armchair" became a household word. Its warm domestic sentiment appealed to the middle class of the whole succeeding generation. The verse was early set to music (*right*) and decades later was still being embroidered on mottoes (*above*), woven on bookmarks (*left*).

Courtesy, Free Library of Philadelphia

TOKENS OF FRIENDSHIP AND LOVE

Right. Greeting card of the 1880's. Gentlemen making New Year's calls left one of these rich creations for each young lady in the family. The recipients pasted them in albums.

Centre. Cut-paper valentine, probably made in Pennsylvania. Roses are cut from pink and yellow papers, mounted on stems of green. Bird of linen and paper.

Courtesy, Free Library of Philadelphia

In the 1840's and 1850's valentine-sending became almost a mania. The prettiest valentine papers were of English make (see *below*). Those who wished to confect their own carriers of sentiment purchased these lacework backgrounds and then decorated them further with painting and pasted-on devices. The latter on being raised disclosed minuscule loving messages.

From the author's collection

From the author's collection

The Ladies' Album. In the first half of the nineteenth century, every young lady had one of these pretty treasuries of sentiment and affection. The volume, elegantly bound and often stamped with the owner's name, was given a place of honor on the centre table. Every lady strove for a high degree of excellence in the contents of "her dearest possession." The paintings were the best her friends could contribute, the sentiments the loftiest, the chirography the most beautiful. In its way the album represented a tiny museum—one eagerly examined by her whole circle.

The best examples of Album Painting were exquisite miniatures. Occasionally album pages featured engraved embellishments of sentimental symbols: the dove, altar, eternal fire, lyre, broken column, and that symbol of hope, the rising sun. Those who could not draw selected from among the pages decorated with these devices one featuring a motif appropriate to the sentiments they wished to inscribe. Pages above from album of young Philadelphian. Her friends, between 1825–1831, adorned its leaves with the most minute painting the author has seen in any album.

ALBUM 12

Of the Beauties of Landscape &
The Passion Therefor
Of Salvator Rosa &
Ruined Castles &
Monstrous Precipices
Of Ladies' Paintings &
Thatched Cottages &
Mother-of-Pearl Moons
Fixed Forever on a Sable Sky
Of Rusticity and the Summer-house
Of Woolen Moss and Autumn Leaves &
Knotted Twigs of Iron

ALBUM TWELVE

❧ ❋ ❧

THE WORLD OF
THE PICTURESQUE

*"O! what can equal the beauties of nature! What enjoyment there
is in them! Albert enjoys it so much; he is in ecstasies here . . .
Really to be able to sit in one's pony carriage, and to see such wild,
beautiful scenery as we did . . . is an immense delight."*

Leaves from the Journal of Our Life in the Highlands,
QUEEN VICTORIA

*"Is that the old church of Castlebar which you were promising to
show me, with its beautiful tower, and the great yew trees? You
are right in your admiration . . . That tower is beautiful, with its
fine old masonry, the quaint fantastic brickwork left, to the honor
of the rector's taste, in the rich tinting of its own weather-stains,
undaubed by whitewash and contrasting with the vivid foliage of
that row of tall limes . . ."*

MISS MITFORD

AND so it goes—from Queen to commoner—for the tendency to express admiration for the picturesque in scenery was general in Victorian life. The Queen's was a simple statement of her feelings, but innumerable passages such as the excerpt from Miss Mitford are witness to the fact that the nineteenth, quite as much as the eighteenth century, looked to its authors and poets to point out the aesthetic values in natural aspects. With sonorous words and phrases the literary profession spread such a glamour over the outdoors that it was never viewed by the educated public except through a dense poetic mist, a fuzziness which persisted until sentimental or analytical absorption in landscape passed completely out of fashion. Today, if described at all, the topographical beauties of nature are minimized in the matter-of-fact accounts emerging from the megaphones of tourist guides, or, in the pictorial field, have become the commonplaces of photography. As a result, only the most stupendous wonders can now elicit even a degree of the admiration which was bestowed in floods upon the most casual bit of picturesqueness by any cultivated Georgian or Victorian.

During the long period when it was a fashionable cult to be enthralled by the beauties of the natural scene, everyone with any pretense to taste collected prints and engravings of landscapes. With the vocabulary of appreciation already detailed for them by their most admired writers, the upper classes were equipped to gush over every prospect. To us, the jargon which they affected seems excessively stilted; at that time it was the common exchange of polite society. English young ladies writing to their friends filled pages of delicate script with conscientious descriptions of landscape, heavily saturated with literary phrases. Promontories were always "lofty," precipices "monstrous," ruined towers "moldering." Their castles invariably "frowned," their cascades "foamed," their trees "withered," and their streams "gently murmured." American satirists were gently amused by young American misses who, aping the English fashion, made brave attempts to adapt this mannered terminology to the landscape of the more settled portions of the United States—a feat which presented insurmountable difficulties. For while this country possessed a terrain rich in natural beauty, it was completely destitute of those firmly cemented keystones of romantic "picturesqueness"—the ruined castle and the sad, abandoned tower.

In fashion's vernacular, no epithet was more tossed about than the word "picturesque." At first the term was applied only to those features in landscape which approximated similar details in the Italian scene—those remote, fanciful and extravagant aspects of nature which characterized all that the English public had been taught to admire. Before the British could be weaned from their long-held allegiance to this type of beauty, it was necessary for English artists to travel about in the British Isles and then to publish their findings detailing the charms of the indigenous picturesque. After the public became more familiar with such works, it was discovered that mediaeval abbeys and castles were quite as "picturesque"—although totally different in character —as any sunlit classic ruin in Italy. And the gentle English landscape was equally worthy of admiration, although it lacked every one of the elements of wild or classic beauty on which all appreciation had hitherto been founded.

The privileged English collected paintings and prints with the same avidity with which the camera fan of today records the sights of travel, and for the identical reason—to preserve memories of those things they had personally observed. As travel facilities expanded considerably in the eighteenth century, the upper-class British on their Grand Tours became familiar not only with the actual topography of the continent, but also with the works of artists which interpreted its noble views. But in their long jaunts through Europe, one country more than any other drew them like a magnet. This was Italy, sunny Italy, dotted with its ruins of the glorious past. When the aristocratic travellers returned home, as first choice they brought back both paintings and engravings of the works of a seventeenth century Italian artist, Salvator Rosa. This artist may well be considered the founder of the whole school of romantic landscape painting. Rosa specialized in portrayals of weird and savage natural beauty. To locate his favorite subject matter, he prowled the rugged Neapolitan coast. His turbulent skies, rough caverns, tortured fantastic trees and overhanging precipices were in profound contrast to the smooth and ordered landscape to which British milords were accustomed and they found the contrast both piquant and emotionally stimulating.

Those who preferred a more tranquil impression of the classic world turned to the works of a contemporary of Rosa's—the Frenchman, Claude of Lorraine. Both artists had innumerable imitators, and, as a result, engravings of the spurious as well as the genuine "Claudes" and Rosas once and for all crystallized the pattern of the "picturesque."

Eventually the craze for the "picturesque" dwindled in the upper levels of society, only to be taken up in the nineteenth century by the well-to-do middle classes, determined to see for themselves the beautiful prospects which had furnished the theme of so much upper-class enthusiasm. Inspired in their turn, these new travellers also went into affected raptures or melancholy meditation on beholding some fine scenic view, especially if its inspirational values had already been highlighted for them by their favorite authors. Ruskin, in particular, contributed much to this voluble appreciation of Nature's beauties. Moreover, he inspired his readers to regard the picturing of landscape as a thrilling and noble expression which, if the artist was sincere in his feeling and in his expression of aesthetic appreciation, would inevitably transmit inspiring and moving sentiments to the beholder. As a result, the substantial buyer of pictures concentrated on landscapes, the ownership of which—for these were then viewed as a mark of culture —at once marked a man as one sensitive to his social obligations. As this cult for romantic scenery gradually permeated the Victorian bourgeoisie, it began to take on a semi-religious quality—a quality to which they gave bland approval, for they always felt more at ease if they could find moral justification for worldly pleasurings. How gratifying it was to the Victorian paterfamilias, his wife, and his brood, when they set out in their new carriage intent on gazing upon some flawless example of picturesqueness, to have assurance in advance that the excursion would result in a heightening of *spiritual* qualities through the uplifting elements inherent in the landscape itself!

All through the eighteenth century as well as in the first half of the nineteenth, art instruction was based on the copying of the works of professional artists. Through faithfully reproducing such models, one learned how to draw and to paint. Formulae for landscape compositions were matters not open to question; they were so well established that some or all of their elements may be found in every painting of the period. From the paintings of Rosa the copyist took the fearful and awesome aspects of natural beauty. For the softer and more peaceful features in landscape, the imitators drew on Claude. It was he who supplied them with the rugged bridges, the winding streams, the distant villas and sunlit hills topped with ancient ruins. From his paintings or those of his imitators, the copyists also abstracted the classic temples and vine-wreathed foregrounds which they introduced to give variety to their compositions. Every young student learned how to draw these separate details according to his ability, and the more ambitious produced compositions into which they managed to stuff practically all of them—with naïve results which we today find engaging.

As it was taken for granted that every well-bred young person should know how to draw, textbooks were prepared for those who found no instructor at hand. Furthermore, the printsellers were equipped not only to sell but even to *rent* prints from which the earnest student could copy. When certain amateurs had learned how to paint landscapes in monochromes of India ink, they were content to rest on this achievement. But those ambitious to go further were warned by the author of one of these stern handbooks not to be too impetuous: they were told "that it would be highly improper to abandon your masters and transport yourself into the country, expecting there to find the colouring laid open at large to every looker-on. Thousands make the journey; but the result for the most part, is melancholy disappointment. Nature only unveils her beauties to those who have perseverance and genius to comprehend her."

The amateur artist whose only instruction was of this negative type might well have become discouraged and might have relinquished all pretensions to what an author, J. W. Alston, in his *Hints on Landscape Painting,* called "one of the first accomplishments in the world." But she who had access to a drawing master was spared disappointment since the drawing master was a business man who planned to satisfy his customers —even though they learned but few truths about art. Before attempting a finished landscape, the pupil received some perfunctory instruction in "touches," an essential feature of all art teaching in the early nineteenth century. "Touches" were artistic exercises based on prescribed patterns of hand movements. These, if docilely practiced until flexibility was acquired, would enable one to depict any type of foliage. There was a special "touch" allotted to each species of tree, among which were connecting radiating lines (these were helpful for ash and elm), fan-shaped zigzags, narrowed scallops, and crisp star-shapes. "Copy it faithfully and imitate

"Touch" for Foliage of the Chestnut Tree.

the touch," the young ladies were told. And imitate it conscientiously the young ladies did. It is these stylized "touches"—executed with more or less dexterity—which give to the landscapes of the first half of the nineteenth century their definite, even if unintentional, quality of decorativeness. Present-day taste delights in this stilted approach to landscape and finds in it much charm. We have even a label for these "works of art" which the girls turned out over a century ago. We call them "American primitives," a term which would unquestionably have sent shudders down the delicate spines of the young lady artists. Desirous of concealing their all-too-recent connections with "primitive America," none had worked harder than they to acquire the "accomplishments"—the gilding—which would help them to obliterate hitherto unavoidable crudities.

Besides the conventional techniques of painting and drawing, other methods of working, long since abandoned or completely forgotten, lent considerable variety to the decorations the young persons turned out. They found ample diversion in constructing picturesque landscapes from curious materials today not accepted as suitable for artistic purposes. Though the embroidered scenic view of silk and chenille had finally ceased to charm, the youthful contemporaries of Queen Victoria found it exciting to make *"sand paintings."* Actually, sand would hardly seem to be a promising material; but as the whole era took delight in surmounting technical difficulties, a method of handling it had been evolved. Vari-colored sands were first collected. Then, after a

Page from Drawing Book. Drawings by fine artists supplied copyists with subjects.

painting had been blocked out very simply in water-color, sand in colors vaguely approximating the desired hues was carefully sifted over selected areas previously coated with mucilage. Details in the paintings were brought out with accents of powdered color mixed with glue.

Such subjects as "Mt. Vesuvius in Eruption" and "The Ruins of Netley Abbey" were popular because they were not too difficult to work out in this muddled technique which seems, for amateurs at least, both clumsy and unrewarding. By certain professionals, on the other hand, the art was practiced with admirable artistic results. Another forgotten but somewhat related technique which lent itself to Victorian decorative purposes was that of "marble dust painting." This was a process by which a gloomy landscape drawing was evolved in black pastel on a ground which had been coated with glue over which marble dust had been sifted and left to dry before using.

In the 1830's and 1840's, England's best artists devoted themselves to seeking out compositions in the British Isles which would set forth their native romantic beauty. For outstanding examples one need but examine the works of those connoisseurs of the picturesque — Samuel Prout and James Harding. So highly esteemed were these artists that certain annuals were devoted en-tirely to their works. Prout was one of the first artists to avail himself of the new art of lithography, that technique so admirably suited to the delineation of land-scape and architectural antiquities. To the amateur and student the drawings of Harding and Prout supplied examples of such perfection that they have never been surpassed. Even today, a century later, the works of Harding are studied in architectural schools as models of highly skilled pencil sketching from nature. But apart from their virtuosity—for no one exceeded Harding in nicety and expressiveness of touch in the pencil medium —they can also be studied as the ultimate in the expression of the romantic. In works such as his *Picturesque Views of Ireland* or *Scotland delineated in a Series of Views* the sentimental young ladies of the period found exquisite models for their hesitant pencils. Here are depicted sturdy remains of castles and moss-covered ruins, undoubtedly set down with all truthfulness. Yet so carefully have the subjects been chosen for their romantic qualities that all ugliness, all unpleasing detail is excluded.

Many similar publications of more or less worth were brought out to satisfy the demand for this type of pic-torial material. After the motifs of romanticism had dominated the pictorial scene for some decades, the young ladies' darling ruins, their abandoned castles, and

204

The Drawing Books disseminated these picturesque architectural bits throughout the world.

their thatched cottages became such symbols of banality that they were finally laughed out of artistic existence. On the other hand, long after the amateurs had turned to something else, the industrial world, instead of allowing oblivion to engulf that favorite artistic cliché, the ruined castle silhouetted starkly against the moon, kept it alive in various other ways. First, manufacturers discovered it to be the perfect motif with which to decorate the blackness of papier-mâché (a mother-of-pearl moon and castle was an item no sentimental romantic could resist). Later on, towards the end of the nineteenth century, this doleful remnant of architecture was painted frighteningly on black velvet; and before the last glimmer of the taste for ruins flickered out, the cloud-shadowed moon and castle were smeared in a slap-dash monochrome of black and gray on wire window-screening. While this ingenious device permitted those behind the screens an uninterrupted view of the street, the lugubrious landscape prevented those outside from seeing in. As consolation, the passer-by was offered a dubious ornamental effect.

The fancy for the picturesque could descend no farther in the social scale, for it had now reached bottom. In two hundred years it had travelled from the art galleries of eighteenth-century aristocrats to its final resting place—the window screens of the most modest citizens of the great American republic.

While this partiality for "the picturesque" endured, the taste for it was expressed in many other departments of living and in curious and ornamental fashions. As an epithet, the term "picturesque" had been subjected to much analysis and definition. Yet in general, its meaning could be reduced to the conclusion that a fondness for the picturesque demonstrated a preference for the untouched, disordered beauties of Nature over those which had been formalized by man. The term, "picturesque" transformed age and decay—characteristics also linked closely with the picturesque — into ideas which were found attractive and acceptable even to the young and lovely. As Victorians became more and more infatuated with the Gothic, they vibrated with pleasure to discover its close relation to certain elements in the picturesque. When feasible, they placed their new Gothic villas in the most romantic locations which could be found for them by their architects, who were, at bottom, not insensitive to the Gothic's implications. When this was not possible, they planted their Gothic conceits on whatever site they happened to own, no matter how inappropriate. To make up for the dissonance between the humdrum terrain and the pseudo-Gothic residence, the Victorians turned, consciously or unconsciously, to another phase of the picturesque. This harmonizing agent was known

205

as the "rustic" style, a curious and long-lived fashion in Victorian decoration. The "rustic" based its designs on inspiration taken directly from the interlacement of branches. In a vague way these intertwined, gnarled twigs suggested the knobby protuberances of formalized Gothic tracery. Though the rustic often introduced a far from agreeable note, all kinds of things were nevertheless constructed in the style. The "rustic" manifested itself in two fashions: either it turned to the actual materials of Nature for its expression, or it imitated Nature's rugged motifs in any substance it chose. Fearful indeed and sometimes wonderful were the decorative imitations.

As a style for horticultural settings, the trend to rusticity had considerable economic justification, for it was at bottom inexpensive. In a "rustic garden," what was in fact actual neglect could blandly be passed over as "picturesqueness." Furthermore, the rustic theme precluded the use of costly appointments—the classic urns and sculptured seats so long linked with formal gardening—and practically invited the homemade variety. The "rustic" gained enormous popularity in the decades between 1840 and 1870—a position in public favor which it has not yet entirely relinquished. Even in a period which prides itself on its functional garden furniture, its serviceable aluminum and metal streamlined pieces, furniture made of natural barked material can still be purchased by those persons sentimentally attached to it. Moreover, these pieces will differ not at all in essentials from the earliest Victorian examples. And what is more surprising, another supposedly Victorian specialty, the *imitation rustic,* cast in weatherproof material, is still with us. Bird-baths of artificial stone modelled to resemble tree-stumps may be obtained today, so

romantically naturalistic in their conception that they might have been fabricated for Queen Victoria's contemporaries instead of for those of her great-grandson.

During the period when the "rustic" dominated the scene, every Victorian property of any pretension, whether in city or country, was adorned with its informal summer-house. Rough porches "prettily thatched with moss" were blithely tacked on to the most stolid of American dwellings to add a touch of Old World charm. And every fine prospect was viewed from a strategically placed seat made of intertwined branches.

In the 1850's the construction of a rustic pavilion was suggested as a pleasant artistic task for gentlemen of leisure and ingenuity; then it was evidently regarded as an occupation not worthy of a skilled artisan's time. But in the energetic United States, it was not long before the "rustic" style was being proposed not only for the arbors on gentlemen's places, but as a style appropriate for the most unassuming of cottages. In addition, it was pointed out that such articles could be put together by the humblest laborer in his few spare hours. A writer in *The Horticulturist* in 1858 finds "this description of furniture very appropriate. In summer bowers, piazzas, and near or in garden walks, it is pleasant to see, if not to rest on, such objects which have an 'expression of purpose' about them satisfactory to the mind."

At the very outset of Victoria's reign, the leading feminine authority on horticulture, Mrs. Loudon, was already suggesting to the English gentlewoman that the designing of informal garden pieces to create picturesque effects would be "an excellent exercise for female taste." To readers who thought of following her advice, Mrs. Loudon stated that even for a *lady* there was nothing at all demeaning in the attempt to convert an old barrel or tea-chest into an elegant rustic support for flowers. (Obviously, even ladies were not immune to the enchantments offered by advice on how to convert a free *nothing* into an artistic *something*.) But lest any such attempt be socially misinterpreted, she adds: "In all cases where the materials employed are of little value, the flowers grown in them should be in the highest possible state of cultivation, *so as to show that the rudeness of the material has been the result of intention, and not of carelessness or poverty.*"

After the Civil War, American writers on home decorating took their turn at trying to inspire their feminine readers to tackle the making of such pieces, referring to it invitingly as a "fascinating domestic employment." As the war had forced many ladies to turn to occupations which they once would have repudiated as entirely inappropriate to their sex (the Americans being very conscious of their recently acquired "gentility"), the advice fell on ears now far more receptive. Converts were warned, however, not to let their enthusiasm for "picturesque" furniture lead them into constructing articles for the indoor embellishment of their homes without taking elaborate precautions to clean and varnish the pieces to rid them of their insect inhabitants.

If the threat of insects kept homemade rustic chairs and cabinets out of the parlor, it did not prevent persons filled with a warm admiration for the style from inventing many other methods to introduce the wild woodland note indoors. That the fondness for these transformations of the natural into the supposedly decorative was general should occasion no surprise, since the average person was being constantly assured that "the beauty of art is not alone for the mansions of the wealthy. Artistic and tasteful adornments are the products of ingenuity and not of wealth." Encouraged by this democratic doctrine, the nimble-fingered became infatuated with the "pleasing devices" which they could make for little or no outlay. One of the most highly regarded of these confections was the rustic picture frame. This, in its commercial manifestation, had such enormous appeal that examples of it can still be located in many an old farmhouse. Constructed of crossed strips of walnut roughly tooled to simulate bark, the corners were ornamented with clusters of carved foliage. Pine cones and acorns were used by the home decorator in lieu of carving.

On the subject of framing the Victorian point of view laid considerable stress on what was then thought of as "suitability": that the motifs used to ornament a frame should be closely related to the subject of the picture.

Fresh spruce twigs freed of needles were made into frames.

There would be greater delight in a rural picture if it were enclosed in a rustic frame, or in a seascape if it were surrounded by one decorated with shells. This conception of "appropriateness" had a long life. Even towards the end of the century, we find the picture dealers selling, as a popular piece of merchandise, a black-and-white print of a lion that is glimpsed through metal bars fastened to the frame to simulate a cage.

Frequently, in a desire to create an ornamental effect at no cost but the effort, borders for pictures were assembled of pressed and waxed autumn leaves. Autumn foliage formed the basis of other fragile bits of decoration. One greatly admired conceit was a wooden cross mounted on a moss-covered base, twined with a dainty garland of small, colorful waxed leaves. In general, the Victorians placed a high value on the decorative qualities of autumn leaves, copying them in wax and embroidery. In 1851 several New England ladies each sent, as "artistic" contributions from their respective States, an ornamental arrangement of "Autumn Leaves" to the Great Exhibition itself.

That the broad field of Victorian fancywork would be affected by "the rustic" was a foregone conclusion. This was to be demonstrated in many fashions. One of these was the period's singular preoccupation with moss, a substance seemingly inseparable from the Victorian conception of hoary and picturesque antiquity. The ladies seemed fascinated by it. Not only did they use moss in its natural state for various projects, but they went to considerable pains to imitate it in wools. One of their favorite fabrications was the "moss mat," to be placed beneath the lamp on the centre table. These mats had a long vogue. Crocheted of several shades of soft green and brown wools, they were first sheared and then subjected to singeing, so that the much-admired brown-tipped mossy effect could be closely approximated.

Early in Victoria's reign, ladies with untrammeled enthusiasm for the romantic used occasionally to paint landscapes in which the inevitable ruin was more than ordinarily prominent. After they had completed the art-work, they covered the painted ruin with fragments of bark; to the painted rocks of the foreground they glued bits of fine moss. These artistic-botanical mélanges in their deep enclosures were regarded as piquant curios-ities even in the eclectic world of Victorian framed decorations. By 1870 the bits of moss were no longer confined to the picture but were transplanted as textural embellishment to the frame itself. Sometimes mosses, after being dried, bleached, and dyed, were clumped into woolly wreaths as frames for photographs. Even the wall-bracket did not escape a coat of this romantic woodland substance. A layer of moss was considered to transform even the most homely bit of wood into a har-monious support for a vase of ivy. This, with a tender thought for "suitability," could be used as an "orna-ment" on outdoor piazza or vestibule wall.

At the height of its popularity, the rustic became the darling of the graphic arts as well, for the illustrators of the period found that nothing was more adaptable to the page layouts then in favor than the branches, twigs, and roots which constituted the working basis of the style. In Germany, where the fashion for interlacing branches into elaborate borders probably originated, the senti-mental rustic held sway for a long period. There it was designated by the term "knuttel," which, if less evocative of poetic imagery than the English epithet, was never-theless exquisitely precise. For "knuttel" can be trans-lated by the word "cudgel" or "gnarled club"—a term of striking expressiveness.

Both furniture manufacturers and foundrymen were attracted by this trend towards the ruggedly naturalistic. At the Great Exhibition in London they were ready to catch the romantic's eye not only with all types of wooden furniture bristling with carved twigs and leaf-age, but with a large variety of "rustic" cast iron garden seats and benches. The designs of the latter were based on as realistic an imitation of bare knotted boughs as was possible, interlaced to form backs, legs, and seats. The fashion for picturesque motifs continued to grow, and by the time of the Centennial Exhibition of 1876, no visitor could escape it. Every path was edged with a neat scalloping of half-hoops of iron, molded in the form of branches—each semi-circle the exact duplicate of its neighboring bent twig. Soon after the first appearance of the arboreal motif on garden furniture, it was also made available to its admirers in the form of cast iron ve-randahs, summer-houses, and fencings.

These architectural whimsies were adopted not only by city dwellers, who, in the midst of endless walls of brick and stone, might be excused for their attachment to symbols of nature, but were fancied quite as much by those living in the countryside. In fact, certain rural property owners derived a particular pleasure from adorning their places with "rustic" embellishments, firmly convinced in their belief that nothing could be more in harmony with Nature's own verdant back-ground than those intertwined branches of iron and those acorns and oak leaves of the same enduring sub-stance.

THE RUSTIC
AND
THE GRAPHIC ARTS

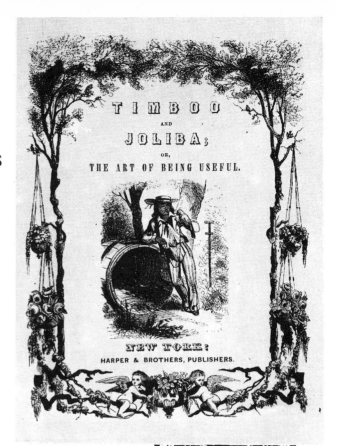

The graphic arts gave endless scope to rustic whimsy—the more improbable, the more admired. For some decades Title Pages of books offered a fertile soil for fantastic growths of trees and roots.

Left. Page Border, *L'Illustration,* 1860. This French fantaisie, entitled "Mélancolie," manages to entrap within its decoratively twisted roots a variety of poses of dejection and symbols of solemn ideas.

The Rustic and the Gothic in entangling alliance.

THE RUSTIC TOUCH
IN
DAILY LIVING

Below. American-made "Rustic" Silver Vase—a presentation piece in 1853. Silver was the preferred medium for naturalistic motifs and textures.

To please the romantic's love of Nature, objects used in daily life were textured to resemble bark, swathed with carved or modelled vines. On the most ornate examples, birds nested in crannies (see French cabinet, *centre*), and perched on the tops of carved caskets.
Left. Lady's Work Table. 1849. A drawing room ornament.

Rustic Plant Holders of vari-colored earthenware. French, 1868. Stylized conceptions of wooden casks encircled with fruiting vines.

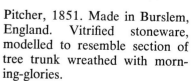

Pitcher, 1851. Made in Burslem, England. Vitrified stoneware, modelled to resemble section of tree trunk wreathed with morning-glories.

THE RUSTIC TOUCH
IN
DAILY LIVING

Centre. German summer-house. 1868. *Above.* American trellised garden retreat. 1855.

By the 1850's every establishment making any pretensions both in city and country had a summer-house, whether it was made of cast iron, of wooden scrollery, or of natural branches roofed with bark.

Upper left. Sketch for Garden Enclosure. 1842. T. J. Ricauti, London. Architects prepared rustic designs for clients so that the fencing would harmonize with the romantic structures they surrounded.

Courtesy, Miss Julia Williamson, Philadelphia

To gratify the taste for the prettily rural, the photographer used rustic pieces, against which he propped his clients for their tedious session.

Photo by Oscar May

Cemetery Bench of a century ago. Its complete lack of structural lines, its languidly intertwined branches, today suggest, not picturesqueness, but the decaying twigs of a brush heap.

From the author's collection

With styles of painting formalized and subjects suitable for pictures clearly stated, landscape painting was reduced to simply making a choice of "picturesque" elements and then applying oneself conscientiously to their rendition. The toiling peasant, the thatched cottage, the contorted tree, the wide-armed ancient oak were pictorial familiars of every wall.

Above, right and left. Watercolor vignettes from lady's album. The antique ruin mantled with ivy and flanked with yew and shattered tree was the commonest of artistic clichés.

Below. Ruined abbeys were choice subjects for experimental ventures in decoration — such as "sand" and "moss" painting. Woodcut from *The Penny Magazine,* 1833.

Courtesy, Mr. Edward Austin Walton

Pricked Work, that eighteenth-century technique, survives in this naive Victorian attempt to depict a ruined castle.

Singularly lovely, Netley Abbey was successfully copied by amateurs and the painting trimmed with moss and bark.

ALBUM 13

Of Weeping Widows &
Weeping Willows
Of Grief Embellished &
Sorrow Adorned
Of Roses and Lilies
Of Marble &
Of Cushions and Bedsteads of Stone
Of the Well-furnished Plot &
Its Iron Lace Boundaries
Of Bereavement in Black &
Assuagement in Violet
Of Memorials in Sculpture &
Of Mementos Bleached and Pallid
In Wax

VERY pleasant Sunday afternoon in countless communities the length and breadth of the land, could be witnessed an identical scene. In this familiar picture walked two persons, one of whom was always a woman Profoundly veiled in black, she leant heavily on the arm of a companion as she moved gravely along a well-kept path. In her hand she invariably carried a neat bouquet of pale sweet flowers. She might be young or old—her age was concealed beneath heavy swathings. But whether her solemn promenade took place in Victorian England, Victorian Maine, or Victorian New Jersey, her destination could be predicated almost with certainty. She was going to pay a weekly visit, not to friends, but to the cemetery.

Going to the cemetery was a favorite outing, one in which duty was mingled with a pleasurable and sensuous melancholy. Without a knowledge of the high mortality which prevailed through most of the nineteenth century, it is impossible to comprehend the Victorian absorption in the world of the dead. Death was a commonplace of daily life, and society was helpless to stave off the dread visitor. Not until 1880 was the world equipped by science to fight diseases which took such a toll of the younger members of families—those large families of our grandparents who never doubted that the coming of ten to fourteen children was the will of God and that the loss of almost all of them, as sometimes happened, was equally His will. For tabulations of such losses one need not even turn to statistics. A visit to any early cemetery will disclose clusters of tiny markers assembled like chicks around the parent stones. To understand this clearly is to erase the current belief

that the Victorians' indulgence in memorials, and their care for the last resting places of their dead, was morbid and overly sentimental. In its essentials, it was a simple acknowledgment of recurrent domestic tragedy—one to which Victorians bowed submissively. And, since the family plot held so much that was close to their hearts, they lavished on it all possible embellishment in outward recognition of their sorrow.

Indeed, a tender concern for the cemetery plots was an important integer in Victorian feminine mentality. To the average woman who had perhaps lost the greater part of her family, the cemetery was the place where her heart already lay interred and where she herself might join her loved ones at any moment. In small communities, which in earlier days offered so little opportunity for diversions, some women visited the cemetery daily, deriving from their very faithfulness a certain mournful satisfaction.

The nineteenth century, one must add, regarded its cemeteries with not only individual but marked communal pride as well, for they were something new. Although conceived as business projects, they were carried out with a tender consideration for the feelings of those who would frequent them. As conditions in general living improved, the subject of insalubrious graveyards, long a concern in cities, became a matter for immediate action. Great transportation improvements now made it feasible to establish cemeteries in localities remote from crowded living areas. In these selected spots, the dead might be interred with complete assurance that their remains would not be ruthlessly disturbed. For there was no question that Victorian sensibilities were far more delicate than those of their predecessors, who, through

Laurel Hill Cemetery, Philadelphia. Engraving by Croome. *Godey's Lady's Book,* 1844. A showplace of the landscape architect's art. The art of the sculptor, too, was well set off by the sombre masses of foliage in which the terrain abounded.

centuries, had become inured to the horrid and barbarous practice of exhuming the dead in order to make room for newcomers within the tightly restricted confines of the churchyard.

First in France and then in England, the landscape architects of the day applied their particular talents to the designing of large suburban cemeteries. Shortly afterwards, the idea was taken up in America. By the 1830's the three chief cities in the United States—Boston, New York, and Philadelphia—had already established great cemetery tracts on sites carefully chosen both for accessibility and for natural beauty and picturesqueness. To these latter features (hitherto not considered at all essential to cemeteries), the managers of the Philadelphia project planned, they announced, to add "the skill of the sculptor, the graceful hand of the florist, the chastened design of the architect, and let the genius and talent of the land throw around the whole their most exalted strains of poetry and religious feeling."

With what today appears to be an amazing readiness, writers and poets of excellent reputation turned themselves into publicity men for these commercial undertakings. In books and articles they rhapsodized over their sentimental beauties. And indeed they were lovely places, for all the great Victorian cemeteries—and through their examples even the lesser ones—were conceived as ornamental parks. So varied were their landscaped charms that they soon became the objectives of fashionable drives. In addition to the sedate enjoyment provided the visitor by their studied elegance, it was suggested by the publicists that the pilgrimage to the family tombs, with its inescapable meditations on the transitoriness of life, might be provocative of pious reflections and of spiritual benefit even to those who quite frankly enjoyed their frequent excursions to these great parks—excursions which so agreeably combined duty with pleasure.

One of the most eulogized of such beauty spots in the whole country was Philadelphia's Laurel Hill Cemetery, established in 1836. No visitor to the city was permitted to pass it by. In fact, the much-travelled author, N. P. Willis, flatly declared it to be—with one exception, and that a Turkish cemetery in Scutari—the most beautiful in the world. At its very entrance one was confronted with an image taken from the world of

216

Contemporary lithograph of "Old Mortality." This group, the work of a Scottish sculptor, was brought over for exhibition in New York's Crystal Palace. Afterwards it was given by the sculptor to Laurel Hill Cemetery, where it may yet be seen.

romance and literature. Immediately on passing through the gateway the visitor faced a wooden Gothic edifice which housed a tale told in sculpture—a tale, moreover, from the works of the period's favorite novelist. This narrative group sets forth not only its own story but also threw in a full-size portrait of the author, the famous Sir Walter Scott. Excellently cut in red sandstone, the group depicted the novelist seated on a tombstone in converse with one of his fictional characters, "Old Mortality," who was engaged in the pious task to which he had dedicated himself—the renewing of the inscriptions on the Scottish martyrs' graves. Mr. Willis viewed this sculptured work with admiration and referred to it as "real life poetry." Furthermore, he considered the development of these areas of loveliness as "delightful indications of a purer growth in our national character than politics and money-making."

Even after a century of use, this venerable cemetery retains its inviting vistas; it is today so redolent of the romantic period in which it originated that it appears almost to be an evocation of an 1840 lithograph rather than a still-prosperous financial operation. Publishers brought out books dwelling on its many charms—books so elegant in their make-up that they were considered "eminently suitable for the centre-table"—a position to which they were assigned without the slightest feeling of incongruity.

Planned as a place of sepulture in perpetuity, Laurel Hill was spared nothing to make it attractive. Originally an elegant country estate, its already well established plantings were further developed as an arboretum; this offered special enticements for the fashionable study of botany. In addition to the hundreds of varieties of trees and shrubs, the exquisitely romantic glimpses of winding river and distant bridges, the rugged descents and shady glens were irresistibly alluring to the lover of the picturesque. Sunny glades offered contrast to masses of dense shade, and the weeping willow—that time-honored arboreal symbol of grief—was everywhere, set in all its languid grace to temper the sunlight over the graves, and incised in symbolic formality upon the tombstones themselves. But for all its popularity, the willow's ancient prerogative to trail in mournful fashion over the grassy mounds was being disputed in many cemeteries by new botanical "weepers." For those who craved the latest thing even in horticultural symbols of grief, there were obtainable weeping birches, weeping ashes, weeping elms, and weeping sophoras. Even the Norway spruce, with its pendulous branches, was recommended for its visual "fitness to purpose." In spite of this range of choice, one of the more poetic among the landscapists, concerned about the subject of appropriateness in cemetery plantings, regrets that no tree in Northern cemeteries ever arrayed itself in that flawless symbol of melancholy—the weird Spanish moss which drips so dolefully from the live-oaks of the South.

In the cemetery the Victorian absorption in sentimental demonstrations of sorrow was given full expression. No longer did the horrid skull-and-cross-bones of Colonial days dominate the necropolis. Gone also were the amusing cherubim which grinned from many an old headstone. In these new cemeteries, mortality was to be glamourized, and the stone-cutter's chisel would depict softer, more acceptable sentiments—those of the ladies' albums. Passing over the many examples of the Gothic (which in truth flowered with considerably more appropriateness in the cemetery than in the home), we find innumerable evidences of the era's sensibility expressed in marble. Filigrees of marble flowers so sharply and beautifully sculptured that the roses, lilies, and dahlias retain all their original delicacy of form in spite of a century of exposure to the elements, wreathe the gravestones with their cold loveliness. Marble ivy, symbolic of the persistence of life in the midst of death, softens the austerity of marble crosses, and marble ivy, together with the real, clambers up stone shafts carved in rustic fashion—those lopped-off tree trunks which were considered most profound and beautiful symbols.

With a view to softening death's asperities, the stone-cutter, in order to give the graves a home-like touch, began to incorporate details taken from the plushy Victorian interior. Drapery which once added grace to

Tombstones in the French style were less harsh in contour.

the severely classic urn of the eighteenth-century cemeteries, now lends its softening lines to the tombstone itself, being looped and tied back in exactly the same fashion as were the parlor curtains. Many stones are topped with a faithfully depicted bit of contemporary upholstery—a marble cushion complete with fringe which simulates the padded top of a *prie-dieu*. Absurd as were these stone pillows which offered not a jot of comfort, physical or spiritual, they must nevertheless have conveyed to the bereaved a certain visual assuagement of sorrow, for they stood high in sentimental favor.

Not only the living quarters, but even the bedrooms of the mid-nineteenth-century house were drawn upon for mortuary decorative inspiration. By the 1850's tombstones in the "French style" became extremely fashionable. These looked exactly like small white marble beds, the head and footstone being connected by side pieces of ornamentally scrolled slabs. Frequently the stylized beds brimmed over with flowers; these lent their spate of sweetness to ameliorate the bitterness of the loss of the loved one.

Symbols, both classical and poetical, add ornamental variety to the tombs. A bridal wreath severed by a dart betokens a bride cut down in her happiness; an infant is indicated by a rosebud with broken stem. A gravestone for the aged is ornamented with a sheaf of wheat, a lamp trimmed and burning, or a shattered urn. The stringless lyre marks the last resting place of a poet, and the broken Doric pillar, the book, the hourglass, the inverted torch, as well as the dart, are at the service of anyone wishing an impersonal symbol of mortality. Sentiments prompted by geographical considerations were also recognized; an accidental death in Egypt would be signalized by Egyptian motifs on one's resting place, and the Northern grave of a Southerner would be marked in tender reminiscence with sculptured palmettos. Stones marked simply "Our Dear Willie," or shapely urns embellished with a touching "Lissie's Grave," are revealing evidence of the era's belief in the coherence of the family as a unit. Moving testimony to the depth of family loss, they also proclaim the overlordship of the Victorian parents who were so profoundly concerned with their own griefs that they allowed their Dollies and Lissies and Willies to rest for all eternity without surnames. Self-complacent as they were, they never doubted that the stones which conveyed their own names might be inadequate to establish the identity of their deceased offspring, each of whom remained, in death as in life, an insignificant integer in the flock of stones which surround the impressive parental markers.

The layout of the Victorian cemetery was characterized by a belligerent individuality. The boundaries of each plot were marked by fencings which jostled their neighbors with a complete disregard for the ensemble, the latter being an idea which remained for the twentieth century to perfect. The well-to-do citizen invested in a formal, enduring enclosure of granite or marble; those with less of the world's wealth were satisfied with fencings of metal. Cast iron enclosures had many things to recommend them. They were adaptable to a variety of topographical conditions, were inexpensive, and the molded iron was capable of pictorial expression to a degree no other type of fencing has ever approximated. There was no end to the pretty fancies it set forth; one could have the most stylish of tracery in the "Gothic manner" or in the equally favored "rustic." On the other hand, the fence which enclosed the last resting spot of one's dearest might be as sentimental in conception as a valentine.

As soon as cast iron appeared on the market, purchasers of the material were told that it would not deteriorate if it was regularly painted. But when this care was withheld and enclosures were neglected, growing vines thrust their living strengths against the inert and brittle material and began actually to rend it apart. Rust hastened this process, and the cast iron decorations were gradually removed from the places to which their disintegrating laciness had long contributed a note of extreme picturesqueness. Because the demand for scrap iron in the recent war made its collection and sale worthwhile, in but a few years the cemeteries were stripped of this most typically Victorian of embellishments.

Before the idea of commercialized care for graves was evolved, each family as a matter of course looked after its own plot. As long as plot owners were governed by the community's ideas of order and tidiness (which were most demanding in the latter decades of the nineteenth century), frequent visits were necessary to maintain these standards. This regular care permitted the installation of a variety of decorative caprices which, according to present-day ideas, added an aesthetically distracting note. In addition to the flowers planted on the graves and any amount of whimsical containers for bouquets, there was usually a cast iron urn. Filled with carefully tended plants, these urns contributed a touch of amusing formality to groupings which, because of the cast iron chairs and benches, sometimes suggested

a most comfortable homelike aspect. In spite of the contemporary vogue for this iron furniture on terrace and in garden, no one who remembers these pieces set within the cemetery enclosures can ever disassociate them wholly from the idea of grief. To such persons they can never be anything but "cemetery chairs," funereal objects which present a bizarre contrast to the worldly backgrounds where they now find themselves admired, whether as salvaged antiques or as reproductions cast in aluminum as well as in iron.

Mourning—in the degree to which it was carried all during the Victorian era—was indeed a new fashion, one which flourished luxuriantly on the fertile soil provided by delicate sensibilities. Besides stressing the attention given to cemetery plots, the custom of mourning established the most rigid controls over the social life of the bereaved. It regulated every detail and texture of costume, decreed the exact length of time the special garb should be worn, dictated the style of stationery (only wide black-bordered stationery was found acceptable), and, according to the intensity of one's grief, even altered the decorations in one's home. As an example of this latter tendency, the most deeply disconsolate signified the profundity of their loss by sometimes making mourning quilts of black and white patchwork to lessen the amount of color about them. No one's conduct better typified the most rigid observance of society's rulings on mourning than that of Queen Victoria herself. In its every detail, her mourning garb and demeanor were a perfect example of the extent to which such customs could be carried by a person resolved to wrap the rest of her days in this particular cloak of sorrowing respect for the dead.

In the one fateful year of 1861, Victoria lost both

Embossed Cards featuring mourning symbols were produced by the manufacturers of the familiar lace-paper valentines.

Courtesy, Free Library of Philadelphia.

Wedding of Prince of Wales. Victoria, gazing at bust of Albert, takes centre. The bride and groom fill in the background.

her mother and her husband. The passing of the Duchess of Kent, bringing her daughter into immediate contact with the mystery and horror of death, made a powerful and morbid impression on the Queen's imagination. This was shockingly aggravated by the death of the Prince Consort at the end of the year. It was said that on hearing the news of the death of "Albert the Good" every lady in England adopted the livery of grief and even little girls went about beribboned and sashed in black in order to show their sympathy for their Queen's great loss. After the Prince Consort's death, the Queen passed into a seclusion of her own choosing from which she emerged, swathed perennially in crape, only to unveil a succession of monuments to the Prince. The dolorous demeanor of the Queen had a widespread effect upon the deportment of widows. Since Victoria never wore anything but mourning colors the rest of her long life, many widows less highly placed followed her sombre example. Although the Queen could indulge herself in this idiosyncrasy ("Osborne seemed like Pompeii, the life suddenly extinguished," one of her ladies noted), her Majesty's actions nevertheless threw a gloomy atmosphere over the whole Court, and for a long time had an extremely depressing effect upon all

the trades which depended for their very existence upon fashion and its changes.

On the other hand, as mourning garb was a universal Victorian custom, there were shops wholly devoted to purveying it. Fashionable mourning put persons who could ill afford it to considerable expense, but it was never evaded, for the Victorians subscribed wholeheartedly to their idea that by indulging in expensive fabrics they were doing honor to the dead. Widow's caps of costly crape shaped like those of Mary Stuart, draped with long, inconvenient veils of the same perishable material were its distinguishing features and became the clichés of both art and literature. The graphic artists never lacked a public for pictures illustrating the subject of mourning and of Christian resignation to one's loss—both widely popular subjects.

As the loss of one's husband was understandably the greatest grief a woman could suffer, the rules for "deep mourning" prescribed that widows, for at least a year, could appear in public only with their faces hidden and their bodies shrouded even more blackly than nuns. After the proper interval had passed, they entered that indeterminate land of "second" or "half-mourning"— a transitional state which tolerated a gradual shading-off, like a drawing in charcoal, from the lusterless black of profound grief to the leaden gray of melancholy, and from there down the scale of sorrow to the wearing of tender violet and soft, retiring heliotrope. After this they could emerge, if they so desired, into the full brilliant color of the world about them. Less poignant losses were recognized by shorter intervals of time with less or no crape.

Mourning conventions dominated even supposedly happy occasions. When the Prince of Wales, he who was to become Edward VII on Victoria's death, was married to Princess Alexandra of Denmark, only fifteen months had elapsed since his father's death. Therefore the occasion was conducted under the conventions of half-mourning. The widowed Queen witnessed the ceremony in extreme privacy from the shelter of the Royal Closet. The bridesmaids, sisters to the groom, were arrayed in white tulle with accents of mauve ribbons, their hair wreathed with lilac-and-white garlands. The guests' costumes, while of great elegance, were uniformly subdued in color: light grays and silvers, lavenders and purples, whites and slates—quiet hues which spoke eloquently to all present of the recent royal loss.

The Queen's intense concentration on all types of memorials channelled the attention of the general public to the art of the bronze-caster and the sculptor. As a result these were busy men throughout the Victorian era. This predilection for statuary encouraged a wide range of sentimental yet questionable artifices for the demonstration of sorrow. Today most of them would be viewed not as evidence of exquisite feeling, but as distressing displays of poor taste. If, in the earlier days of the nineteenth century, one paid a visit to the resting place of Queen Louise of Prussia in Charlottenburg near Berlin, one found the tomb to be a fair white Doric temple encircled by mourning cypress and willow. "Upon a sarcophagus," says a visitor, "lay a sheet and the outline of the human form was plainly visible beneath its folds. The person with me reverently turned it back, and displayed the statue of his Queen. It is a portrait-statue recumbent, said to be a perfect resemblance—not as in death, but when she lived . . ."

Since Victoria in her expressions of personal feeling always preferred the plastic to the graphic, she was surrounded by marble and bronze facsimiles of her babies' hands, models of her favorite animals, and statuettes of objects dear to her heart. Albert's picture topped with a memorial wreath was hung on the headboard of every bed in which she slept, over the empty pillow next to hers. When she mounted the staircase at Osborne, she passed a monumental statue of the late Prince Consort portrayed as a Roman citizen. A magnificent marble bust of the dearly lamented stood by the mantel in the sitting room. Before it was daily placed a wreath of fresh flowers.

Published accounts of the royal widow's faithfulness could not fail to have an effect on sentimental persons who felt it beseemed them also to adopt—in addition to perennial "widow's weeds"—as many other outward manifestations of feeling as their means would permit. Though they could not command the best sculptors in the land to create statues, and had neither gardeners nor greenhouses to supply them daily with exquisite floral chaplets, they could at least make an attempt to preserve certain of the funeral sprays or fabricate others which would serve as permanent symbols of their loss. To keep the souvenirs of these sad occasions intact, various techniques were devised. If the flowers were white (and white and violet were the only colors permissible at Victorian funerals), they were subjected by a domestic treatment to coatings of white wax which was rendered more opaque with bismuth. But sprays of commercially prepared white artificial flowers made of wax were also frequently sent by mourners as a floral tribute, so that they could afterwards be kept under glass as a memento. Not only were these actual souvenirs of the funeral respectfully preserved, but symbolic devices were also fabricated by the sorrowing as additional memorials of Death's visit: among them were harps, anchors, and crosses. Executed in pure white wax, such objects were garlanded with blossoms which themselves had emotional significance. Especially attractive for the purpose were white roses, passion flowers, and ivy. These waxen funereal mementos were set against black velvet in the favorite recessed frame. Occasionally they were placed under glass shades just as were the flowers of colored wax; in which case they contributed their own distinctive aura of melancholy to the already cheerless parlor of the post-Civil War period. Funereal souvenirs which have survived are conclusive evidence of the unquenchable springs of Victorian emotion which could dredge up from its deepest griefs the ornamental decorations for its daily life.

221

Above and right. Courtesy, Index of American Design, National Gallery of Art

Memorial. 1881. Belated example of Paper-Cutting. Motifs were set by custom but lack of skill blurred traditional forms.

Panel of Cemetery Gate. *C.* 1845. Wood and Perot, Philadelphia. The willow, lambs, and dove in familiar melancholy amity.

The Weeping Willow was the emblem of elegant sorrow; no painted or embroidered memorial was without one. After the pressure of Victorian life increased, women had less time to devote to these sad ornaments, and the tree then lost its long-held importance in decoration.

Left. Currier and Ives lithographs replaced the hand-drawn memorial, with space reserved on the impressive monument for vital statistics.

Courtesy, Free Library of Philadelphia

A white cross wreathed with snowy ivy made an admired parlor ornament.

Above and right. Courtesy, Chester Co. Historical Society, West Chester, Pa.

Top. Memorial in watercolor. 1822.

Courtesy, Miss Marie Granger

Above. Birth, Marriage, and Death Record. Memorial of Quaker family, unusual for its elaborateness, its Pennsylvania German fractur decorations colored by a Victorian prettiness which is heightened by the frivolity of the ribbon ruching framing the notations.

Above, right. Page from an Album. 1843. "Reflections in a Churchyard," beautifully inscribed and painstakingly detailed down to the last gravestone. Such lugubrious selections were not at all unusual, for on the album's pretty pages Art, Friendship, and Death were closely allied.

Right. Young ladies wishing to paint a weeping willow could usually find a model in their drawing books from which to copy.

223

SYMBOLS
OF
BEREAVEMENT

Photo by Oscar May

Stately urns surmounting the encroaching ivy lend a classic note to a thickly wooded corner.

Below. Characteristic Victorian union of the naturalistic and Gothic.

*Courtesy, Index of American Design,
National Gallery of Art*

Though of mid-nineteenth-century origin, the Grave Markers shown here preserve a degree of eighteenth-century formality and grace.

Lower right. A variety of symbols are happily amalgamated on this valentine cut in stone: the ivy, oak, rose, wreath, book, and fluttering dove. The Gothic touch creeps in by way of the finial and crockets which perch like fat robins upon the stone's upper edge.

Photo by Oscar May

Centre. Gate for Cemetery Plot. Weeping cupid, reversed torches (symbolizing life extinguished), arabesques of poppy pods (sleep), were united to form a design fraught with emotional significance.

Photos by William Riedel

Left. Life and Death were closely interwoven. Fully aware, therefore, that it was touching a universal chord, a ladies' periodical presented—as its frontispiece for December, 1869 —that popular scene, the snowy graveyard lit by the moon. This was titled "The Last Night of the Old Year."

Right. Plot Enclosure. Simulations of the upholsterer's cords, tassels, and (*below, left*) lambrequins and cushions added softness to iron's rigidity, to marble's coldness.

Lower right. Iron Furniture Pieces, for practicality outdoors, were openwork affairs. That the grapevine design, recently revived, was an early favorite is shown by a woodcut of 1856 and by the settee, a surviving original.

Courtesy, Index of American Design, National Gallery of Art

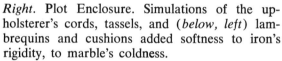

Above and left. Photo by Oscar May

GONE BUT NOT FORGOTTEN

Decorations made of the hair of loved ones were cherished mementos. Preserved under glass, they varied in scale from mere boutonnières to large wreaths made from hair of all colors. The latter were impressive, if misguided, monuments to persistence in collecting and to patience in execution.

At bottom. Flower spray of hair set off in handsome gold frame.

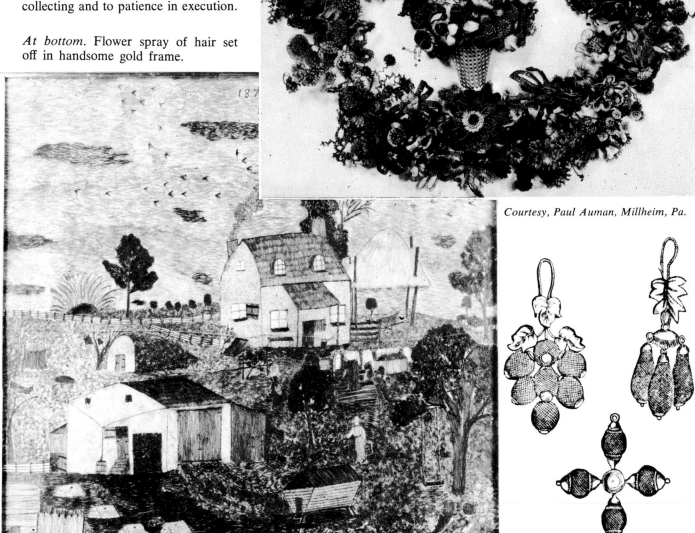

Courtesy, Paul Auman, Millheim, Pa.

Courtesy, Montgomery Co. Historical Society, Norristown, Pa.

Jewelry made of hair.

Courtesy, Philadelphia Museum of Art

Left. Centre. Primitive monochrome landscape, "The Old Homestead," 1876, executed solely with glue, strands and clippings of hair. This belated example of an outmoded technique—worked by a Pennsylvania German woman with charming fidelity to every detail—was probably prepared to be exhibited at the Centennial in 1876. Compared to this ambitious undertaking, the old-time memorials, painted with a pigment which incorporated clippings of hair, were dainty but insignificant achievements. In the early Victorian decades, hair was used (by those who delighted in a medium for the challenge it presented) to embroider portraits and decorations.

226

ALBUM 14

Of the Parlor Bedizened
With Pampas-grass, Pleatings, Tassels and Fringes
Of the Artistic Revolution
Where Beauty Contended
With Tradition
Of the Centennial &
The All-conquering Orient
Of Bric-a-brac, Rogers Groups, &
The Jap Fan Triumphant
Of Eastlake, Morris, Wilde
Sage-green and Peacock-blue
Of Aesthetes, Palettes, Rushes, Cat-tails and Cranes
Of Sunflowers Rampant &
Of Sweet Kate Greenaway
Of the Drapery-slung Cozy Corner
Where the Era
Expired

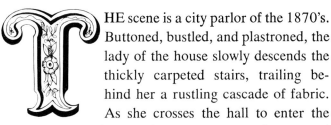

ALBUM FOURTEEN

≈ ❋ ≈

THE ARTISTIC WORLD

OF

MR. EASTLAKE

THE scene is a city parlor of the 1870's. Buttoned, bustled, and plastroned, the lady of the house slowly descends the thickly carpeted stairs, trailing behind her a rustling cascade of fabric. As she crosses the hall to enter the parlor—for she is expecting a guest recently returned from England—her train catches in one of the cloth petals of the door-rug, that thickly layered article designed to battle with drafts which creep insidiously beneath all doors. The rug's many petals, each cut and bound by her beauty-loving fingers, offer such resistance to the stiff, pleated flounces of her train that it is disengaged only with effort.

The parlor is her poem, dedicated to Beauty and the Social Graces. Glancing about appreciatively, she reassures herself that all its appointments are in the precise spots designated for them: the centre-table bears its up-to-date paraphernalia—the stereoscope and tray of cards, the kaleidoscope, and the albums, both photograph and autograph.

How much prettier the table looks since she has concealed its old marble top with the richly braided and embroidered cover. Only a close examination of its supports, now fortunately hidden beneath the cover's full circular sweep, will reveal its out-of-dateness. She twirls the piano stool, rapt in admiration of the new *couvrette* she has just completed for it, an ornamental protective sheath spotted with lumpy flowers crocheted of red and black wools firmly fastened down on a white net ground. Already vastly impractical, it has been rendered even more so by an edging of fat tassels which bounce vivaciously in response to the twirling.

Her glance falls approvingly on the mantel dressed up for the first time in its new velvet lambrequin—the best quality velvet, of course! On this superb appliqué decoration she has lavished many weeks of work, but she is most amply repaid by the results, for nothing could have added a note of greater elegance. At the ends of the mantel the marble scrollings of acanthus escape from the heavy velvet swathings and confirm what the mistress of the house has striven to conceal: that the mantelpiece, too, is of white marble, a substance which to her generation seems unpleasantly stark and cold.

As the lady herself is wrapped in many layers of material, she must do the same for her possessions. To veil the basic simplicities of the brick-colored flowerpots at the windows she has shrouded them with admirably crocheted skins of shaded wools. And the slender walnut stands which support the flowerpots are likewise fitted with their own elegant coverings made to match the lambrequin.

One of the picture frames hangs slightly askew; she moves over to straighten it, admiring, as she does so, the summer frame-covers. To be sure, it is a bit early in the season for these protections, but her daughters have been so eager to confect them (each green leaf cut by hand from tissue paper) that she has not had the heart to forbid their premature installation. Thus equipped, the parlor is ready for summer and its pest of flies; these plagues will have no opportunity to bespeck *her* gold frames, at least! Let the lazy among her contemporaries content themselves with their ugly summer swathings of tarlatan on picture frame and chandelier; she herself prefers the pretty old-fashioned paper adornments made by her girls. In fact, there is no end to the delightful

229

things they contrive to protect surfaces, to disguise function, and, in addition, to contribute notes of "elegant refinement" to articles of domestic use. Each summer the girls adorn the fireplace in a different fashion. This year they have installed a "cataract screen"—a veritable Niagara of frayed strips of tarlatan. This inflammable object is fastened in the chimney breast in such a manner that it streams gracefully over the grate —a triumph of the romantic fancy over the ugly and utilitarian.

Noting something in one of the more distant reaches of the long room which needs a corrective tweak, she sweeps toward her objective, the crisp pleatings of her train overturning in their passage one of the many footstools which constitute a never-ending hazard in the tortuous route she must follow between the chairs, the small tables crowded with knickknacks and all the other stylish appurtenances. Having righted the footstool she replaces the embroidered and tasseled cloth doily which serves as protection to its beaded velvet covering. With anticipation she turns to a corner of the room which, until lately, has annoyed her by its emptiness. But now that she has installed a pedestal, and on it a female statuette, she receives a thrill of aesthetic pleasure from the sight of that sprightly draped figure, its immaculate whiteness of breast and back glimmering through the veiling of soft *tulle* she has recently added. This last fastidious accent has won the praise of all her friends, themselves specialists in ultra-refinement in decoration.

And now just a touch to the colored plumes of pampas grass in the pair of elaborate vases on the mantel shelf and a tender flick of the finger to the tassels dripping from her new gilded bamboo workstand. At last she seats herself to await her visitor. Nervously she adjusts a fold of her costume, delighting the while in its bizarre color scheme—that bold alliance of azure and olive which she would never have dared adopt had she not read that the great Monsieur Worth employed it frequently. Then she wonders whether her visitor—this young architect fresh from his studies overseas—will approve of her and her parlor.

Suddenly he is announced and she rises to greet him, not a kilt-pleat of her many flounces out of place, not a wrinkle added to her panier poufs, for she has been sitting and moving with considered discreetness. Not for an instant has she forgotten to maintain the stiff perfection of the puffs, loopings, ribbon bows, cascades of ruffles, and other elaborate manipulations of material in which she is enveloped.

The visit is over. On his way back to his hotel, the young architect tries to shake off the impressions of airlessness, of the layerings and veneerings and all the earnest but misguided strivings towards beauty with which the house is crammed. To what extremes would women not go in their eternal desire for embellishments! How idiotic that fluffy hearth curtain! It suggested nothing so much as a fashionably dressed young lady with the upper part of her body caught in the chimney! What is wrong with the world that it is so afraid of simplicity and repose, so terrified of the word *bare?* Why does this word convey nothing but starkness to his feminine contemporaries—why, in fact, does it seem to be only a synonym for *nudity?* To the contemporary mind, nudity seems intolerable, whether disclosed by the human form or by anything else which parades its elementary structure unadorned. To escape the implication of *bareness,* women, besides covering themselves with layers of stuffs, seem driven to superimpose bearskin rug on figured carpet, drapery on drapery, and to hang fringes and tassels on everything.

But why censor only the women? Certainly much of the ugliness of manufactured articles resulted from a like urge on the part of industry to embellish its products, hoping by bedizenment to cover up a hopelessly bad foundation. When would the revolution in taste which had recently originated in England begin to clear out the stuffiness which was cluttering up the interior of the Victorian house? When would American women learn of this new movement which was going to change the whole style of their decorative furnishings? Certainly it was time for some alteration.

To William Morris, the English architect, must be given credit for creating the movement which effected a reform in public taste. Most persons had no chance to see, much less own, any of the articles which were produced under his supervision for they were far too expensive for the average purse. Nevertheless, the influence of his ideas eventually became inescapable in the whole field of decorative arts. Any interest today in Arts and Crafts is directly traceable to the sound aesthetic principles laid down by this remarkable Victorian and his associates.

By temperament William Morris was spiritually akin to mediaeval life and methods. As a child he rode about in a toy suit of armor, and at the age of four he began to saturate himself in the romances of Sir Walter Scott. An avid naturalist even as a boy, he developed his taste for botany through a careful study of Gerard's great *Herbal.* By this study he did more than advance his botanical knowledge; his close examination of the magnificent woodcuts in this volume furnished him with a form of stylization which he adapted with great success in later life to the wallpaper and textile designs for which he became widely noted. In 1857, when Morris wished to marry, he could find nothing on the market which he considered fit to place in the simple, original house he was planning for his future home. Everything was vulgar and ugly. A man of many talents and a master craftsman, boldly he faced the task of designing and creating all of its interior furnishings.

So successful were Morris's innovations that he was inspired to enter the decorating field as a professional. In 1861, he and certain sympathetic pre-Raphaelite painters set up in business, ready to undertake the entire furnishing of a house. Established firms of decorators resented the intrusion of this new organization with its utterly novel ideas—and were no doubt further displeased when the young firm took space to display its wares at the Exhibition of 1862. Here its unique productions could be examined by millions instead of by the few who were already patrons of the firm. The displays could not have failed to make some impression for nothing like them had been seen since mediaeval days. The feminine eye was particularly drawn to the beautiful embroideries—the portières, furniture coverings, and wall panels executed by certain ladies in the families of the firm. Although these pieces were produced by techniques with which the lady visitors were perfectly familiar, the designs and the fabrics on which they were worked—the coarse serges and rough linens—were utterly different from anything to which fashion had hitherto given its approval.

But the world of the 1870's was not to be given time to allow the healthy winds of Morris's doctrines to blow away the inane antimacassars and lambrequins. Nor was the decade to be given an opportunity to replace these things with even modest demonstrations of attempts to follow Morris's famous rule—"Have nothing in your house that you do not know to be useful, or believe to be beautiful." Had the latter part of the Victorian era followed Morris's injunction, it might have escaped much of the censure heaped upon it for its astounding tastelessness. But Morris's ideas had scarcely begun to infiltrate the public mind when they were contested by other far more powerful influences, those backed by industry and commercial expansion. Unable to choose

among all the aesthetic contradictions presented to her by industrial competitiveness, the average Victorian homemaker let herself be overwhelmed by the whole combination.

Prior to 1872, no one in Europe had ever crossed the ocean for the express purpose of carrying the gospel of "the beautiful" to that "uncouth" and "bombastic" American public which so sadly lacked aesthetic enlightenment. But in that fateful year the bearers of European culture appeared here for the first time in person to brave audiences composed of hordes of extremely receptive "barbarians." The pronouncements of the overseas visitor which were to work the greatest change in the American home, however, were imparted not from the platform but from the pages of a book which appeared on American bookstore shelves in that same year of 1872. In view of the uproar it was to create, the title of this work was pleasantly unpretentious, merely a tactful *Hints on Household Taste,* presented by Charles Locke Eastlake, a well-known English architect. Published first in England in 1868, Eastlake's propaganda for decorative reforms had probably not created much of a furor in his own country, for the ideas he voiced had been advocated for some years by other thoughtful members of his and allied professions. But none had hit on so effective a title—a title which would take his reforms directly to the householder.

After *Hints* made its American bow, Eastlake's ideas had an enormous influence. Every young couple with any pretensions to culture owned a copy which they studied avidly, for the work dealt in a chatty manner with their own problems. From the front door to the roof, the book pointed a critical finger at the shortcomings of the average house, and in so direct a fashion that it left no doubt as to the decorative revolution its author intended. Furthermore, this volume introduced into the American vocabulary of home-furnishing two hitherto unused words: "artistic" and "inartistic," which were now applied to a whole new set of values, and soon those old and tried measuring rods, "elegance" and "refinement", went into the discard. As an architect, Eastlake examined everything from the point of view of common sense. He was hopeful that good furniture could be turned out at prices the public could afford and that—even though produced by machines—it would emerge from its multiple processes not too degraded in style. None of the period's shams and refined affectations escaped him—neither the fake reproductions of Jacobean and Gothic antiques which were then being turned

231

Philadelphia's new Academy of the Fine Arts and the "Eastlake Organ" both made their bow in 1876. Strikingly suggestive of each other, they exemplify the period's idea of strong design.

surface were difficult to harmonize with the low-toned color schemes on which fashion now beamed. Mr. Eastlake looked upon the cheaper encaustic tile and found it good. He indicated that it should be used not only for flooring in hall and vestibule but for wainscoting as well.

But the manufacturers were not content to restrict themselves to encaustic's rather modest effects. At once they plunged into a veritable orgy of all varieties of tile production for domestic uses. After the public saw the tile exhibits at the Centennial Exhibition, tiles became enormously popular decorations. Not only were they used in fireplaces, but they were also introduced into furniture and set into interior woodwork, window boxes, and brick housefronts. Encaustic tiles, dull-finished and quiet in tone, were in themselves unobjectionable; but when industry brought out the majolica tile, not only highly colored but in addition embossed in reliefs which shattered the glaze into a monotonous and irritating series of reflections, it produced an object for which there is no artistic defense.

Eastlake asked his readers to reflect upon the absurdity and unsanitariness of draperies which untidily swept the floor, and of dust-holding cornices. To those who were convinced by his arguments, he suggested an idea for their decorative as well as sanitary salvation—the use of easily cared-for washable textiles, such as cretonnes and the new striped fabrics then coming out of the Orient. Backed by Eastlake's authority, the progressives discarded the massive draped valances, and, furthermore, boldly adopted another of their mentor's proposals, the radical notion that they hang their new curtains in straight folds instead of the ostentatious loopings so dear to the decorator. And that they daringly suspend them in mediaeval fashion by means of rings sliding frankly on a visible brass or wooden rod. Unquestionably practical, this simple idea was nevertheless subjected to a type of vulgar exaggeration in scale. This can be credited only to the Victorian preference for an effect of massiveness and solidity in everything—even in such minor objects as curtain poles. Though poles often supported nothing heavier than lace, both rod and rings suggested visually that there was no weight—not even that of the heaviest velvets—which they were not capable of sustaining.

All the readers of Eastlake's *Hints* piously abjured gaudy wallpapers, covered their floors with small patterned rugs, and painted or papered their rooms in the low tones advised by their authority. Furthermore, no ornament was placed, no bracket chosen, no picture

out in quantity for those who were fleeing from the "vulgarities" of rosewood, nor the painted imitations of marble which served as wall decoration in hall and vestibule. In this latter area of the domestic interior, Eastlake had to wait only a short time to see what he considered improvement, for a new manufactured product, the encaustic tile, was about to supplant that old favorite, marble, whose light hues and uncompromising

232

hung, without consulting *the book*. But when they had studied the fine sketches which the architect improvised to illustrate his ideas of simplicity and honesty in design and construction, and then demanded "Eastlake furniture" at the warehouses, they were told flatly that there was no such style. But Eastlake's converts were insistent; had they not seen the pictures in his *Hints*? Finally, in order to satisfy repeated demands of this character, the manufacturers were forced to invent a complete line of furniture "after Eastlake," basing it entirely on the few admirable illustrations he used to embellish his literary effort. "Eastlake" then became the name of a style, and the term was attached to pieces which violated every principle of the quite sensible reforms the English architect advocated. When the trend in furnishing swung over to something else, the term "Eastlake" became—and still is—an epithet of reproach, a memorial quite undeserved by one who was fundamentally a sincere opponent of all industrial shams.

To manufacturers, always on the search for new ideas, the demand for this non-existent style came as a godsend—particularly welcome since the style was fitted with a good sturdy English name which anyone could enunciate. No longer need their customers struggle with the pronunciation of *Louis Quatorze* or *Louis Seize*. Eastlake himself never gave his style a name. Some of his professional contemporaries referred to it as "domestic Gothic"; others called it "the homelike style."

Since Eastlake laid stress on the principle that function should be accented, not hidden, he gave particular emphasis to metal fitments—those fine bold hinges and escutcheons which added so much to the decorative quality of mediaeval furniture. Easy to imitate, these characteristic features of Eastlake's designs were woefully caricatured by the furniture manufacturers who reproduced them cheaply in stamped iron or irrelevant brass. As ornaments they became almost as reprehensible an embellishment of the furniture dubbed "Eastlake" as were the glued-on scrollings and unnecessary curvings and shapings of the popular so-called "French" furniture so deplored by this architect. Study of Eastlake's sketches discloses a further attachment to the ancient mortise-and-tenon joint. This he transformed into a decorative accent, as he did the bandsaw's scrollings and the honest turnings of the lathe. The conservative eye, trained to curves and French polish, discerned no beauty whatsoever in his rectilinear innovations. To its unsympathetic view, his stained or oiled (never varnished) oak furniture trimmed so brazenly with

Eastlake, in proferring a sketch showing how draperies might be sensibly hung, used an antique weapon as curtain rod—a suggestion which resulted in startling parodies. See *below*.

ugly metal hinges resembled nothing so much as a section of an old barn.

Though the American conservatives continued to live in their houses filled with ponderous walnut scrolleries while the young moderns went over wholeheartedly to the newer version of solidity put forward by Morris, Eastlake, and their supporters, neither type of householder could insulate himself entirely against the decorative influences which permeated every corner of the

country as a result of the Centennial Exhibition, held in 1876 in celebration of the anniversary of American Independence.

Fifty-one countries brought their arts and manufactures to Philadelphia, and, before the exhibition closed, almost ten million visitors beheld them. In this enormous group was a larger proportion of the middle and lower classes than had ever before attended any similar show—a circumstance which could not help but work a change in taste. Though one of the obvious benefits of a visit to the Centennial was an intangible harvest of culture, this great section of the American public, unfamiliar with the higher reaches of cultural attainment, vastly preferred the concrete. Thus, they returned to their homes laden with haphazard selections of the unique arts which emanated from all corners of the world. Among this influx, by far the most insidious, the most pervasive, were the Japanese goods.

Only a few years before the Centennial—in 1866, to be precise—Japan, after long deliberation, made up her mind to become part of the modern Western world— and then entered it with amazing speed. Very shortly, Oriental bazaars began doing business in the large cities, and through the Centennial every corner of the country acquired a superficial acquaintance with the arts of the East. The Oriental exhibits drew enormous crowds, and as a result myriads of lacquered boxes, embroideries, carved pieces of ivory, miniature pagodas, and countless fans were carefully packed in portmanteau and telescope to be added to the happy confusion of bric-a-brac already installed on whatnot or mantelpiece. Through the medium of the Centennial, other objects seemingly almost as alien as Japanese goods were introduced into the staid Victorian home. Such were the German cuckoo-clocks, the hand-carved brackets, and innumerable other examples of Swiss handicrafts which the sentimental promptly fell in love with. Large carved Swiss bears presenting card trays, or circling their forepaws to hold umbrellas contributed a terrifying note to dimly lit hallways; while in innumerable sitting rooms or parlors, glum wooden images of the Lion of Lucerne were made to lie down sentimentally on the mantelpiece with the Staffordshire lambs already in residence.

As at all other international shows of industrial arts, the ceramic exhibits aroused vast interest, inspired equally by pyramidal displays of grotesque water jugs from the hands of Spanish or Turkish potters, and by a broad counter of exquisitely decorated Austrian porcelain. The German ceramic exhibits included examples of German steins. As novelties, these caught the public's eye and soon the German beer stein was introduced as a decoration in the middle-class American home, certainly a curious object to be found in that frequently "temperance" locale. To be sure, the decorative use of the stein appeared to have the endorsement of Eastlake, for he featured one or two, together with other pieces of artistic pottery, as ornaments on sideboard and on overmantel shelving illustrated in the *Hints*. But the Americans who, trusting to this pictorial authority, purchased German steins did not realize that those specimens to which Eastlake gave his approval were antique examples of sound craftsmanship and not the cheap, slovenly decorated article which Germany, because of this new fad, now began to ship over here by the boatload.

Eastlake's sketch for the overmantel just mentioned solved a problem: how to provide a central spot on which to display examples of decorative objects which were really worthy of collection. For its day the idea of the overmantel was a sound one, for it was hoped that its adoption would wean the Victorian householder from her attachment to trivial ornaments and to the innumerable small tables on which she exhibited them. It should not be laid to Eastlake's account if the less discriminating of his readers used this new architectural feature not to display the best in decorative accessories but rather as a more palatial housing for the gewgaws removed from the whatnot—a piece which promptly went out of style after the overmantel came in. Eastlake's overmantel was comparatively simple in design, but the architectural monstrosities it spawned were probably the worst decorative eyesores of the period. For some decades the late-nineteenth-century house was presided over by this monumental "gallery chimney-piece" (as it was also called). Its intricately shaped shelves and brackets were frequently backed with bevelled mirrors to add a further showy note.

As the century waned, it became necessary to invent a further architectural feature—its use restricted fortunately to the dining room—in order to cope with the ever expanding collections of steins, china, and bric-a-brac. This was the plate-rail, a grooved wooden molding which made a separation between the body of the wall and the frieze. The plate-rail cost but little to install, and, until women tired of caring for the rows of plates and steins it supported, it had an enormous popularity which lasted far into the present century.

At the Centennial, those who studied the Japanese

235

ceramics viewed them set within an ornamental enclosure of bamboo. To a public which had never before seen it, this giant grass was in itself quite as unique, as interesting, as were the ceramic displays. Bamboo was taken at once to the public's heart, and articles made of this golden reed—or even shaped in imitation of it—were all the rage in the latter part of Victoria's reign. Painted, gilded, or left *au naturel,* chairs, cabinets, and stands of this frail-looking material introduced in the midst of the somber solidities of the Victorian interior were testimony that the Oriental invasion of the Occident had been completely successful. Seen here, also for the first time, were Japanese folding screens embroidered with exquisite delicacy; these dazzled the feminine public and suggested hitherto undreamed-of possibilities in needlework. Novel inspirations for embroidery would also be engendered by a display sent over by Great Britain, an especially impressive show being contributed by the recently established Royal School of Art Needlework. This organization, founded to encourage a taste for decorative art, operated with the Queen's particular approval. Among its exhibits were pieces designed by William Morris as well as by Walter Crane—artist, designer, and illustrator—whose influence was equally notable in many fields of late Victorian decoration. Royal needlework was represented by a cheval fire screen and an embroidered tablecloth made by Victoria's daughters. Of particular interest in this rich display were screen panels embroidered on purple velvet, on which bloomed an English garden of lilies, campanulas, poppies, and foxgloves. Adorned with graceful arrangements of lilies certain curtains of dark chocolate drew every feminine eye as well.

For those who found these richly surfaced screens, curtains, and bedspreads a little too radical for their taste, and who derived pleasure only from that with which they were already familiar, there were satisfying displays of traditional Victorian crafts. Conservative needleworkers were reassured to see that other women had not yet given up stitching woolwork portraits of George Washington or of the Queen. Here, as in the Crystal Palace in 1851, visitors could again marvel at portraits worked in human hair; and those who sought for leather or wax flowers, illuminated texts, moss pictures, frames made of pressed leaves, or articles made of fish-scales were not disappointed. A hint, however, that the time-honored arts were about to make way for something new might be deduced from a few exhibits of wood carving done by women, and of oil painting on satin and on velvet "tidies." Innocuous in themselves, these latter decorations nevertheless pointed to the ultimate extinction of the older crafts. For when women turned to painting on textiles—a quick and comparatively easy method of achieving an effect—it was in tacit acknowledgment of the fact that they no longer had either the patience or the deftness to execute as tedious and highly skilled works as did their immediate forebears.

The Oriental decorative approach, its novel selections and arrangements of Nature's materials caught the Occident's attention immediately. As a result, Victorian taste, which till now had been wholly engrossed with hothouse flowers and pampered garden darlings, would turn for ornamental purposes to the American wildings, plants hitherto completely ignored. And in this re-examination of the floral world, interest would center on species with a perpendicular habit of growth, tall plants being more adaptable for compositions on the kind of objects which were coming into fashion—the screen panels, portières and silken banners, all Japanese-inspired. Among tall plants, conspicuous favorites were the giant sunflower, iris, hollyhock, and long-stemmed lily. Surpassing even these, however, in general appeal was the cat-tail or bulrush. All these soaring plants flourished weedily within their rectilinear confines—the cat-tails in such immoderate profusion that their numbers might well have filled the Great Dismal Swamp. In fact, so universally was the modest cat-tail used, not only in domestic but also in industrial design, that, together with the heron (another Japanese introduction) it might easily stand as a pictograph of the whole post-Centennial period. In its very simplicity of line lay the cat-tail's artistic doom; its brown velvet cylinder and the green swords of its foliage were so fatally easy to depict—even by the most unskilled of amateurs—that they were eventually caricatured out of existence.

Only rarely did the decorators of the post-Centennial period depart from their vertical floral favorites; when they did, their choice fell upon trailing plants, a selection again influenced by Japanese art. Under the determined guidance of the ladies, trumpet flowers or blackberry vines straggled with studied nonchalance across the hand-painted, plush-framed china plaques, wrapped themselves around the shoulders of jars and punch-bowls, sprawled across the glass of mirrors or languidly draped themselves over the glossy blackness of long narrow wood panels—another modish decoration inspired by the Japanese *kakemono*. Before the home decorators of the seventies and eighties ceased to play with ideas borrowed from the Orient, they diverted themselves further by the fabrication of some appallingly tasteless travesties of the beautiful embroidered screen panels of the Japanese. Most degraded of all were paintings on plush or velvet, stroked on in thick oil with a pen to simulate the needlework they found too tedious to attempt!

Those who recall late Victorian furnishings can always evoke amusement by relating their memories of the humble articles—the rolling-pin, flatiron, shovel and coal scuttle which, after undergoing a beauty treatment, became "ornaments" which were used to decorate the middle-class interior. For the Victorian woman to move these utilitarian pieces from the kitchen into the parlor seems today a singularly incomprehensible gesture, as there was nothing about these objects which could be regarded by *her* standards either as "elegant," "artistic," or "refined." But if one considers them as symbols, their elevation to the rank of "ornaments" was indicative of the change which had taken place in the social status of their owner. Having herself become a "lady"—at least in her own estimation—she could signalize her attainment of that ineffable state by glorifying these tokens of her former servitude.

But let us not view these ladies of the gilded flatirons and rolling-pins with too great a sense of superiority, for women at the present time are doing a parallel thing. Only today instead of "artistic" they term it "amusing" when they employ an honorably battered shoemaker's bench as a tea or cocktail table, or transplant a time-scarred wooden kitchen-sink from an old farm shed to their "early American" dining rooms, unaltered except for cleaning and waxing. Indeed, the ladies of the "eighties" were far more fastidious; none of their common utensils was given a decorative rating until it was made seemly with a coat of gold bronze, which then was ornamented with painted floral sprays; sometimes instead it was covered in great part with a layer of embroidered plush. Furthermore, in its passage from kitchen to parlor, each piece was detained for additional embellishment—the ribbon bows and streamers which added the final bewitchment. In their fondness for such gewgaws, Americans went even further than their English prototypes, who thought it *chic,* in 1880, to gild a milkmaid's stool, cover it with a satin cushion embroidered in apple blossoms and use it, quite in the tradition of Marie Antoinette and Le Hameau, to give a piquant touch of rusticity to their elegant drawing rooms.

In the mysterious mélange of latter-day nineteenth-century decoration, it would be difficult to separate the influence of the Japanese arts from the equally powerful effect of the "aesthetic movement" which sprang up in England in the late seventies. Actually, there was no such movement. But as Whistler had already called the public's attention to the beauties of Japanese art, and Morris to the virtues of the mediaeval craftsman, the term was both an appropriate as well as a useful one with which to label the complex synthesis derived from the union of Oriental inspiration with mediaeval artistry. And so it stuck. The most conspicuous proponent of the aesthetic movement was Oscar Wilde. Even while studying at Oxford, he brought much ridicule upon himself by espousing a violent interest in "Art for Art's sake"—doctrine again already promulgated by Whistler. In his rooms at college Wilde made a decorative feature of "aesthetic objects"—sunflowers, peacock feathers, lilies, and old blue china. Whistler had long collected Japanese porcelains and he was to paint his famous "Peacock Room" in 1877 while Wilde was still in the University. But it was Wilde's lively genius for publicity which would draw the attention of the world to these innocent objects of decoration and plant one or another of them, either as actualities or as decorative images thereof, in practically every house in the land.

Wilde acquired a genuine following in London, an artistic group that enthusiastically took up the new decorative ideas he championed. The feminine members of the aesthetic cult went in for dress reform, a necessary and a long-overdue movement. These new garments clung to the figure in long, simple, mediaeval lines. With such earnestness did Wilde's followers take up the new modes that by 1880 both their appearances and affectations were furnishing Du Maurier, *Punch's* gifted illustrator, with a rich mine of subjects for caricature. Every little while that talented artist's pencil detailed for readers of that estimable journal the concerns of the world of the aesthetes—a world which, at least in his drawings, revolved entirely around "artistic" colors, wallpapers, "dadoes," Japanese fans, sunflowers, and sprays of white lilies in jars of blue china.

As leader of the aesthetes Wilde was never restrained in his aims by diffidence. In fact, in order that he might never fail to catch the public eye, he wore in his buttonhole either a lily or a sunflower—blossoms which invariably succeeded in administering the shock he intended. Though this innovation in boutonnières was never adopted by his scandalized contemporaries, other ideas of Wilde's were later taken on by persons who would have utterly disavowed them had they known where they originated. Such was the old-time fashion of painting woodwork white. Wilde revived it while still in Oxford; two decades passed before it was in general use. And the spotlight which *Punch* turned on his harmless pieces of blue china was so powerful that it had the opposite of the effect intended; indeed, it set the whole world to collecting examples of similar-hued porcelains.

A Philistine*

Take away all your adornments aesthetical,
Plates of blue china and bits of sage green,
Though you may call me a monster heretical,
I can't consider them fit to be seen.
Etchings and paintings I loathe and abominate,
Grimly I smile at the name of BURNE JONES
Hating his pictures where big chins predominate—
Over lean figures with angular bones.

Buy me what grinning stage rustics call "farniture,"
Such as was used by our fathers of old:
Take away all your nonsensical garniture,
Tapestry curtains and borders of gold.
Give me the ancient and solid mahogany,
Mine be the board what will need no repairs;
Don't let me see, as I sit at my grog, any
Chippendale tables or spindle-legged chairs.

Hang up a vivid vermillion wall-paper,
Covered with roses of gorgeous hue,
Matching a varnished and beautiful hall-paper,
Looking like marble so polished and new.
Carpets should all show a floral variety,
Wreaths intermingling of yellow and red
So, when it enters my home, will Society
Say, "here's a house whence aesthetics have fled."

On the stage Gilbert and Sullivan's *Patience* travestied the absurdities of the "aesthetes" out of existence. But the publicity of comedy and of caricature was not able to wipe out the beneficent decorative influences set in action by the movement—for the reforms for which it agitated were the wholly legitimate offspring of the artistic revolution sponsored years before by Morris and the Pre-Raphaelites.

Although Wilde is credited by the satirists of the 1880's with having first introduced the peacock feather, the lily, and the sunflower into the world of decorative art, he actually only directed the public's attention to motifs which, in truth, had been in ornamental use for

Punch, Nov. 20, 1880.

"Aesthetic Lady and Woman of Fashion." From *Punch,* 1881.

some years. Two decades before Wilde ever wore his first sunflower, Morris had perceived its ornamental possibilities when he turned to those coarse and easily painted golden disks in order to fill up the troublesome foreground of a mural. At the Centennial the sunflower was a motif of consequence for its flaunting blossom was conspicuously featured on "The Queen's Curtain," a simply hung pair of rich brown velvet portières topped with a flat, straight-edged valance. Planned to be used at Windsor, the sunflower design had been suggested for the curtains by none other than her Majesty herself. With the stamp of royal approval on this certainly bucolic motif, future popularity was assured. The English Exhibit also displayed a magnificent sunflower quilt worked in the same appliqué technique.

The simple forms of sunflower and lily lent themselves so easily to this new technique (appliqué, as now used, was really a revival of an antique Renaissance craft) that their attraction was irresistible. By the time Wilde lectured in the United States in 1882, his audiences were filled with women engaged in working on the latest vogue, the "Oscar Crazy Quilt." To make this new variation in the familiar field of folk art, women centered blocks of fabric with appliqués of sunflowers worked out in a yellow fabric of more or less elegance.

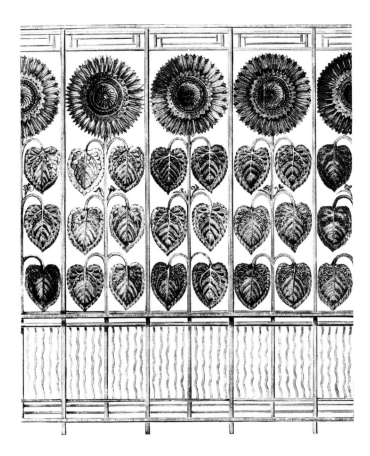

Screen of iron sunflowers was an innovation in design.

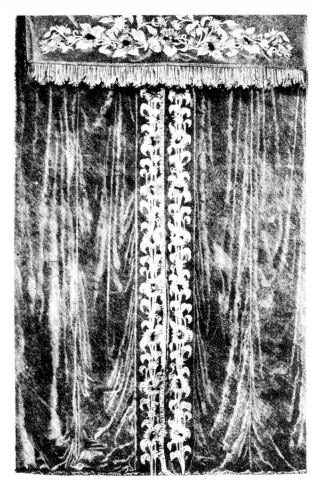

"The Queen's Curtain." Simple lines became fashionable.

These were set against a background of the fashionable "crazy-quilt" texturing.

Another earmark of post-Centennial decoration is the lavish use of the fan as ornament. In 1867, Whistler, when decorating his own house, introduced a few purple fans on the walls and ceiling of a blue room. A few years later, ladies at social gatherings displayed a fleeting affection for really gigantic fans. By the late 1870's, Japanese fans, together with cat-tails and sunflowers, were solidly entrenched as reigning decorative royalties. In informal interiors both flat and folding fans were tacked up as friezes or were crossed and placed, trophy fashion, over doorways. Dutifully following Oriental example, the Occidental world copied the simple forms of fans in various types of fancywork. Japanese fans were wedged behind nearly every picture frame and mantel ornament, for in this fashion the ladies who considered them "artistic" could indulge in a spree of cheap "art." In order to supply the demand, Japanese fans of paper and of silk were imported so lavishly and were marketed so cheaply that, after an extended period of popularity, they inevitably palled. Indeed, so satiated did the world become with the very idea of fans that it is now difficult to picture the time when they were thought of as a fascinating novelty.

On the "aesthetic" cult is laid the responsibility for immersing the whole late Victorian period in a bath of "artistic" hues—a term then applicable only to the tertiaries of the color scale. No primary color was ever allowed to penetrate this select "aesthetic" circle: no honest reds, or pure yellows, or frank blues. Instead, their legitimate place in the decorative arts was usurped by a large and poetically named group of low tones—reduced colors which then enjoyed a popularity never again regained. This range included every variety of rust, ochre, peacock-blue, citron, olive, and sage green.

The inception of the vogue for subdued hues can be credited to William Morris. As a sensitive colorist, Morris could not bring himself to use the brilliant aniline dyes which were then the only thing available for his purposes; not only did they fade quickly, but they were too intense to fit into his schemes. His only alternative was to experiment with vegetable dye-stuffs, and the neutral tones mentioned above were the result of these early trials. When Morris finally achieved the pure, fast colors he was seeking, he discarded the dull colors of his early ventures, in fact, repudiated them completely. And though he grew to loathe the very sound, not to mention the sight, of "sage green," the public, together with his many imitators, forever associated with him

"Aunt Perlina's Bedquilt is returned as Not Suitable for Exhibition at the Centennial."

Omnes: "Not sootable, indeed!—not sootable! My 'pinion is, that show will be a failure." *Harper's Bazar*, 1876.

Victorian artistic eclecticism, while embracing nearly everything, had only scorn for "the primitive."

these bilious hues.

As a result of this definite alteration in color schemes, even the assortment of plants selected for interior embellishment underwent a change. Since the aesthetes shuddered at the blatant cheerfulness of fuchsia, geranium, and begonia, they had of necessity to turn to non-flowering plants whose foliage was of a decorous dullness. Choice fell upon the aspidistra—a plant never quite dead and never quite alive—and on palms fashionably olive in hue. The fringed arcs of the latter were always useful to break the vertical lines of straight-hanging portière and curtain—those austere lines to which the generation was not yet accustomed.

Other curving lines were provided by the drooping fern fronds which were supported in soft splendor by the majolica jardinière set on its matching pedestal—these articles most often being a pair of gaudy and horrible examples of ceramics.

In the midst of the antagonistic decorative influences which made such a seething whirlpool of latter-day Victorian taste, sentimentality, that once lusty growth, ran great danger of disappearing entirely. There seemed little for the tender and delicate heart to feed upon.

Though it supplied an endless world of inspiration, Japanese decoration, since it represented an alien civilization, offered nothing but aesthetic sustenance. Even if one stuck Japanese fans behind every picture frame; even if one centered one's interest on the fashionable dragonflies and insects, these were nevertheless cold creatures with no Occidental emotional associations, and left one's heart quite unmoved.

Some comfort for the emotions, however, and even a decided improvement in one's surroundings could be extracted from the new fashion for collecting the furniture of an earlier America. This particular "mania," supposedly aroused by the Centennial Exhibition, is credited with interesting Americans in their historic background. Those who already possessed or had "picked up" specimens of Colonial furniture (at this time called "Revolutionary") derived considerable sentimental as well as aesthetic pleasure from these fine specimens of craftsmanship. And at the same time they discovered that an interest in one's own background could be quite as productive of romantic and stimulating emotions as was the imagined world of Scott's novels. As usual, the idea was soon taken up by the less discriminating. Down from their attics came the spinning wheel and grandmother's splint-bottomed chair, to be dressed up with bows of ribbon and "tidies" of silk and plush. Bedecked in this patronizing manner, the simple old pieces were posed as frivolous decorations before the coal-burning grate, itself a feeble mockery of the great flaming logs which had once furnished them with a warm background.

Other less fortunate sentimentalists, attached even in the swirling seventies to outmoded moss-rose buds and forget-me-nots, were saddened when they found their modest favorites pushed aside by the vulgar cat-tails, the gaudy sunflowers, and other bold decorative newcomers. Fortunately for these folk bereft of their world of the sweetly pretty, there suddenly appeared on the horizon an artist whose work filled not only all their artistic needs but soothed their hearts as well. These were the delightful illustrations of Kate Greenaway, the young woman whose pictorializations of children, landscape, animals, and flowers had enormous popularity during the last decades of the Queen's reign. Artists and public alike were charmed by the sincerity and delicacy of these children who moved sedately, or romped rhythmically, on Christmas cards and picture books—children dressed in the simple, quaint, and utterly forgotten costumes of the early nineteenth century. Credit must be given to the world of fashion for at once perceiving the charm of these costumes. Around 1880 it introduced the Kate Greenaway styles, the first example of a trend towards simplicity in children's dress. These new costumes were an immediate success, and during the next decade or so the most tastefully garbed children on both sides of the ocean were those arrayed in this picturesque, becoming mode.

But even the artistic flawlessness and innocent graces of the quaint Greenaway drawings were not adequate defense against that kind of commercial manipulation which always vulgarizes a motif in order to render it more acceptable to that great section of the public which invariably prefers the exaggeratedly sugar-coated to the plain and wholesome. Since they were a *novelty*, the world of industry pounced at once on Miss Greenaway's defenseless children, for it knew a gold mine when it saw one. With complete unconcern, it pinned Kate Greenaway's pretty, melodious name to a wide range of mediocre mass-produced objects, and thus eventually succeeded in destroying all interest in what is still as delightful a picture-book world as it was on the day when the drawings of the young English girl

first captivated the public fancy. Lithographers grew rich with colored prints imitating her very individual style, and industrial designers found her books a fresh source of ideas. Soon fanciers of commonplace bric-a-brac were able to purchase a motley crew of caramel-colored bisque Greenaway figurines to add to their collection of ornaments. And those who were by this time flooding the market with atrocious designs suitable for home embroidery stamping discovered that the Greenaway illustrations furnished endless subject matter for their patterns. Women stamped Kate Greenaway motifs on all kinds of textiles—"tidies," towels, tablecloths and lambrequins, to mention but a few. The contours of the little figures were so easily defined in simple outline stitch that the good little girls of the eighties often received their elementary home instruction in needlework in this pleasant fashion, instead of by means of the tedious sampler of their mothers and grandmothers.

In the last decades of the nineteenth century, patterns produced for popular taste were sometimes of an extraordinary silliness. Stately walnut beds flaunted pillow shams which carried sentimental pictures, etched with a needle in red cotton, touchingly labelled "Good Morning" and "Good Night," and other supposedly dignified interior adornments displayed idiotic kittens and birdies, daisies, and comedian bullfrogs. The latter were featured with cat-tails on that essential of bedroom furnishing, the linen "splasher" which—on the wash stand of the pre-bathroom era—presented so seductive a temptation to embellishment.

Although the aesthetic movement stressed the use of plaster casts of impeccable classic ancestry in decoration (nothing was considered greater evidence of culture), the sentimental together with the prudish would have none of them and carried on a petty war against the nude in art. In catering to such scruples, Victorian sculpture began to take on a domestic playfulness, both in order to be acceptable and to be comprehended. In addition to serving the purpose of objects of art, sculpture was being incorporated into articles of daily use. During the Centennial period, the average citizen wholeheartedly admired garden fountains of the type which dripped spray on the most realistic of umbrellas under which crouched the chubbiest of infants. And he was equally intrigued with soda fountains—a recent innovation—crowned with glass domes which housed a bisque trifle of nude femininity over which water fascinatingly and endlessly played.

Even the bronze warrior who had formerly posed

THE BUTTER
WOMAN—THE
FORCED PRAYER

with such hauteur on the mantel shelf now joined the ranks of utilitarian sculpture. Owing to great progress in metal casting, these formerly costly figurines now disdainfully supported highly ornamented globes of gas jets, not only as table lamps but also as "gaseliers," those lighting fixtures which sprouted from the newel posts in the halls of every late Victorian city house.

Another manifestation of popular sculpture shown at the Centennial was the "Rogers Groups," those inexpensive plaster statuettes which by this time were already widely known. These had been definitely planned to fill the demand for sculpture from social levels which were unable to afford an example from Carrara, yet were eager to own a piece of plastic art. The "Rogers Groups" were executed by John Rogers, an American sculptor, who always referred to his unpretentious statuettes by this term. Besides the familiar and humorous subjects of everyday American life which told their stories with such clarity, there were groups depicting incidents in the recent Civil War, as well as plastic presentations of well-known literary and historical themes. A "Rogers Group" constituted a superb wedding gift, an always welcome addition to the standard wedding presents—the silver cake-basket, teapot, cruet-stand, or swinging ice-pitcher. The group most favored for this purpose—named with such appropriateness that its selection was almost inevitable—was that of an awkward couple labeled "Coming to the Parson." With the exception of the cast iron soldier which topped monuments of the Civil War, often the first, and frequently the only, impression of plastic form received in Victorian days by the average American remote from cities, came from the Rogers Groups. It has been estimated that at one time almost 100,000 of them held

places of honor in the parlors and bay-windows of the East and Middle West—the lace curtains pulled crisply apart so that these accepted witnesses to one's good standing in the community might be glimpsed in all their putty-colored glory, since they were never tinted in anything but this uncompromising drab.

The most popular piece of sculpture shown at the Centennial (for it was voted as such) was that which pictured a rebellious Italian three-year-old with folded hands, called "The Forced Prayer." Though the Italians outdid all other nations with their engaging genre pieces, equally well liked was an example of a domestic American venture into the plastic arts. This was a bulging bas-relief of a woman's head, modelled incredibly—of all things—in butter! This artistic creation was the work of an amateur lady artist from Arkansas and was officially known as the "Dreaming Iolanthe." The summer of 1876 was an extraordinarily hot one, yet all through that overwhelming heat the "Dreaming Iolanthe," in her deeply recessed frame, was maintained in her golden buttery perfection. This circumstance so impressed the sweltering visitors that even today the "Butter Woman," as she was popularly known, remains indelibly engraved on one nonagenarian's memory—the only object of "art" which she can now recall!

The Victorian emotional attachment to the "picturesque" in Nature endured only so long as contacts with her beauties remained infrequent and difficult of attainment. After railroads had been in operation for several decades, the Victorian world discovered that one of its most agreeable diversions, the romantic appreciation of landscape, was no longer productive of the same intense pleasure as formerly, since the beauties of Nature could now be noted on every journey. In 1872, when certain descendants of the earlier devotees of the "picturesque," dripping with lace veils, scarfs, and attired in the fashionable trailing skirts, competed with each other on a special putting course in the first ladies' golf match ever played in England, (or elsewhere,) they were also marking the spot where the "romantic" fondness for Nature perished. After this unique event, outdoor games were to alter all social behavior; gone forever were those delicate encounters with "Nature" which were the only alfresco experiences permitted the earlier feminine Victorian. From now on, landscape, instead of being an ethereal background about which one rhapsodized, became a reality, something solid on which one might play games and enjoy oneself in other wholesome fashions.

If one ignores equestrianism and certain polite attempts at archery, the idea of sports as such first entered the life of the average woman in 1856, the date when croquet was introduced in England. From all angles, the game appealed to Victorian tastes. Generous in its provisions for group participation, it was inexpensive, and—most important of all—it could be enjoyed without departing from the hallowed precincts of the home. Its tempo was so gentle that it need not disarrange the most fragile ruffle or fluttering ribbon on the most elaborate of crinolines, every line of which was prettily set off against the cropped surface of the greensward. And everyone might share in its pleasures—curates and coquettes, young and old. Croquet immediately became popular, and, by the end of the Civil War, the painted balls were being knocked about even in American villages far from the main stream of fashionable life.

As Victorians moved out of doors in pursuit of this new amusement, the interest in the "picturesque" moved indoors, in which locale it was transformed in the minds of the romantics into a synonym for the "artistic." The "picturesque artistic," as construed by the novel-reading romantic, was capable of a wide variety of interpretations which added mounting confusion to the already murky stream of post-Centennial decorative ideas. But, primarily, it seems linked with the artist and his environment. For some years the "artist," his ideas and standards, had been a subject of considerable public interest. Painters dependent on fashionable approval had learned how to centre public attention upon themselves and their surroundings. And the affairs of contentious artists, such as Whistler, were brought to the notice even of persons who had probably never seen—or ever would see—either an artist, an oil-painting, or a studio. Articles began to appear in the popular periodicals which dwelt on the *artist's* taste in arrangement, his ignoring of fashion, and his clear preference for beauty wherever he saw it, whether in handsome old pieces of furniture from every corner of the world ("second-hand stuff" ignored by the majority), or in forgotten artistic knick-knacks.

Fascinated by these novel ideas so weighted with "romantic" associations, the world of women turned to them with gusto and eagerly inserted "studio" touches into the amazing medley of furnishings already installed in their houses. Scarves of old embroidery or of Oriental silks were draped with cautious carelessness over screens, vases, pianos, pedestals, easels, and even picture frames. In further imitation of studio décor, the home decorator of the eighties planted gigantic Japanese vases in the corners of her rooms. In order to break up the murky shadows which tended to collect there, she stuck large specimens of dried vegetation into these alien ceramics—fan-leaved palms or cat-tails—if she had the courage to pass over the ubiquitous peacock feather. In interior arrangements, the young modern would have none of the set garnitures of the preceding generation. After having studied the painter's still-life compositions of fans, drapery, and pottery, she piled her own interpretations of the ideas in uncertain clumps on every mantelpiece and cabinet. Another of the notable features of any artist's workroom was the screen, with its suggestive allusions to models who divested themselves of their garments behind its decorated surface. Prior to the Centennial, screens had been an old-fashioned —in fact, forgotten—article of luxury. But when the folding screen was revived in the 1870's, every form of it was adapted by fashion—not only the beautiful embroidered Japanese examples, but many other varieties painted or worked by the home needlewoman, who found in screen panels a greater area for embellishment than was heretofore available on the ordinary piece of fancywork.

Delighted with the variety of outlets which this new "artistic" trend furnished for their romantic ideas, the ladies indulged themselves to their hearts' content. Indeed, not satisfied with having adopted practically all the furnishings of the studio, they took over even the artist's palette itself. Introduced into their carefully casual arrangements, nothing ranked higher as a modish piece of decoration than the palette; but the palette, like every other practical object at that time, was never used for ornamental purposes without embellishment. Its normal blobs of color were allowed to remain, but it was bedecked further with little painted landscapes or sprays of flowers. A handful of grasses or peacock feathers thrust through the aperture intended for the thumb added an exquisite touch of picturesqueness to this utilitarian professional article. Sometimes the palette was mounted on a plaque of deep-toned velvet or plush, for even at the time when they were steeling themselves to accept the rough dull-surfaced crashes of the aesthetes, the ladies found it difficult to relinquish these richly piled textiles.

Those sections of the public which had not gone over to the craze for the aesthetic and its approved wall decorations—the coldly correct etching and photograph of classic ruin and statuary—displayed instead a marked

243

preference for "chromos." Though deplored by the more cultivated portion of the public, these brightly colored pictures, manufactured by a process loftily titled "Chromo-Lithography," were highly satisfactory to the masses, for they served to fill the need for a cheap simulacrum of an oil painting. Now, for the first time, everyone who had a few dollars could purchase large facsimiles of oil paintings, "complete," said the publishers, "with brush marks and all the texture of the canvas." The first chromos the manufacturing lithographers brought out were of sentimental subjects—"The Dead Linnet" and the "Dead Bulfinch," for instance. As these pretty colored prints attracted customers at once, it was not long before the field of "Chromo-Lithography" was widened. Soon it included well-liked "Old Masters" such as "Beatrice Cenci" as well as colored pictures of all the Presidents, Christian emblems, religious subjects, and landscapes which ranged from "Moonlight on the Nile" to "A Home on the Wabash."

The most unusual series in a line of chromos was one called "Classic Pictures." These "Works of Art," said the publishers at the outset, "were created to fill a demand." Let us understand at once that these "Classic Pictures" were not the images of pallid Venuses and Mercurys which the phrase usually evokes. Instead, they were lithographs of opulent, almost nude, ladies, glowing with warm and lifelike color, invariably posed in richly furnished interiors on elaborately curtained and draped divans—the latter in itself a suspect décor.

To ensure that the benefits of "Art" reached every village and farm, the "chromo" companies employed local canvassers as agents, and through those neighborly contacts the innocuous, lifelike panels of fish and of strings of game were introduced as dining room decorations into every middle-class home. But to acquire the particular appreciation demanded for the less publicized portions of their line—the highly colored "Art Pictures" —the agents sought for a market not in the home, but in these purely masculine nineteenth-century haunts, the livery stable, the barber shop, and the saloon. In these regions where no "pure" woman of the middle classes would have dared venture without sacrifice of her womanly character, these "works of art" found lodging and were protected from her scathing censorship, for her muffled upbringing would never have permitted her to allow pictures of the big-thighed, big-bosomed ladies admittance to even the most obscure corner of her genteel environment.

Although the average woman would tolerate no

chromo portrayals of Oriental luxuriance within the chaste four walls of her dwelling, the time was far closer than she realized when, of her own volition, she would install that distillation of Eastern luxurance, the *cozy corner,* in her own establishment—and, in so doing, be regarded as in the vanguard of fashion.

She took her first steps in that direction in the late seventies when, to forward the "artistic" idea in home furnishing, she introduced another piece of studio equipment, the *divan.* This article created an enormous vogue for Eastern handworked textiles to cover it and the mound of pillows which it supported, and so put an end to much tedious, indigenous handwork. No longer would women slave over cushion tops of Berlin-work and any lingering inclination to use patchwork for the same purpose was considered shockingly reactionary. So fashionable did the divans become that the exporters of Oriental stuffs were encouraged to flood the Western markets with them.

To utilize this surplus of Eastern textiles, the "Turkish cozy corner" was evolved. The "cozy corner," which used the divan as a base, was an accommodating item of decoration which could be fitted into any odd corner of the house; it was perfect for alcoves, for under stairs, and for irregularly shaped spaces. Above this padded nest of Oriental fabrics was fastened a gingerly balanced canopy constructed on supports formed of crossed antique weapons. From this was looped a twisted conglomeration of richly patterned Bagdad hangings and softly colored Persian scarves. To carry out the Oriental note even more convincingly, an inlaid tabouret supporting a Turkish *narghile* was placed before the cushion-heaped divan, and a pierced swinging lamp, one or two jardinières of Benares brass standing about, and some papier-mâché war trophies fastened on the wall helped to accentuate the Eastern atmosphere.

The Turkish cozy corner was the ultimate nineteenth-century manifestation of the taste for "the picturesque," the fancied tissue of romance itself. Was it not the very image of the setting for Byron's harem beauties, accounts of which had so fascinated the sheltered grandmother of the fin-de-siècle romantic? And though the former lady savored the picturesqueness of such exotic settings only by means of the steel engravings in her cherished Annuals, the latter, thanks to invading commerce, could take her studied ease in the transplanted actuality itself. In the divan's seductive comfort lay the doom of such Victorian stiffness which might have been tempted to linger on, whether in demeanor or furnishing.

Having mastered the art of lounging gracefully—for it had to be studied—the satisfied amateur decorator of the 1890's, seated in her cozy corner, let her gaze stray to the usual archway, the opening of which was pencilled over with a flimsy portière put together of clattering strands of beads and tiny sections of bamboo. Although but a translucent apology for a portière, the bead strands nevertheless served to conceal the future which lay immediately beyond, the future which no woman, even though seated in her canopied shelter (so like a fortune-teller's booth), could descry.

For the Queen still sat on the throne; it seemed as if this venerable personage held back the hand of Time—as if nothing could ever really change. . . .

But in January of 1901, Queen Victoria passed out of her world. The ancient hand of Time, clasped so long and so firmly by her Majesty, felt itself suddenly released! Gleefully it reached out to rid the new century of all the stuffy elaboratenesses. With an authoritative gesture it ripped down that supreme dust-catcher of all—the cozy corner—and ruthlessly snatched the tinkling bead portières from their latticed wooden moorings. To the attic it consigned the tottery bamboo cabinets, the fragile gilt chairs, the bronze statuettes, the plush-framed panels, the embroidered lambrequins, the Japanese fans, the fancy silk-petticoated lampshades, and most of the bric-a-brac. In the areas it had gleefully cleaned out, it firmly set down the severest of brown oak "Mission" furniture, covered the walls with plain papers wholesomely labelled "oatmeal," and hung up dull, ascetic draperies of "monk's cloth" for the housewarming to which the new century was invited.

As the years rolled on, the lines and shapes of things became simpler and simpler, until the most modish furnishing of all was reduced to a mass of cubes, a series of unadorned plane surfaces, and a framework of bent metal tubings.

The world looked on approvingly, acknowledging the practicality of it all—and yet felt vaguely ill at ease. Then, slyly but unhesitatingly, Time's gnarled old hand reached into the attic, grasped once again the delicate "Parian hand" it had so long ago consigned to that dusty retreat, filled this vase as before with the palest of blush roses, and tenderly placed it upon the most uncompromisingly rectangular of modern cabinets in loving memory of the Queen.

245

Left. Interior of a Boudoir, a Victorian decorator's dream. Shown at the Centennial, its Louis Quatorze draperies, its decorated ceilings, its walls of tufted brocade established, for the millions who beheld it, an ideal of luxurious—if unattainable—elegance in furnishings.

The thickly padded and tufted furniture pieces of the 1870's offered a satisfactory support to the similarly padded, tufted, fringed, shirred and draped lady of the period. Some of these pieces were curious departures from the customary idea of seats. Nevertheless, they functioned adequately for their purpose—which was to permit a woman to sit on them sidewise. In this far from easy position she could display not only the full glory of bustle and train, but the painfully acquired elegance of her tiny, tiny waist.

To add to the impressiveness of their but recently acquired "art pieces," the nouveaux-riches festooned the supporting pedestals and easels with luxurious draperies characteristic of the Louis XIV style. This idea was immediately debased; soon there were easels of the cheapest bamboo, which supported the ubiquitous crayon portrait. In every "best room" these solemn likenesses peered out from beneath tasseled loopings of tawdry silks.

Right. Basic pieces of Parlor Suite. *C.* 1870. These units were multiplied according to need. The Louis Quatorze style satisfied the love for richness, carving, gilding.

247

LEVIATHANS OF WALNUT

Left. Pier Glass. 1870. Frivolous gilt mirrors made way for stately walnut pieces. These were trimmed with incised gilt lines and with moldings and chamfered corners stained the color of ebony.
Right. Chandelier of the 1870's.

THE SIDEBOARD presided like an unwieldy matriarch over the Victorian dining room. Improvements in preparing veneers made it possible to employ a variety of curving surfaces to diversify its bulkiness. Its real function was often set aside in favor of an extravagant display of glued-on ornamentation.

Left. Carved Buffet. Walnut. *C*. 1868. Germany. Behind France and England in aesthetic ideas, Germany clung to magnificence, not simplicity, in furnishing.

Above. American simplification of this German design resulted in pleasing contours and agreeable placing of motifs.

Courtesy, The Library Company of Philadelphia, Ridgway Branch

248

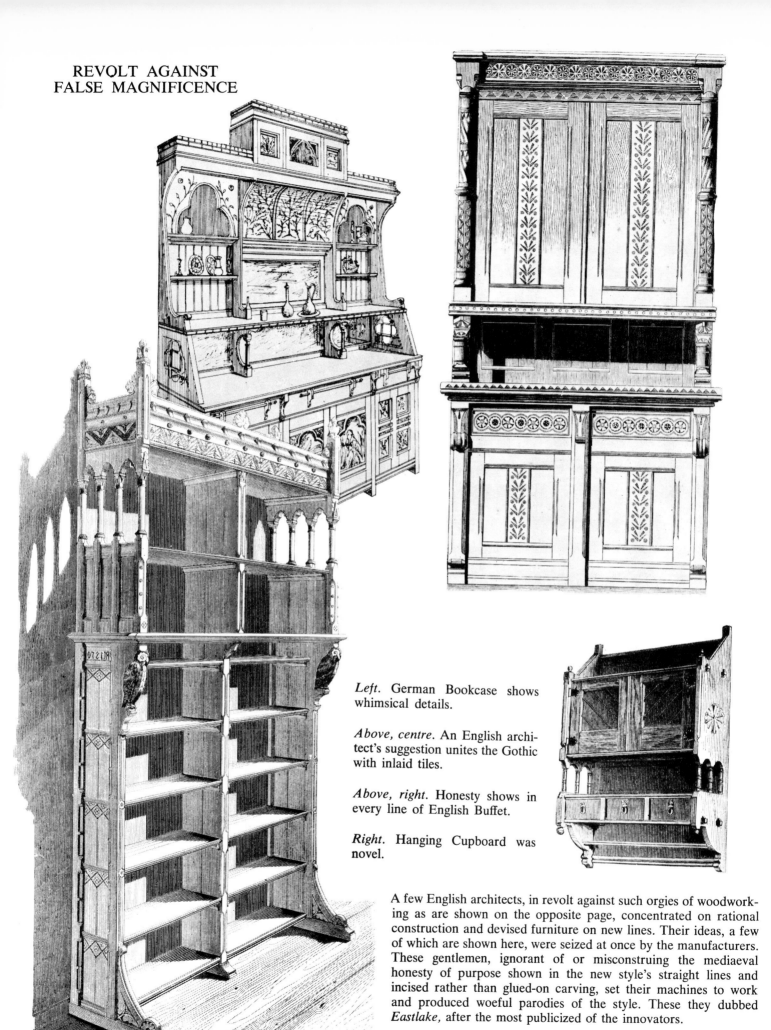

Left. German Bookcase shows whimsical details.

Above, centre. An English architect's suggestion unites the Gothic with inlaid tiles.

Above, right. Honesty shows in every line of English Buffet.

Right. Hanging Cupboard was novel.

A few English architects, in revolt against such orgies of woodworking as are shown on the opposite page, concentrated on rational construction and devised furniture on new lines. Their ideas, a few of which are shown here, were seized at once by the manufacturers. These gentlemen, ignorant of or misconstruing the mediaeval honesty of purpose shown in the new style's straight lines and incised rather than glued-on carving, set their machines to work and produced woeful parodies of the style. These they dubbed *Eastlake,* after the most publicized of the innovators.

Courtesy, Victoria and Albert Museum

Printed Cotton. "Cray" pattern, by Morris.

Right. Courtesy, Metropolitan Museum of Art

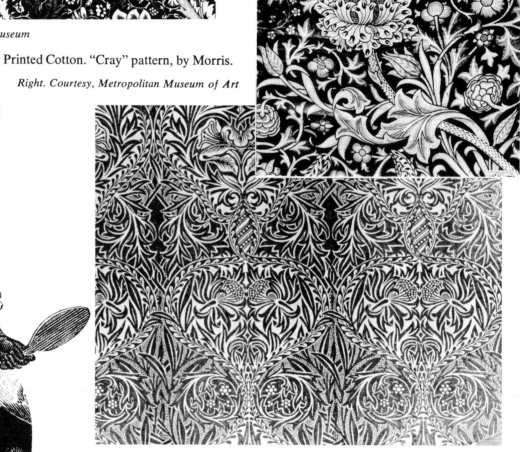

Courtesy, Victoria and Albert Museum

"Sweet Little Buttercup" or
"Art Embroidery." From
Punch, 1879.

William Morris, through his intense study of antique patterns, established an impeccable precedent in design. Though his production was small, it nevertheless altered the whole trend of later Victorian ornament. To use a Morris cretonne or wallpaper, with its flower forms stylized beyond identification, provided the discriminating with a reason for a new snobbishness—a superiority over those whose tastes kept them chained to the "vulgarly naturalistic."

Morris's activities in laying stress on well-designed embroideries for decorative uses did not escape the satirists of *Punch.* The drawing reveals not only the newest ideas in needlework, but also the female form emancipated from its cocoon of bustle and ruffles. Sleek contours, then so startling, are by now so familiar that there is no longer any point to the satire.

250

Walter Crane, an excellent English designer, introduced a strain of sentimental classicism into the welter of Centennial cat-tails. His distinctive style was soon imitated, and, though degraded, his influence on decoration was unmistakable. His were the severely profiled ladies posed in classic draperies or in the romantic costumes of an earlier day. His, too, were the peacocks and Japanese cranes. Indeed, he probably contributed greatly to the latter bird's regrettable popularity.

Right. Wine Cooler with Embroidered Panels. Crane. 1876.

THE INFLUENCE OF WALTER CRANE

Illustration by Crane for *The House Beautiful.*
For its day, an informal yet well-composed synthesis of antique and modern pieces. *Left.* Screen by Crane, 1876, was the inspiration for a horde of lesser attempts in needlework.

KATE GREENAWAY CREATES A TREND

"FIVE LITTLE SISTERS WALKING IN A ROW." Illustration by Kate Greenaway. Her drawings not only revolutionized the style of children's books but were also the stimulus for delightful improvements in children's dress. The little figures became so popular and were used with such banality in machine-produced types of decoration that their intrinsic charm was worn practically threadbare.

Left. Good Little Girl of the Gay Nineties, dressed in her Sunday best. Courtesy of the author, who granted herself permission to publish this revealing portrait of herself.

Right. Bisque figurine in Kate Greenaway style, the most commonplace of ornaments.

Trade Cards bearing Kate Greenaway figures, imprinted with name of New York merchant. *C.* 1880.

Right. Linens embroidered with the little figures were general.

Courtesy, Miss Eleanor Graham

Courtesy, Free Library of Philadelphia

TRADE CARDS

In the 1870's those fond of collecting were given a new incentive. They began to gather up trade cards—a new product of that rapidly growing industry, lithographic color printing. Used as an advertising medium by all manner of commercial enterprises, these small but colorful picture cards brought much pleasure to a public then unsatiated with mass-produced color work.

253

Those who disliked Bentwood's simplicity, yet desired lightness, chose pieces of wicker and rattan. These inoffensive materials were tortured into furniture of indefensible ugliness.

Above. Wicker, at the World's Fair, 1893, forms a background for the Princess Eulalia and that queen of the hothouse, the "American Beauty" rose. Introduced in 1886, this much lauded flower was idolized for her size, perfume, and extravagantly long stem.

Also called "modern" were grotesque pieces of upholstered furniture, like the above.

Austrian Bentwood chair, shown at the Centennial, found its way into American homes.

Bentwood Furniture (a Victorian *modern*) exemplified Eastlake's dictum on good design: that furniture should, at first glance, proclaim its purpose. First exhibited outside the country of its manufacture, Austria, in 1862 by the firm of Thonet. Any ornamental effect Bentwood presented was the result of functional necessities.

Pattern for Ingrain Carpet. "Corn" design created by a young woman which won her a prize in a contest. *Right.* Truly up-to-date was a cretonne which mingled tennis with roses, for women and sports were just getting acquainted.

Above and below, Courtesy, Index of American Design, National Gallery of Art

American designers, depending mainly on Europe for cultural ideas, rarely attempted to use native material for decorative inspiration. When they did, they were apt to turn to Indian corn. *Right.* Parian Pitcher. Corn stalk is twisted into a grace not native to it. *Above.* Fencing of cast iron, a picturesque tangle of corn and pumpkin. Designed by the Philadelphia firm of Wood and Perot. *C.* 1850.

255

A GLIMPSE AT THE MULTIFORM WARES OF VICTORIAN CERAMISTS

The desire for novelty resulted in endless variety in ceramics. No style was too bizarre to copy, no idea too preposterous to attempt. *Above.* Saccharine bisque statuettes were goddesses of the hearth. *Above, right.* In the 1870's, Royal Worcester went Oriental. *Above, left.* Caryatid Fruit Dish of shining white. Copeland, *c.* 1870.

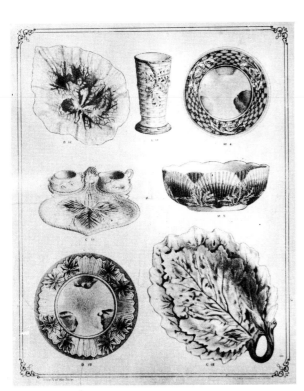

Courtesy, Chester Co. Historical Society

Left. Catalogue page of "Phoenix-ville Majolica," *c.* 1890. A bright ware which appealed to popular taste.

Above and at left on facing page. Majolica Stands, *c.* 1870, made by Minton, England. Showy pedestals for plant or lamp, reminiscent of earlier magnificences in bronze or polychromed wood, were produced in majolica. This ware was streaked with color and glistened unpleasantly because of a too brilliant glaze which blunted every crisp edge and gathered in pools of strong color in every hollow. As a result of this blurring of forms, majolica, even when excellently modelled, presented a curiously tasteless effect.

DOULTON
AND
OTHER WARES

To achieve an elaborate texture, Doulton Ware, a salt-glazed pottery, was incised, carved, and also dotted with ornaments in relief. *C.* 1876.

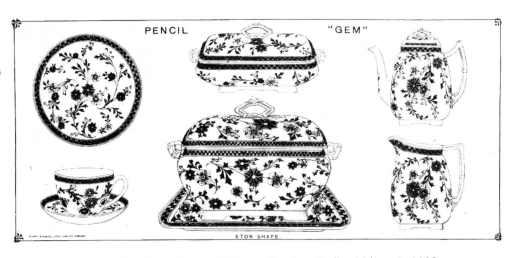

Catalogue Page of Dinner Service. Staffordshire. *C.* 1880. All-over effects were the mode.

Woodland plants painted on Mantel Tiles, Minton, 1876. Besides the obvious uses, this great manufactory promoted the use of its products as decorations for furniture.

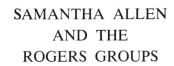

THE FAVORED SCHOLAR

THE TAP ON THE WINDOW

Left. A Rogers Group, properly displayed, was set in the window on a small fancy table, to be glimpsed between the lace curtains by every passerby. An elaborately worked Lambrequin interposed between the statuette and its fancy support heightened the smart effect.

Right. "Hide" and "Seek" (on facing page), companion pieces by J. A. Rogers, told their innocent story to millions.

Marietta Holley through her vastly popular mouthpiece, Samantha Allen, expressed the sentiments of the American middle class. When Samantha speaks, it pays to listen: "I stood . . . a lookin' at some beautiful little statutes [Rogers Groups at the Centennial] . . . They was perfectly beautiful, though middlin' small sized, and they all had clothes on, which was a surprise to me, and indeed a treat." To a public unfamiliar with, or embarrassed by, the nude in art, the garmented figure, together with low cost and familiar subject matter, may well have been a factor in the enormous appeal of the dun-colored Rogers Groups.

SAMANTHA ALLEN REPORTS ON SCULPTURE AT THE CENTENNIAL

Italian Terra Cotta. 1876. The idea was soon adapted to a fountain finial (with water dripping eternally from the umbrella). A group which never lacked admirers among those who considered the playful justly within the province of the arts.

"What lovely forms and faces was round me on every side . . . all carved out of hard stun marble for my delight; all painted out on canvas and hung up for me to smile upon and weep over—for beauty always affects me dretfully. . . . Oh what beautiful little white stun childern there was before me, in every beautiful posture that childern ever got into—a laughin' and a cryin', and a feedin' birds, and a pickin' thorns out of their feet and a hidin' and a seekin'." Samantha Allen.
Above. Fountain, Boy with Fish. *C.* 1870. J. L. Mott & Co.

Latter-day Victorians reduced art to a domestic ritual. In a corner allotted to art's mysteries, devotees practised their beliefs: that every useful article could be made decorative, and that every useless one could be changed into an ornament. The lady decorator was beguiled by gilt paint; with it she wrought amazing transformations. An ear of dried corn, gilded and ribbon-tied, became a support for a thermometer; a gilded palm-leaf fan, touched up with ostrich tips, was quickly changed into a chaste decoration. Searching about for other trivial objects to metamorphose, the home decorator dripped gilt and painted flowers on rolling-pins and flat-irons, palettes and coal-shovels. The results were so grotesque that those qualified to judge showered the poor ladies' efforts with ridicule.

THE FEVER FOR RIBBON

Wall Pocket made of two fans laced together with ribbon.

Courtesy, *Index of American Design, National Gallery of Art*

Detail of Crazy Quilt.

THE PLAGUE OF PLUSH

Standing Work Basket, made from rush basket and discarded arrows.

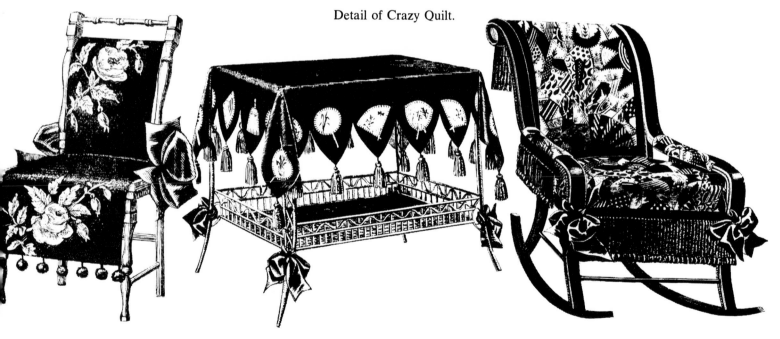

Then, as now, many horrors in decoration were the result of thrift unguided by taste. In this type of reclamation project, our grandmothers, ever respectful of substance, never dreamed of simplifying structure with saw or hatchet. Instead, they preserved it intact, mantling it with covers of embroidered felt or marbled plush which were fastened on with perky ribbon bows. Even in the most sedate circles, bows fluttered in butterfly fashion on everything, since the fad for them was universal.

Centre. "New beauty" added to dainty rattan table. Cover is of dark red felt, appliquéd with fans.

Left. Fancy chair. Made from old piece, gilded, then covered with scarf of embroidered plush, fringed with plush balls!

Above. Aspirants after elegance were assured that an old chair, varnished and decorated with a piece of "crazy work," would look like new.

THE COZY CORNER OF THE GAY NINETIES

The craze for the Turkish Cozy Corner ran like a forest fire through the homes of the nineties. A house was indeed out of date which did not boast at least a modest semblance of this Oriental idea. The most elaborate were constructed of fantastic loopings of Oriental textiles, caught up here and there with decorative bits of Eastern metalwork. Pierced metal lamps shed a dim glow over a shadowy mountain of embroidered pillows, and furniture inlaid with pearl added to the cozy corner's invitation. The appeal, however, was short-lived; while seductive, the cushioned pile was an unsurpassed dust trap. Maintenance became such a problem that finally even the most romantic of homemakers lost patience with this stuffy nook and forced the cozy corner to make its dusty exit.

BIBLIOGRAPHY
AND
INDEX

The works here listed are but a few which contributed to the background of this book. They only point a finger, however, at a field so crowded with material that every researcher can compile his own listings. Fiction and memoirs are rich in details, and any searching through the better periodicals, no matter what the subject matter, is invariably rewarding.

ARCHITECTURE

The Architecture of Country Houses . . . , A. J. Downing. New York, D. Appleton & Co., 1850.
Deals with the American farmhouse, cottage, and villa. Includes furnishing and decoration. Modestly illustrated.

An Encyclopaedia of Cottage, Farm & Villa Architecture and Furniture, J. C. Loudon. London, Longmans, Brown, Green, and Longmans, 1846. Copyright, 1833.
A comprehensive volume. Contains small but clear cuts of simple cottage furniture in general use in 1830–40's. Has glossary of terms.

A History of the Gothic Revival in England, Charles Eastlake. London, Longmans, Green and Co., 1872.

Pompeiana; the Topography, Edifices and Ornaments of Pompeii, Sir William Gell and John P. Gandy. London, Rodwell and Martin, 1817–1819.
A well-illustrated work which introduced Pompeian material to the English designer.

Sketches for Rustic Work, T. J. Ricauti. London, 1842.
Drawings in lithograph by architect for garden houses, bridges, fencing, and furniture.

The True Principles of Pointed or Christian Architecture, A. Welby Pugin. Edinburgh, John Grant, 1895. First published in 1841.
Two lectures on the subject. A foundation work. Has fine clear illustrations.

Voyage dans la basse et la haute Egypte, Baron de Dominique Vivant Denon. Paris, 1802.

ORNAMENT AND DESIGN

Art Journal Illustrated Catalogue of the Industry of all Nations. London, George Virtue, 1851.
A key to the best ornamental design of the day. Illustrative material was discriminately selected and depicted by wood engravings of unusual excellence for the time.

Book of Specimens of Plain & Fancy Printing Types. Philadelphia, L. Johnson, 1869.
Beautiful examples of long-established type foundry's fonts, borders, ornamental initials. Earlier edition published in 1853.

Guter und schlechter Geschmack im Kunstgewerbe, Gustav E. Pazaurek. Deutsche Verlags-Anstalt, Stuttgart und Berlin, 1912.
German Victorian curiosities of decorative art. A valuable background for similar American examples.

Illustrated Catalog of Statuary, Fountains, Vases, Settees. New York. J. L. Mott Iron Works, 1873.
Well-illustrated volume picturing cast iron appointments fashionable in mid-Victorian days. With the exception of the Gothic, which was out of date by 1873, the volume contains every familiar object and decorative trend.

Oxford Drawing Book, The, Nathaniel Whittock. New York, 1852 (published originally in England, *c.* 1825).
Illustrated with rather primitive lithographs of the pictorial subjects then in favor with amateur painters.

Studies in Pen Art, W. E. Dennis. A. N. Palmer Co., 1914.
Large clear pictures and good explanatory text. Alphabets and Victorian scrolled birds executed by "the master, W. E. Dennis."

EXPOSITIONS

Asher and Adams Commercial Atlas; Pictorial Album of American Industry. New York, 1876.
Large, well-illustrated volume. Deals with manufactures at time of the Centennial.

Dickinson's Comprehensive Pictures of the Great Exhibition of 1851, London, 1854.

1851 and the Crystal Palace, Christopher Hobhouse. London, J. Murray, 1937.

Frank Leslie's Historical Register of the U. S. Centennial Exposition, 1876 . . . ed. by Frank H. Norton. New York, Frank Leslie's Publishing House, 1877.

Gems of the Centennial, D. Appleton & Co. New York, Appleton, 1877.
Excellent illustrations and fine selection of material.

Great Centennial Exhibition, The, Phillip T. Sandhurst, Philadelphia, 1876.

Illustrated Catalogue of the Universal Exhibition of 1867. Published with the Art Journal, London and New York, Virtue & Co.
The Art Journal has reported no fewer than seven Great Exhibitions of Art Industry.

Illustrated History of the Centennial Exhibition, James D. McCabe. Philadelphia, 1876.

Illustrations of furniture, candelabra, musical instruments from the Great Exhibitions of London and Paris, John Braund. London, 1858.
Braund was a designer of furnishings for royal houses. The illustrations are large clear engravings; the selections shown, when not of French inspiration, are rustic in character.

Les Merveilles de l'Exposition Universelle de 1867, Jules Mesnard. Paris, Imprimerie Générale de Charles Lahure, 1867.
Beautiful engravings of the best furniture, jewelry, silver, etc. Selections are showpieces, not characteristic of articles in general use.

Official Descriptive and Illustrated Catalogue of the Great Exhibition, 1851. Vol. II and III, Spicer Brothers.
Describes many manufacturing processes and is clearly illustrated.

Report on Design . . . Richard Redgrave. London, William Clowes and Sons, 1852.
An excellent book, reviewing the work in the field of applied art at the Great Exhibition. Judgments expressed on design were incontrovertible. Author very critical of public's bad taste.

Tallis's History and Description of the Crystal Palace and the Exposition of the World's Industry in 1851. London, 1852.

The World of Science, Art, and Industry in the New York Exhibition—1853–4, ed. by Professor Benjamin Silliman, Jr., and Charles P. Goodrich. New York, G. P. Putnam & Co., 1854.

FURNITURE AND INTERIOR DECORATION

Art Decoration applied to Furniture, Harriet Prescott Spofford. New York, Harper & Brothers, 1877.
For its day a dignified treatment of the subject.

L'art industriel, recueil de dispositions et de décorations intérieures, Leon Feuchère. Paris, Goupil et Compagnie, 1839–48.
Useful only for comprehending the taste for elaborateness. Interiors are those of palaces. No text accompanies the illustrations.

Art in the House, Jacob von Falke. Boston, C. Prang & Co., 1879.
Very thorough analysis of style and styles. Chapter on Woman's Aesthetic Mission.

Beautiful Homes, Henry T. Williams and Mrs. C. S. Jones. New York, Henry T. Williams, 1878.
Aimed at improving the taste "of the great and highly respectable middle class" of America. A convenient compendium of the startling decorative ideas which kept the homemaker busy.

The Book of American Interiors, Charles Wyllys Elliott. Boston, James Osgood and Co., 1876.
Useful for descriptions of textiles and color schemes.

The Cabinet Maker, Richard Charles. London, E. & F. Spon, 1868.
Slender volume without letterpress. Full of rather thin drawings of furniture and valances, many of them in mediaeval style (bad Eastlake). Includes material labelled "Neo-Grec."

Cabinet Maker and Upholsterer's Guide, George Smith. London, Jones and Co., 1826.
Very good work on the Greek influence. Text is unimportant but illustrations are clear, plentiful, and hand-colored.

Cabinet Maker's Album, a selection of choice designs in rich and plain furniture for the use of cabinet makers and upholsterers . . . E. Steiger. New York, 1871–1872.
American edition of a German work.

Cabinet Maker's Album of Furniture, comprising a collection of designs for the newest and most elegant styles of furniture. Philadelphia, Henry Carey Baird, 1868.
An American work, planned for use of the cabinet maker. Contains forerunners of golden oak monstrosities.

La Décoration et le Mobilier a l'époque romantique et sous le Second Empire, Albert Keim. Paris, Éditions Nilsson, 1930.

Decorations for Windows and Beds, T. King. London.
Book of designs prepared for upholsterers' use. From
it clients made their selections of styles.

The Decorative Painter's and Glazier's Guide, Nathaniel Whittock. London, Virtue, 1827.
Treats of decoration of apartments, with detailed instructions in imitating woods and marbles in painting.

An Encyclopaedia of Domestic Economy, Thomas
Webster. New York, Harper and Brothers, 1845.
1st English ed. 1844.
Amended to conform to American needs. Over 1200
pages of minute letterpress take care of all phases of
domestic economy. Has many small clear engravings
of furniture.

Gothic Furniture, Augustus Charles Pugin. London,
Ackermann, 1827.
First regular work to illustrate a style rising in favor.
Very striking engravings, hand-colored, of furniture
and draperies, with descriptive letterpress.

*The House Beautiful; Essays on Beds and Tables,
Stools and Candlesticks,* Clarence Cook. New York,
Scribner, Armstrong and Company, 1877.
Stresses simplicity, individuality and taste in furnish-
ing. Reflects the trend towards antiques as furnish-
ing.

The Laws of Harmonious Colouring, adapted to interior decorations, etc., David Hay Ramsay. Edinburgh, 1829. American ed. Henry Carey Baird,
1867.
Author was Sir Walter Scott's decorator.

Modern Dwellings, H. Hudson Holly. New York,
Harper & Bros., 1878.
Deals with exteriors and interiors. Has "profited by
Eastlake"; written in chatty fashion, but material is
unattractive.

Rustic Adornments for Homes of Taste, Shirley Hib-
berd. London, new ed., Groombridge and Sons,
1870. 1st ed. 1856.
Illustrations are of good quality. Author protests in
1870 that his work was copied by Edward Sprague
Rand in "Flowers for Parlor and Garden." Tilton,
Boston, 1863.

*Specimens de la Décoration et de l'Ornamentation au
XIX Siècle,* Edouard Liénard. Charles Claesen,
Liège et Leipsic, 1866.
Handsome volume of illustrations by the designer,
Liénard. As well-drawn as it could possibly be.
Source-book for the best design of the 1870's.

The American in Paris, Jules Gabriel Janin. London,
Longmans, Brown and Green, 1843.

The American Woman's Home, Catharine E. Beecher
and Harriet Beecher Stowe. New York, J. B. Ford
and Co., 1869.
Gives a fine picture of what was wrong with the
housekeeping of that day and many suggestions for
bettering it.

America Revisited, George Augustus Sala. London,
Vizetelly & Co., 1883.
Very chatty book by journalist. Illustrated with contemporary prints. Good for aspects of social and
economic life.

As We Were; a Victorian Peep Show, E. F. Benson.
London, Longmans, Green and Company, 1930.
A worldly and interesting record of life from 1860
to 1914.

A Book of Remembrance, Elizabeth Duane Gillespie.
Philadelphia, J. B. Lippincott Company, 1901.
Born about the same time as Queen Victoria, the
author depicts the life of early Victorian days on this
side of the Atlantic.

Country Living and Country Thinking, Gail Hamilton.
Boston, Ticknor and Fields, 1862.
Mid-Victorian living, as seen through the eyes of a
noteworthy woman writer.

Fifty Years Ago, Walter Besant. New York, Harper &
Brothers, 1888.
A picture of society when Victoria ascended the
throne—informal style which treats of all levels of
life.

Les Fleurs Animées, Jean Ignace Grandville. 2 vol.,
Paris, 1847.
Translation of above called *The Flowers Personified,*
N. Cleaveland, Esq. New York, R. Martin, 1847.
Same material used in *The Family Circle & Parlor
Annual,* James G. Reed, New York, n.d.

Flora's Dictionary, Mrs. E. W. Wirt of Virginia. Baltimore, Lucas Brothers, 1855.
Large book, filled with hand-colored lithographs of
flowers and finely detailed floral borders surrounding
letterpress, treating of the "flower language."

Grandmother Brown's Hundred Years, 1827–1927,
Harriet Connor Brown. Boston, Little, Brown and
Company, 1929.
An epic of American life of a Victorian pioneer.

Ladies Magazine of Gardening, Mrs. Loudon. London, 1842.
Charming book with clear woodcuts. Good accounts of travel in Scotland.

The Lady of Godey's—Sarah Josepha Hale, Ruth E. Finley. Philadelphia and London, J. B. Lippincott Company, 1931.
A well-rounded picture of nineteenth-century life.

Literary Annuals and Gift Books—A Bibliography, Frederick Winthrop Faxon. Boston, The Boston Book Co., 1912.

A London Family, 1870–1900, M. Vivian Hughes. London, Oxford University Press, 1946.
Pleasant picture of middle-class family life.

The Maclise Portrait Gallery of Illustrious Literary Characters, New York, Scribner and Welford, 1883.
Excellent line portraiture of literary Victorians (1830–1838) with backgrounds providing much detail of furniture and accessories.

Modes and Manners of the Nineteenth Century, Dr. Oskar Fischel and Max von Boehm. Vol. III, London, J. M. Dent & Sons, Ltd., 1909.

Our Mothers, ed. by Alan Bott. Text by Irene Clephane. London, Victor Gollancz, Ltd., 1932.
Illustrations from early periodicals with lively text.

Parks, Promenades and Gardens of Paris, William Robinson. London, J. Murray, 1869.

Philadelphia as it is in 1852, R. A. Smith. Philadelphia, Lindsay and Blakiston, 1852.
Early example of a type of publication which prefigured the operations of the present-day Chambers of Commerce.

Pictures of the French, a series of literary and graphic delineations of French character . . . Jules Gabriel Janin. London, Orr, 1840.

A Ragged Register, Anna E. Dickinson. New York, Harper & Brothers, 1879.
A lecturer's impressions of people and places in the United States. Chatty.

Rural Essays, A. J. Downing. New York, G. P. Putnam and Company, 1853.
A posthumous work, containing all his essays published in the Horticulturist.

A Victorian Village, Lisette Woodworth Reese. New York, Farrar & Rinehart, 1929.
Picture of a Victorian childhood spent in a middle-class family in Maryland.

Victoria Royal, Rita Wellman. New York, Charles Scribner's Sons, 1939.
"The flowering of a Style." A brilliant summary of the Victorian era and its decorations.

Village Life in America 1852–1872, Caroline Cowles Richards Clarke. New York, Henry Holt and Company, 1913.
Charming book on village life. Diary of a girl in New York State. Includes period of Civil War.

Window Gardening, ed. by Henry T. Williams. New York, Henry T. Williams, 1872.
Devoted to the culture of flowers and ornamental plants for indoor use and parlor decoration.

The Young Ladies' Friend, Mrs. John Farrar. New York, Wood, 1849.
Book on etiquette.

NEEDLEWORK AND LADIES' ARTS

The Artist or Young Ladies' Instructor in Ornamental Painting, Drawing, etc., B. F. Gandee. London, Chapman & Hall, 1835.

Art Recreations, Levina Urbino. Boston, J. E. Tilton, 1860.
An invaluable and instructive volume on techniques.

Elegant Arts for Ladies. London, Ward & Lock, n.d.
Very informative about a wide range of arts.

Fret Cutting and Perforated Carving, W. Bemrose, Jr. London, Bemrose & Sons, n.d.
Full-scale patterns adequate for the purpose.

The Handbook of Needlework, Miss Lambert. New York, Wiley & Putnam, 1842.

Household Elegancies, Mrs. C. S. Jones and Henry T. Williams. New York, Henry T. Williams, 1875.
Horrific hints for the embellishment of the American home; includes all the techniques favorable for the production of "dust-collectors."

Ladies' Fancy Work, Hints and Helps to Home Taste and Recreations, Mrs. C. S. Jones and Henry T. Williams. New York, Henry T. Williams, 1876.
Material outdoes even the preceding volume.

Ladies Handbook of Fancy Work, Florence Hartley. Philadelphia, G. G. Evans, 1859.
A manual on the subject, with many illustrations.

Ladies Work Table Book. Philadelphia, G. B. Zeiber, 1845.
A very moralistic work, planned for the instruction of young maidens.

The Lady's Manual of Fancy Work, Mrs. Pullan (Aiguillette). New York, Dick and Fitzgerald, 1859.
An exceedingly clear work with a glossary of terms. The author, editor of at least eleven magazines and fancywork departments, says that she is the source to which all the plagiarists turn.

Needle and Brush—Metropolitan Art Series. The Butterick Publishing Co., Ltd., 1889.
Quick and easy ways to perpetrate late Victorian fancywork atrocities.

Phantom Bouquet, Edward Parrish. Philadelphia, J. B. Lippincott & Co., 1862.
"A popular treatise on the art of Skeletonizing leaves and seedvessels, and adapting them to Embellish the Home of Taste."

Pretty Arts for the Employment of Leisure Hours, Ellis A. Davidson. London, Chapman & Hall, 1879.
Deals with the less ladylike techniques which were coming into vogue: wood-carving, fret-sawing, lithography, etching, etc.

Woman's Handiwork in Modern Homes, Constance Cary Harrison. New York, Charles Scribner's Sons, 1881.
An earnest striving to expound the theories of good taste and to raise the standards of women's handwork. Informative about textiles and furnishings.

The Young Ladies' Treasure Book, Daniel McCoy. London, Ward, n.d.

The Young Lady's Book—A Manual of elegant recreations, arts, sciences, and accomplishments. London, Henry G. Bohn, 1859.
Many of the arts expounded were those of an earlier day, as the work had been brought out originally around 1840.

Wax Work—Lessons in Modelling Flowers and Fruit in Wax, J. H. Mintorn. London, George Routledge & Sons, n.d.
The author, "Modeller of Flowers in Wax to the Queen," taught the art and sold the materials needed.

PERIODICALS

The Art Journal . . . Vol. 1 to 74, Feb. 1839 to Feb. 1912. London, Virtue & Co.

The Crayon: a Weekly Journal devoted to the Graphic Arts. New York, 1855–1861.

Carpentry and Building. New York, Vol. I–XXXI, 1879–1900.

Decorator and Furnisher. New York, Vol. I–XXXI, 1882–1898.

The Englishwoman's Domestic Magazine. London, Vol. I–XXVII, 1852–1879.
A somewhat more worldly version of "Godey's."

The Garden. London, Vol. I–CXI, 1871–1927.

Gleason's Pictorial Drawing Room Companion. Boston, Vol. I–VII, 1851–1854.

Godey's Lady's Book and Magazine. Philadelphia, 1839–1898.

Graham's American Monthly Magazine of Literature, Art, and Fashion. Philadelphia, Vol. I–LIII, 1826–1858.

Harper's Bazar, New York, Vol. I, 1867, *et seq.*

Horticulturist and Journal of Rural Art and Rural Taste. Albany, N. Y., Vol. I–XXX, 1846–1875.

Illustrated London News. London, 1842, *et seq.*

Frank Leslie's Illustrated Newspaper. New York, 1855–1891.

Frank Leslie's New Family Magazine. New York, 1857–1860.

Peterson's Magazine. Philadelphia, Vol. I–CXIII, 1842–1898.

QUEEN VICTORIA

Albert the Good, Hector Bolitho. New York, D. Appleton and Company, 1932.

The Childhood of Queen Victoria, Mrs. Gerald Gurney (Dorothy Frances Gurney). New York, Longmans, Green and Co., 1901.

Drina, England's Young Victoria, Marion W. Flexner. New York, Coward-McCann, Inc., 1939.

The Girlhood of Queen Victoria, a selection from Her Majesty's diaries between the years 1832 and 1840, ed. by Viscount Esher. London, John Murray, 1912.

Leaves from the Journal of Our Life in the Highlands, from 1848–1861 . . . Victoria, Queen of Great Britain, ed. by Arthur Helps. New York, Harper and Brothers, 1868.

Letters of Lady Augusta Stanley—A Young Lady at Court, 1849–1863. New York, George H. Doran Company, 1927.

Private Life of the Queen, The, By a Member of the Royal Household. D. Appleton and Co., 1897.
A factual though not analytical account, written during the Queen's lifetime. Gives detail of her habits and surroundings.

Queen Victoria, Lytton Strachey. New York, Harcourt, Brace and Co., 1921.

Victoria, Queen and Ruler, Emily Crawford. Bristol, Arrowsmith; London, Simpkin, Marshall, 1903.
An engaging feminine approach to the subject by a writer who was foreign correspondent for the English press. Her material comes from her memories and from her acquaintance with people who knew the Queen.